Wilson Language Basics

Teacher's Manual

Levels K-1

WILSON®

Wilson works.

FIRST EDITION

Wilson Language Training Corporation
www.wilsonlanguage.com
www.fundations.com

Fundations® Teacher's Manual Levels K-1

Item # TMANK1

ISBN 1-56778-166-7

FIRST EDITION

Fundations is published by:

Wilson Language Training Corporation
175 West Main Street
Millbury, MA 01527
United States of America

(800) 899-8454

www.wilsonlanguage.com

Printed in the U.S.A.

Acknowledgments

Many people contributed to the development of Fundations®. First and foremost, we thank the principals, teachers and students in the elementary schools that implemented the Wilson Reading System® in their general education classrooms. Their work confirmed that WRS instruction is successful in whole class settings and set the foundation for Fundations. In particular, we thank Robin Carlo, Maryann Previti, Meg Kursonis, Alice Riordan and Karen Kontulis at St. Peter's Elementary School in Worcester, MA; Erica, the St. Peter's student who brilliantly named Echo the Owl; Georgia LaFortune and the principals, teachers and students in Lynn, MA; Gail Mikolaycik and the students in Douglas, MA; Eileen Harris and the Kennebunk, ME schools; and Ellie McGarry, Mary Moran, and the teachers and students in Rutland, VT.

Fundations is the culmination of many years of experience teaching youngsters to read and write. Barbara A. Wilson led the writing project in scope and vision. Janet R. O'Connor nurtured the idea for years and developed the Home Support Packet. Edward J. Wilson brought the publishing and logistical resources together.

Our gratitude and appreciation go out to our Contributing Editors: Robin Carlo, Cheryl Koki, Georgia LaFortune, Gail Mikolaycik and Alice Riordan for their efforts. Special thanks to Mary Ann Bonneau, Deanna Nadeau and Cara O'Connor for supporting customers through the Fundations development process.

Fundations could not exist without our partners at New Territories, Inc. Todd Grant and Keith Deinert led their staff and vendors in designing, manufacturing and delivering a beautiful new program. We thoroughly enjoy working with them and the talented illustrators at Mediaweave. Andy Deal at Ocean One Productions produced the videotape and Animation Technologies developed the multimedia CD-ROM. Many thanks to Robin Carlo, Cheryl Koki, Lisa Murphy, Karen Kontulis, Gail Mikolaycik and Alice Riordan for their master teacher performances.

Thanks to everyone at Wilson Language Training involved with delivering Fundations, from Customer Service to Shipping. Thanks to Diane Armstrong, Bert Baldarelli, Judy Nicholas and Paula Mariani for their unending support. Special recognition is due for a few folks who put in a lot of extra time to complete this project. Deirdre Perry, Danielle Ferreira, Lisa Dennett and Suzy Collette typed and edited the manuscript. Alan Donati guided the multimedia CD-ROM through a maze of technical challenges. Tony Pepin led the logistical support. A standing ovation is due Fernando Botelho, Creative Director, who put all the pieces together in his first project with WLT. Finally, thanks to all the dedicated teachers and trainers of Wilson Reading System for making the dream of Fundations come true!

Contents

Preface   vi

Implementing Fundations   1

Introducing Fundations   2

Supplemental Activities   8

References   12

Lesson Activity Overview   15

Level K Orientation & Units 1-5   49

Orientation   52
Unit 1   60
Unit 2   112
Unit 3   126
Unit 4   136
Unit 5   146

Level 1 Orientation & Units 1-14   157

Orientation   160
Unit 1   164
Unit 2   174
Unit 3   186
Unit 4   200
Unit 5   214
Unit 6   226
Unit 7   240
Unit 8   256
Unit 9   270
Unit 10   284
Unit 11   298
Unit 12   314
Unit 13   326
Unit 14   338

Appendix   353

Preface

Building a foundation for reading and writing is key! It is also important to have fun while doing this - Fundations®.

Fundations is an adaptation of the Wilson Reading System® authored by Barbara A. Wilson. The Wilson Reading System, published in 1988, has been implemented in school districts throughout the United States for more than a decade.

The Wilson Reading System is a remedial program based on the principles of Orton-Gillingham methodology. It is a systematic, sequential, multi-sensory method of teaching reading and writing skills to students who struggle, including those with a language learning disability or dyslexia.

The instructional principles for teaching reading and writing have been identified by NICHD research and the National Reading Panel. Both the Wilson Reading System and Fundations provide teachers with programs that incorporate these important principles. The Wilson Reading System is an intensive program for the more challenged readers, whereas, Fundations provides the foundations for life-long literacy for all children.

Implementing Fundations®

Fundations can be implemented in one of three ways, depending upon a school district's comprehensive language- arts program.

1. Whole Class General Education Instruction with Targeted Instruction for Children with Difficulties

Fundations can provide all students with a foundation for reading and spelling. It is delivered to general education classrooms in 25-30 minutes lessons per day. This is appropriate when the core language arts program does not present a systematic phonics approach. Fundations should be combined with literature-based instruction to provide a comprehensive language arts program.

In addition to the daily whole class lesson, the students who struggle in general education classrooms (in the lowest 30th percentile) should also have additional Fundations targeted instruction in a small group setting.*

2. Students In the Lowest 30th Percentile

In schools where Fundations is not used in the general classroom, it is appropriate to select Fundations as an intervention program for students in the lowest 30th percentile. Students should have Fundations for 40-60 minutes each day, completing the 20-25 minute daily lesson, plus supplemental activities, as appropriate.*

3. Students with a Language Learning Disability

Students with a language-based learning disability require explicit, cumulative, and multisensory instruction due to a difference in learning style. Fundations can be combined with a literature-based program to provide this type of required instruction as an alternative to the district's core language arts program. Lessons should be scheduled daily and students should receive:

- Fundations 25-30 minute daily lesson
- Fundations targeted small group or 1:1 instruction (25 - 30 minutes) with supplemental activities.*
- Literature-based comprehension instruction and other decodable text instruction (30 minutes - 1 hour)

Students in grades 2 and 3 that need more intensive 1:1 instruction should be tutored in the Wilson Reading System by a certified Wilson Instructor.

See the Supplemental Activities Section (Pages 8 - 11) for further guidance.

Introducing Fundations®

HOW TO PROCEED

This manual, along with the corresponding CD-ROM, provides the guidance necessary to successfully teach Fundations for either Level K or Level 1. To gain an overview, read the general Introduction section:

- Fundations Skills
- Fundations Principles of Instruction

Note the Lesson Activity Section which provides the procedures for all Fundations lesson activities listed in alphabetical order. You will be directed to these activities as needed throughout the program. There is no need to read through all of these at this time. When directed, however, be sure to study and master the lesson procedures.

Read the Introduction and Orientation for your appropriate Level. This will direct you to prepare your material, view the CD and study the lesson activities needed for Unit 1.

Though it is essential that you take seriously the critical task of setting a foundation for life-long literacy, it is just as important to remember to have FUN! Enjoy Fundations.

Fundations SKILLS

Letter Formation

The Wilson Font provides a basic manuscript form of print. Often students come to kindergarten or Grade 1 with an ability to write upper-case letters of the alphabet. To begin reading and spelling instruction, however, lower-case letter knowledge is key. Rather than reinforce or teach the upper-case letters first, Fundations begins with lower-case.

Letters are practiced with sky writing. Gross motor memory helps students learn the letter formation. In kindergarten, sky writing and tracing are strongly emphasized throughout the first half of the year. Students master letter formation with verbal cues, repetition, sky writing, tracing and writing practice (all described in the lesson activities).

It is important to establish good writing habits. You will teach pencil grip and writing position. The students should write with their chairs pulled in and their feet on the floor. If a child can not reach the floor, you might put a box under the table for them. The student's elbow should be on the table with their "free" hand holding the paper in place.

Phonological Awareness

Phonological awareness is a broad term. It is the understanding that spoken language consists of parts:

- A spoken sentence consists of separate words. (Word awareness)
- A word consists of separate syllables. (Syllable awareness)
- A syllable consists of separate sounds, or phonemes. (Phoneme awareness)

Phonological awareness can be taught and learned. In Fundations this is done sequentially, beginning with word awareness.

In kindergarten, students will learn:

1 Word awareness then,
2 Syllable awareness, and lastly
3 Phoneme awareness.

Phoneme awareness involves several sequential skills: isolating sounds, identifying sounds, categorizing sounds, blending sounds, segmenting sounds and manipulating them.

By the end of kindergarten, students will blend, segment and manipulate sounds in words containing up to 3 sounds.

In Level 1, phonemic awareness instruction continues and students learn to blend, segment and manipulate sounds in words with up to 6 sounds in a syllable.

Sound Mastery

The introduction for letter formation and sounds is sequenced to minimize confusion between like sounds. Students learn more common sounds first, including consonants with continuous sounds that can be held. The sound of **m**, **/m/**, can be continued **/mmm/** or held, whereas the sound of **/t/** can not.

Fundations sound instruction is initially linked to letter formation. Students learn the letter name, its formation and its sound simultaneously. This creates an important link and uses motor memory learning to associate letters with their sounds.

To remember a sound, students also learn a keyword. This word is used consistently. For example, for the letter **a**, the keyword is **apple** (**a-apple-/a/**). The / / marks represent the sound associated with the letter.

Another important aspect to sound mastery with Fundations is the teaching of sounds in two directions:

1 **Letter to Sound**

In this direction, students **see** the letter and identify the sound.

2 **Sound to Letter**

In this direction, students **hear** the sound and identify the corresponding letter(s).

Students do a daily drill of sounds, saying the letter-keywords and sounds. The daily 2-3 minute Sound Drill is the only "drill" aspect of Fundations. This is designed to create fast and efficient neurotransmitting pathways to access sounds. Students have lots of opportunities to practice the sounds with a variety of activities.

Phonics

Sound mastery is a key component of phonics. Phonics instruction, however, must go beyond this sound-symbol knowledge. In Fundations, students are explicitly taught how to blend sounds into words. This is systematically done following the six basic syllable patterns in English. (See Appendix.)

In Level K, students learn to read and spell CVC or consonant-vowel-consonant words. Students begin with blending words that start with the continuous consonants **f**, **m**, **n**, **l**, **r** and **s**. These are more easily blended since the consonant sound can be held into the vowel **/mmm/ /a/ /t/ - mat**.

In Level 1, students learn to read and spell short vowel and vowel-consonant-e words in both one and two syllable words. They progress systematically from the CVC words to words with 4 then 5 sounds to words with more complex patterns including multisyllabic words and vowel-consonant-e.

Students learn how to blend words with the finger-tapping procedure used so successfully in the Wilson Reading System. To blend the sounds /m/ /a/ /t/ into a word, students are taught how to say each sound as they tap a finger to their thumb. As they say /m/ they tap their index finger to their thumb, as they say /a/, they tap their middle finger to their thumb and as they say /t/ they tap their ring finger to their thumb. They then say the sounds as they drag their thumb across their fingers, starting with their /m/, index finger.

Students apply phonics skills to decode words, phrases, sentences and stories that contain the specific letter-sound relationships that they are learning. There are multiple opportunities within lessons for students to apply skills and read words.

Vocabulary

In Level K, students develop vocabulary from reading aloud and classroom discussions.

In Level 1, students also study vocabulary more explicitly. Students learn a "Word of the Day" selected to correspond with the word structure being studied and its high frequency of use. Some multiple meaning words are included. Words are used in sentences and are put onto flashcards to be reviewed frequently. Students enter the word and a sentence into a vocabulary dictionary, which is a section in their Student Notebooks.

Students begin dictionary skills by learning the following 4 quadrants of the alphabet:

1	a	b	c	d	e	f
2	g	h	i	j	k	l
3	m	n	o	p	q	r	s
4	t	u	v	w	x	y	z

Note that the letter arrangements on your magnetic Standard Sound Card Display and the students' Letter Boards reflect these four quadrants. You will also see these quadrants in the Level 1 Student Notebook. Help students think of the letters in these quadrants to begin their successful dictionary work.

Sight Word Instruction

Words that are phonetically irregular are taught as words to be memorized. These "sight words" (or Trick Words in Fundations), are taught separately from phonetically regular words.

Fundations Trick Words were selected due to their high frequency of use in English schoolbooks according to the American Heritage Word Frequency Book. These words are important for students to master for both reading and spelling since they are quite common. A small number of these words are phonetically regular (such as the word **for**). These phonetically regular words have been included because they have phonetic elements taught in higher levels of Fundations.

Students are introduced to three new sight words per week. Lots of repetition is needed to master these words so they are added cumulatively and are reviewed often. When students complete Level 1, they will know the 150 most frequent words according to American Heritage Word Frequency Book.

Motor memory, with sky writing and tracing, is used to learn phonetically irregular words. Students enter these into a Trick Word dictionary in their Student Notebooks. This section is also divided by quadrants (see Vocabulary) to help develop the students' skill at finding words in the dictionary. Note that in this section in their Notebooks words are entered in columns, rather than left to right. Show students dictionaries to demonstrate how words are listed from top to bottom in columns.

Fluency

Fluent reading is an essential reading skill necessary for comprehension. Automaticity is a term that refers to the quick and automatic recognition of words in isolation. It is necessary for fluency, but it is not sufficient. In addition to automaticity, students need to develop prosody (phrasing) and expression.

In Fundations, students have multiple opportunities to develop quick and automatic word recognition. They also work to develop prosody and expression.

Students do both echo and choral reading of stories to help develop fluency. During echo reading the teacher reads a sentence and students repeat. During choral reading the teacher and students read together. Teachers help students with phrasing by scooping sentences.

In Level 1, additional fluency work is provided with the Fluency Kit. There are timed exercises for sounds, word lists, trick words, and phrases. The controlled text material is used for repeated reading. Children chart their progress on an individual recording form. The students work toward a goal of 60 words per minute by the end of grade one. The Fluency Kit also provides a controlled story (95 - 100% decodable) for each Unit and 4 decodable text stories for fluency as well as comprehension.

Comprehension

Students begin to develop comprehension by listening in kindergarten. Oral stories are acted out with Echo and Baby Echo puppets. Students learn to re-tell the stories in their own words. The stories are then transcribed and read with both echo and choral reading.

Students in Level 1 read short, narrative, controlled stories that are 95-100% decodable. They continue to develop their ability to re-tell stories in detail using their own words.

Students are introduced to the difference between narrative and expository text. Discussion of narrative text includes:

- Setting and characters
- What happened first, next, etc.
- What happened in the end and how did the characters feel

Although Fundations includes the above aspects of comprehension, for a comprehensive program, combine this with more formalized literature instruction.

Written Composition

Handwriting and spelling difficulties in later grades affect the composition quality and amount that children write. These skills are directly taught and reinforced in Levels K and 1 so that students set a foundation for writing.

Students learn to segment and spell words in correspondence to decoding patterns. They learn to segment and associate letters with sounds rather than memorize these words. Students also systematically learn punctuation, capitalization and proofreading skills. In both Level K and 1, students dictate short passages. It is recommended that students also keep a daily journal in Level 1.

Throughout the day, hold students accountable for the skills that have been taught. Reinforce spelling, punctuation rules, etc. Have students refer to their Trick Word Dictionary to proofread sight word spelling.

Invented spelling is acceptable (and expected) for emergent writers. Allow this for words that do not contain the elements of word structure taught thus far.

PRINCIPLES OF INSTRUCTION

The principles of instruction are key to the success of Fundations. These principles, basic to the Wilson Reading System, are also identified by research as effective teaching principles.

Explicit Instruction

Instruction is visible and explicit. Unlike many programs where students work independently on phonics worksheets, all Fundations instruction is interactive.

The teacher directly teaches all skills to students through modeling and active learning. The owl puppets, named Echo and Baby Echo, are used to encourage students to model the teacher and repeat sounds and echo read sentences.

Students blend and segment sounds with a finger-tapping procedure. They actively manipulate sounds by moving magnetized letters to form words and they learn basic sentence structure by constructing magnetized sentence parts.

All learning involves active participation. This provides learning through various modalities and also helps maintain the students' focus.

Systematic Instruction (Sequential and Cumulative)

Fundations presents all skills in a systematic and sequential manner in four levels: Level K, Level 1, Level 2 and Level 3. Due to the sequential aspect of the program, students must complete each Level. The Level K is the only level that can be skipped if students begin in Level 1.

The four levels will most often correspond to the students' grade level (Level 1 for grade 1 students). However, the program can also be used sequentially with students in other grades. For example, if introducing Fundations to a second grade group of students, they would need to begin in Level 1 if it was not previously completed. Children then, must master the skills for each level before progressing.

Each of the four levels presents skills in Units. These Units build on previously taught skills, presenting all new information explicitly. This is true for all areas of instruction. This direct and systematic instruction provides the greatest impact on children's reading and writing achievement.

All previously taught skills are brought forward in a cumulative way. Students have ample opportunity to apply these skills for reinforcement. Instruction continually spirals back to relate the new concepts with previously mastered ones. In this way, students are able to develop a deeper understanding of the structure of English words.

Motor-Memory Learning

Much of the "doing" is in the form of motor-memory learning. Students use sky writing to learn letter formation and the challenging trick, or sight words. Gross motor memory is more memorable than fine motor memory. Students use a straight-arm and wrist when sky writing in order to maximize the gross-motor learning.

Students also use their motor memory when tracing letters. A letter's corresponding sound is linked to the letter formation when tracing. This helps to facilitate the association between the letter and its sound.

Students also use motor memory and tactile learning when they tap sounds to blend and spell words. This has proven successful for over a decade in the Wilson Reading System. The tapping of fingers to thumb greatly enhances the students blending ability. If students are unable to tap in this manner, have them tap their fingers to another surface, such as the tabletop. The tapping procedure is fully described in each applicable unit. You will also find it demonstrated on the CD-ROM.

Repetition

Fundations provides a high frequency of skill presentations. Students have multiple opportunities to practice and reinforce all skills. The same information is presented in different ways and with varying activities.

Feedback

Students' correct responses are given immediate positive feedback. Students' errors are also corrected "on the spot" so that the students learn from mistakes. It is important to do this in a supportive way. Provide the student with an immediate opportunity to give a correct response to a similar item after a correction is made.

Supplemental Activities

In addition to whole-class instruction, students who are in the lowest 30th percentile, those with specific areas of weakness or a diagnosed language disability should work with support personnel in small groups or tutorial settings.

Title 1, speech therapist, special education staff or other school staff can provide the targeted supplemental instruction for students who need additional support. Classroom assistants or paraprofessionals can also assist with some of the supplemental activities with guidance from a specialist.

Use the Fundations Basic Kit to provide the instruction. You will also need the students' materials and the Fluency Kit (Level 1) from the classroom, as needed.

LEVEL K
SUPPLEMENTAL ACTIVITY GUIDE

Group Size

The small group targeted instruction in kindergarten can range from 1:1 to 1:3.

Frequency

Students who struggle need lots of repetition and practice. Do this routinely, providing a daily supplemental lesson of 15-20 minutes, if possible.

SUGGESTED ACTIVITIES / FALL (UNITS 1 & 2)

See the Activity section in this Manual for the specific lesson activity procedures. Adjust frequency of supplemental activities as needed.

Letter Formation/ Sound Mastery
(Two to Three Days per Week)

Follow the schedule of letters introduced in the classroom. Practice 2-3 letters, completing the following three activities:

Sky Writing

Have student(s) trace the letter on your classroom board or overhead screen while you verbalize the letter formation. Then have the student sky write and say the letter, keyword and sound.

Student Notebook

Have the student(s) re-trace the letter in their Notebooks. Say the letter-keyword and sound while they trace it. Be sure they follow the correct letter formation (according to the verbalization) when they trace each letter.

Echo/Letter Formation

Dictate sounds and have the student(s) write the letter on the Dry Erase Writing Tablets.

Sound-Symbol Correspondence
(One to Two Days per Week)

Drill Sounds

See Activity Procedure.

Echo/Find Sounds

See Activity Procedure.

Keyword Puzzle

Make this together. Be sure to reinforce letter-keyword-sound as a match is made. As an alternative, you can spread out only the pictures. You then select a letter and have the student find the corresponding keyword picture.

Phonological Awareness
(One to Two Days per Week)

See each Unit's Word Play activity suggestions.

SUGGESTED ACTIVITIES / SPRING
(UNITS 3 - 5)

Letter Formation
(One to Two Days per Week)

Continue with the Letter Formation sequence of activities listed above, as needed.

Word Blending/Spelling
(Two to Three Days per Week)

See Unit Resource List for words.

Build words with Magnetic Letter Tiles

Follow the procedures described in the Unit's Introduce New Concepts to build words. Help students tap and read them.

Echo/Find Sounds and Words

See Activity Procedure.

Dictation/Dry Erase (Sounds and Words)

See Activity Procedure.

Phonological Awareness
(One to Two Days per Week)

See each Unit's Make It Fun activity suggestions.

LEVEL 1
SUPPLEMENTAL ACTIVITY GUIDE

Level 1 students who have reading difficulties and did not have Fundations in kindergarten may benefit from supplemental work in letter formation and sound mastery as described in the supplemental activities guide.

Do this at the beginning of the year and extend your time in Units 1 and 2, as needed. To do the kindergarten Notebook activity, these students will need the Level K Student Notebook as well as the Level 1 Student Notebook.

Be sure to follow the Lesson activity procedures demonstrated on the CD-ROM. These are listed alphabetically in the lesson activity section of this manual.

Group Size

The small group targeted instruction in Level 1 can range from a 1:1 to 1:6 teacher-to-student ratio, depending upon the student need.

The supplemental activities can be categorized into 3 areas of instruction:

1 Phonics/Spelling
2 Vocabulary, Trick Words, and Comprehension
3 Fluency

Select the activity focus as appropriate. Students will often benefit from additional support in all three areas. However, some students might only need extra help in one area. If all three areas are needed, use the recommended frequency noted beside each area of focus as a guideline.

Frequency

Students should have a 30-minute supplemental lesson 3-5 times a week.

Fundations®

Phonics/Spelling
(15 minutes, 3 days per week)

Students with difficulty need sufficient practice not available in the whole class. Provide practice by dictating additional sounds, words, and sentences, including both current unit words and review. (See each Unit's Resource List).

Do the following lesson activities:

- Drill Sounds (with Standard Sound Cards)
- Echo/Find Sounds and Words
- Dictation (Composition Book; worksheets in Appendix)

Vocabulary
(10 minutes, 2-3 days per week)

Whenever students have a Word of the Day in class, they add it, with a sentence, to their Student Notebooks.

Help students write the sentence for their Word of the Day, as needed. The sentence is not phonetically controlled and will therefore be challenging to copy from the board. You can either write the sentence for the student, or provide a sentence written on paper to be copied (rather than off the board).

Make a set of Word-of-the-Day flashcards. If possible, laminate these so that students can "mark up" the words. Make another set, but this time rather than writing the word, draw a simple picture that illustrates the sentence used for that word in the Students' Notebooks.

Have students read your entire Word of the Day packet as flashcards (chorally or in a round robin). You can also time this activity.

Other Activities
(Be selective)

- Fan cards out for a student to select a word. Ask students to come up with the meaning of the word or to use it in a sentence. When the students give you a sentence, help them by elaborating and providing the picture clue, as needed.

- If your card is laminated, ask a student to "mark up" the word and discuss the word structure.

- Make two columns of flashcards. In one column put the word and in other column put corresponding cards with pictures. Have students match the word with the picture and use it in a sentence.

- Have students put words into piles according to categories. For example, make a pile of words that have a digraph. Other possible categories:
  - Words with a bonus letter (Unit 4-14)
  - Words with welded sounds (Unit 4-14)
  - Words with a base word and suffix (Unit 6-14)
  - Words with a blend (Unit 8-14), etc.

- Select a student to read each pile.

- Spread out cards and have students find the word you are thinking of, as you provide them clues with synonyms or other indications of meaning.

Trick Words
(5 minutes daily)

Trick Words require lots of practice. Sky write and finger-write trick words, but do not tap them out. Listen to the student read each trick word written in the Student Notebook.

Have each student make a personal set of Trick Word flashcards. These can be hole-punched and put onto a ring. When a student demonstrates mastery for reading and spelling, the mastered word can be removed from the ring. However, it will remain listed in the Student Notebook for reference, as needed. Hold the student accountable for any word listed in the

Trick Word dictionary.

Comprehension
(10-15 minutes, two to three days per week)

Read, visualize, and replay. Help the students develop comprehension skills by reading short stories aloud. Stop frequently and help the student "make a movie" in their heads. You can draw pictures to represent the words. Model retelling the story in your own words. Have the students retell it to you, using their movie or the pictures as a guide.

Fluency
(Daily, 2-3 minutes per student, 5-10 minutes for group activities)

In each Unit, use the Fluency Kit to copy a set of charts for each student. See the Level 1 Fluency Kit for complete directions.

Time each student individually in four separate sessions on each chart. Then transfer the students' best score to their recording form.

In between sessions, you can practice with students as a group with echo or choral reading. It is most important to help students with phrasing. To do this, model reading the phrases while scooping under each phrase with your finger.

Model reading the stories with correct phrasing. Have students read the stories independently with your assistance and modeling, as needed.

References

Adams, M.J. 1990. *Beginning to Read: Thinking and Learning about Print.* Cambridge, MA: MIT Press.

Anderson, R. et al. 1985. *Becoming a Nation of Readers: The report of the Commission on Reading.* Washington, DC: National Academy of Education, Commission on Education and Public Policy.

Brady and Shankweiler (ed.) 1991. Phonological Processes in Literacy – A Tribute to Isabelle Y. Liberman. Lawrence Erlbaum Associates, Hillsdale, NJ.

Bredekamp, S. and C. Copple, eds. 1997. *Developmentally appropriate practice in early childhood programs.* Rev. ed. Washington, DC: National Association for the Education of Young Children.

Bursack, William D. and Dickson, Shirley V. 1999. *Implementing a Model for Preventing Reading Failure: A Report from the Field*, Learning Disabilities Research and Practice, 14 (4), 191-202.

Chall, J.S. 1983. *Stages of Reading Development.* New York: McGraw-Hill.

Childs, S.B. (ed.) 1968. Education and Specific Language Disability: The Papers of Anna Gillingham, M.A. 1919-1963. Monograph No. 3. Baltimore: The Orton Society.

Fuchs, D., and Fuchs, L.S. 1999. *Monitoring student progress toward the development of reading competence: A review of three forms of classroom-based assessment.* School Psychology Review, 28, 659-671.

Gillingham, Anna, and Stillman, Bessie. 1956, 1963, 1977. Remedial Training for Children with Specific Disability in Reading, Spelling and Penmanship. Cambridge, MA: Educators Publishing Service. (These three editions are now in print. Earlier editions, beginning in 1932, were privately printed.)

Kame'enui, E.J. and Carnine, D.W., eds. 1998. *Effective teaching strategies that accommodate diverse learners.* Columbus, OH: Merrill, Prentice Hall.

Kavenaugh, James F. (ed.) 1991. The Language Continuum from Infancy to Literacy. Parkton, MD: York Pres.

Lyon, R. 1997. *Report on learning disabilities research at NIH.* http://www.ldonline.org/ld_indepth/reading/nih_report.html, 1-11.

Moats, L.C. 1995. Spelling Development Disability and Instruction. Baltimore: York Press.

National Reading Panel. 2000. Teaching children to read: An evidence-based assessment of the scientific research literature on reading and its implications for reading instruction: Reports of the subgroups. Bethesda, MD: National Institute of Child Health and Human Development.

Neuman, S.B., C. Copple, and S. Bredekamp. 2000. *Learning to read and write: Developmentally appropriate practices for young children.* Washington, DC: National Association for the Education of Young Children.

Neuman, S.B. and K. Roskos, eds. 1998. *Children Achieving: Best Practices in Early Literacy*. Newark, DE: International Reading Association.

O'Connor, J. and Wilson, B. 1995. *"Effectiveness of the Wilson Reading System® used in Public School Training."* In McIntyre and Pickering eds. Clinical Studies of Multisensory Structured Language Education. Salem, OR: International Multisensory Structured Language Education Council.

Shaywitz, S.E., Escobar, M.D., Shaywitz, B.A., Fletcher, J.M., and Makuch, R.W. 1992. *Evidence that dyslexia may represent the lower tail of a normal distribution of reading ability*. New England Journal of Medicine, 326, 146-150.

Simmons, D.C., Kame'enui, E.J., and Good III, R.H. 1998. *What reading research tells us about children with diverse learning needs: Bases and basics*. Mahwah, NJ: Lawrence Erlbaum Associates.

Snow, C.E., M.S. Burns, and P. Griffin, eds. 1998. *Preventing reading difficulties in young children*. Committee on the Prevention of Reading Difficulties in Young Children, Commission on Behavioral and Social Sciences and Education, National Research Council. Washington, DC: National Academy Press.

Stanovich, K.E. 1986. *Matthew effects in reading: Some consequences of individual differences in the acquisition of literacy*. Reading Research Quarterly, 21, 360-406.

Stanovich, K.E. 2000. *Progress in understanding reading: Scientific foundations and new frontiers*. New York: Guilford.

Strickland, D.S., and L.M. Morrow, eds. 2000. *Beginning Reading and Writing*. New York: Teachers College Press, and Newark, DE: International Reading Association.

Strickland, D.S., and L.M. Morrow, eds. 1989. *Emerging literacy: Young children learn to read and write*. Newark, DE: International Reading Association.

Torgesen, J.K. and Wagner, R.K. 1987. The nature of phonological processing and its causal role in the acquisition of reading skills. Psychological Bulletin. 101 192-212.

Torgesen, J.K. 1998. *Catch them before they fall: Identification and assessment to prevent reading failure in young children*. American Educator, 22 (1), 32-39.

Whitehurst, G.J., and C.J. Lonigan. 2001. *"Emergent literacy: Development from prereaders to readers."* In S. Neuman and D. Dickinson eds., Handbook of Early Literacy Development. New York: Guilford.

Wilson, B. 1988. Wilson Reading System. Millbury, MA: Wilson Language Training.

Wilson Language Basics

Lesson Activity Overview

The Fundations® Lesson Activities are listed on the following pages in alphabetical order. Some Activities, (Word Play, Make It Fun and Storytime), are variable and are described on the last page of this section.

Some Activities are for Levels K and 1, while other Activities are specific to a Level (as indicated by a **K** and or **1** at the top of each activity page).

These Activities provide the students with lots of repetition but in varied ways. The repetition is key to student mastery. The variation allows for learning with different modalities and also helps to maintain interest.

You will need to master these activity procedures to help your lessons go smoothly. However, there is no need to learn them all at one time. Lesson Activities will be gradually added as you progress through the Units.

How To Prepare For An Activity

- Read the Activity description (in this Overview Section).
- Refer to the Activity Cue for reference.
- View the corresponding Teacher's CD-ROM.
- Prepare the appropriate Activity Plan Cards to help develop your lesson plan. These cards, along with other resources, are available at **www.fundations.com**.
- Practice the Activity.

Alphabetical Order

SYNOPSIS

Once students have learned a letter, they add the corresponding Letter Tile to the Alphabet Overlay on their Letter Board. Eventually, students should have all 26 letters of the alphabet. Students then practice placing and naming the letters in alphabetical order.

PROCEDURE

- Have students start with the magnetic Letter Tiles on their blank Building Boards.

- The Alphabet Overlay is placed in the upper left hand part of the Letter Board.

- Students put Letter Tiles in alphabetical order on their boards, matching them to the Alphabet Overlay. They should match and place letters in order (**a** first, then **b**) rather than randomly.

- When students have their tiles placed, say the alphabet altogether. Use the Baby Echo pointer to point to your Standard Sound Card display and have students point to their Letter Tiles. Emphasize each row, pausing for a deep breath at the end of each one.

Say

a-b-c-d-e-f (breathe).

- You can also say a row and have students echo. Alternatively, you can have a student come up and use the Baby Echo pointer to do a row.

In a Nutshell

- Students match Letter Tiles onto their Alphabet Overlay (which is placed on the Letter Board).

- This is done in alphabetical order.

- You say the alphabet as students point to the Letter Tiles.

TEACHER MATERIALS

- Standard Sound Cards
- Baby Echo Owl Pointer

STUDENT MATERIALS

- Magnetic Letter Tiles
- Letter Boards
- Alphabet Overlay for Letter Boards

VIEW THE CD-ROM

LEVEL K
Unit 2

ESTIMATED ACTIVITY TIME

10 MINUTES

Activity Cue Alphabetical Order

Teacher Does	Teacher Says	Response
Hand out the Letter Boards and Magnetic Letter Tiles.	**Match the letters to set up your boards.**	Students get boards and tiles out.
Point to the first row: **a-b-c-d-e-f**	**Which row do you set up first?**	The top row.
	That's right. Set up the top row first. Don't forget to say the names of the letters when you put them on your board.	
Assist students as needed.		Students set up boards.
Once boards are set, use Baby Echo pointer to say alphabet together. Pause at end of each row. Variation: Student uses Baby Echo pointer to do a row.	**a-b-c-d-e-f, breathe. g-h-i-j-k-l, breathe. m-n-o-p-q-r-s, breathe. t-u-v-w-x-y-z.**	As they get more proficient, students can point to their own boards while you do this.

Dictation/Sounds

SYNOPSIS

Students practice both sound-symbol correspondence and letter formation with this activity.

This is a teaching time, not a testing time.

PROCEDURE

- You say a sound.
- Students echo the sound when you hold up Echo.

Say

/m/ (hold up Echo and students echo /m/)

Write /m/.

- Then everybody writes the letter(s). Have a student do it on the classroom board or overhead.
- Have the student at the board provide the letter name when you ask, **"What says /m/?" (m)**
- Have students check their work and correct it immediately. If doing this on the Dry Erase Writing Tablets, they should erase and write the correct answer. In the Composition Books, they can put a line through the incorrect response and write it correctly.

In a Nutshell

- You dictate sounds, students write the corresponding letter.
- Students always repeat dictations of sounds.
- When using the Dry Erase Writing Tablets, do 3 sounds.
- When using the Composition Books, do 3 sounds.

TEACHER MATERIALS

- Echo the Owl
- Classroom Board or overhead of composition paper (see Appendix).
- Unit Resources (Echo Sounds List)

STUDENT MATERIALS

- Dry Erase Writing Tablet or Composition Books
- Student Notebooks (for reference as needed)

VIEW THE CD-ROM

LEVEL 1
Dictation Dry Erase
Composition Book - Sounds

ESTIMATED ACTIVITY TIME

5 MINUTES

Activity Cue Dictation/Sounds

Teacher Does	Teacher Says	Response
Select a sound from the Echo Sounds list in the Unit Resource.	/t/	
Hold up Echo the Owl.		/t/
	Write the letter that says /t/.	Students write the letter(s). Have one student do this at the classroom board or overhead.
	What says /t/ (student name)?	Select the student at the classroom board to name the letters.
	Check your work.	On the Dry Erase Writing Tablets, students erase to fix any errors. In the Composition Book, students cross out errors and write in corrections.

Dictation/Words

SYNOPSIS

Students develop the skills of phoneme segmentation and the matching of letters to the segmented sounds. Students independently spell words and reinforce their understanding of word structure by marking up the word.

This is a teaching time, not a testing time.

PROCEDURE

- You say a word (selected from Words list in each Unit Resource).
- Students echo the word when you hold up Echo.

Say

mat (hold up Echo and students echo **mat**)

Elbows up, lets tap it /m/ /a/ /t/.

- Students then write the word independently. Select a student to write the word on the classroom board or overhead and spell it orally.

Say

Check your word and fix it if you need to.

- After review and current words are completed, have a student read back all the words and then direct the students to "mark up" their list of words. (e.g. underline the digraphs, circle suffixes, etc.)

In a Nutshell

- You dictate words, students segment sounds and write the word.
- Students always repeat dictations of words.
- When using the Dry Erase Writing Tablets, do 3 words.
- When using the Composition Books, do 2 current, 2 review words.

TEACHER MATERIALS

- Echo the Owl
- Classroom Board or overhead of composition paper (see Appendix).
- Unit Resources (Review and Unit Words List)

STUDENT MATERIALS

- Dry Erase Writing Tablets or Composition Books
- Student Notebooks (for reference as needed)

VIEW THE CD-ROM

LEVEL 1
Dictation Dry Erase
Composition Book - Word Dictation

ESTIMATED ACTIVITY TIME

5-10 MINUTES

Activity Cue Dictation/Words

Teacher Does	Teacher Says	Response
Select a word from the Words list in the Unit Resource.	**mat**	
Hold up Echo the Owl.		mat
	Elbows up. Lets tap it /m/ /a/ /t/.	Tap the word with the students.
	Write mat.	Students write the word(s). Have one student do this at the classroom board or overhead.
	Who can spell mat?	Select a student to spell the word orally, or have the student at the classroom board do it.
Check the word on the classroom board.	**Check your work.**	On the Dry Erase Writing Tablets, students erase to fix any errors. In the Composition Book, students cross out errors and write in corrections.
Direct students to **"mark up"** words (For example, underline digraphs).		

Dictation/Trick Words

1

SYNOPSIS

Students practice the spelling of high-frequency non-phonetic words.

This is a teaching time, not a testing time.

PROCEDURE

- You say a word (selected from Words list in each Unit Resource).
- The students echo the word when you hold up Echo.
- The students write the word with their fingers on a surface, saying the letter names.
- Students write the word. (Students can check spelling in the Trick Word Dictionary section of their Student Notebooks if needed.)

In a Nutshell

- You dictate words, students write them from memory.
- The students always repeat dictations of words.
- When using the Dry Erase Writing Tablets, do 3 trick words.
- When using the Composition Books, do 2 trick words.

TEACHER MATERIALS

- Echo the Owl
- Classroom Board or overhead of composition paper (see Appendix)
- Unit Resources (Trick Words List)

STUDENT MATERIALS

- Dry Erase Writing Tablets or Composition Books
- Student Notebooks (for reference as needed)

VIEW THE CD-ROM

LEVEL 1

Composition Book - Trick Word Dictation

ESTIMATED ACTIVITY TIME

5 MINUTES

Activity Cue Dictation/Trick Words

Teacher Does	Teacher Says	Response
Select a word from the Trick Words list in the Unit Resource.	These are trick words. Can we tap them?	No.
	What do you have to do?	Have our eyes (and fingers) memorize them.
	Dictate trick word: **what**	
Hold up Echo the Owl.		what
	Let's write it with your finger on the table. Ready? **What** **w - h - a - t**	Students write with you on table surface.
	Okay, now write it. Remember to have your mouth tell your hand the letters to write. Let your mouth be the boss.	Students write the word. Have one student do the word on the classroom board or overhead.
	Check your word: what. **w - h - a - t**	On the Dry Erase Writing Tablets, students erase to fix any errors. In the Composition Book, students cross out errors and write in corrections.

Dictation/Sentences

SYNOPSIS

Students independently write a sentence from dictation. This helps them develop their auditory memory for words. They also develop their proofreading skills with guidance.

Teach students to leave a finger space between words. Every sentence must begin with a capital letter and end with a punctuation mark.

Students should work independently when writing sentences. If they need help, they can check their Student Notebooks for sounds, rules, or trick words. Give guidance, but have the students work toward correcting their own errors.

PROCEDURE

- Dictate the sentence (selected from Sentences list in each Unit Resource). Emphasize phrases by using a pause. Use somewhat of a sing-song voice to help students remember the sentence.

- Students echo the sentence when you hold up Echo.

- Students independently write the sentence in their Composition Books. Circulate among students and guide with questioning.

- You may have one student write the sentence on the Blue Word Frames at the front of the class. Explain that high edged frames are for words with upper-case letters, small punctuation squares are for periods, and tall punctuation rectangles are for a question mark or exclamation point.

- Re-dictate the sentence as students point to the words on their papers, making sure they have all the words. Ask if they have a capital letter at the beginning and punctuation mark at the end.

- Have students check the spelling of any trick words.

- Have the students check the spelling of the other words by tapping. After students tap each word (not trick words), give them time to check their words.

- Have students fix any mistakes.

- Have them "mark up" the words, as directed.

In a Nutshell

- You dictate sentences, students write independently and proofread.

- Students always repeat dictations of sentences.

- When using the Composition Books, do one sentence.

- This Activity is used in Level 1.

TEACHER MATERIALS

- Echo the Owl
- Blue Sentence Frames
- Unit Resources (Sentence List)

STUDENT MATERIALS

- Composition Books
- Student Notebooks (for reference as needed)

VIEW THE CD-ROM

LEVEL 1
Composition Book
Sentence Dictation

ESTIMATED ACTIVITY TIME

5 MINUTES

Activity Cue Dictation/Sentences

Teacher Does	Teacher Says	Response
Select a sentence from the Sentences list in the Unit Resource. Be sure to say it in phrases.	**The cat is on the bed.**	
Hold up Echo the Owl.		**The cat is on the bed.**
Repeat the sentence as needed to individual students. Circulate and guide students with questioning.		Students write the sentence. If a student forgets the sentence, he/she should raise hand. Have a student write the sentence on the Blue Word Frames.
Repeat the sentence.		Students point to the words they wrote and add words if needed.
	Do you have a capital letter at the beginning? Do you have punctuation?	Students check.
Direct students to check any trick word spelling.	**Proofread your trick words,** (word) **and** (word)**.**	Students check spelling. They can check in their Student Notebooks if needed.
Direct students to tap and check other words.	**Tap and look at your words.** **Tap out** /each word/**.** Do not tap trick words.	Teacher and students tap each word. Students correct their work.
Check the sentence on the Blue Word Frames.	**Check your work.**	Have the students check their sentence with the one on the Blue Word Frame and make corrections.

Drill Sounds

SYNOPSIS

Every lesson starts with a quick, warm-up sound drill. Students must memorize the letter-keyword-sound. Eventually, students should be able to say the letter name, keyword and sound when the sound card is presented without modeling.

PROCEDURE

Large Sound Card Drill

First practice some sounds with the Large Sound Cards. Model sounds and have the students echo.

Standard Sound Card Drill

Next, point to the Sound Cards with the Baby Echo pointer. Students say the letter-keyword-sound. Have students look at other reference tools (their Desk Strips, the Posters) for keyword assistance.

Do all of the consonants at the beginning. As students get to know their consonants, be selective. Do the new consonants and include any other new or difficult sounds. Be sure to say the letter, the keyword and then the sound (**m-man-/m/**). End with the sound, using the keyword to help them remember the sound.

As a new sound is taught, the Standard Sound Card is added to your card display to be drilled at each lesson.

Teacher as Drill Leader with Standard Cards

Initially, you should model the sounds and have the students repeat. Say letter-keyword-sound as you point to the card and have the students echo.

Student as Drill Leader with Standard Cards

Once students are familiar and comfortable with the format for drilling sounds, a student can lead the drill. The **"drill leader"** can change daily allowing each student a turn. The drill leader says the letter-keyword-sound (**m-man-/m/**) and the class repeats. This allows you an opportunity to assess the students' level of mastery and fluency with the sound drill.

Direct the student to select all vowels and any new sound. In addition, you can have her or him select 4-5 of their choice. (If there are troublesome consonants or any you want to assess for accuracy, direct the student to include those as well.)

In a Nutshell

- Students practice sounds, saying Letter-Keyword-Sound.

Vowels
- Always do vowels: **a-apple-/ă/**

Other Sounds
- Be selective (include new sounds, trouble sounds, and rotate others for review).

TEACHER MATERIALS

- Large Sound Cards
- Standard Sound Cards (magnetized for use on classroom board)
- Baby Echo (on a pointer or ruler)

Level 1 Standard Sound Cards have the keywords on the back for each sound. Be sure to teach each sound and keyword as directed in the Unit. If more than one sound has been taught for a letter, the students should give all the taught responses for that letter.

VIEW THE CD-ROM

LEVEL K and 1
Drill Sounds

ESTIMATED ACTIVITY TIME

3-5 MINUTES

Activity Cue Drill Sounds

Teacher Does	Teacher Says	Response
Show students a Large Sound Card.	**Say** letter-keyword-sound (for example, **t - top - /t/**)	**t - top - /t/**
Point with Baby Echo to Standard Sound Cards on your magnetic display.	**t - top - /t/**	**t - top - /t/**
Variation: Students can be drill leader when they become more proficient.		

Echo/Find Letters

SYNOPSIS

Students reinforce their skill of matching a letter with a given sound.

PROCEDURE

- Have the students start with the magnetic Letter Tiles cleared off of their Letter Boards.

- The Alphabet Overlay is placed in the upper left hand part of the Letter Board.

- Say a sound and hold up Echo. This is the students' cue to echo the sound. For example:

Say

/t/ (hold up Echo and students echo /t/).

Find /t/.

Students then point to the Letter Tile that has the letter representing the sound (**t**).

What says /t/?

Call on a student to answer ("**t**") by naming the letter that makes that sound.

- You then direct students to **"match it"** and they place the Letter Tile on the corresponding letter on their Alphabet Overlay.

- Students can also make the letter(s) with their index fingers on their Letter Building Boards or desks to add a tactile-kinesthetic reinforcement.

- Call on individual students to come to the front of the class to find and point to letter(s) on the Standard Sound Card display.

- Be sure they repeat the sound before answering. This **"echoing"** of the sound helps you know the students have heard it correctly, and helps them to better process the sound.

- Students need to name the letter, not just point to it.

In a Nutshell

- Dictate new sounds, review some previously taught sounds, and target trouble sounds.

TEACHER MATERIALS

- Standard Sound Cards (magnetized for use on magnetic board display)
- Echo the Owl

STUDENT MATERIALS

- Letter Board
- Alphabet Overlay
- Magnetic Letter Tiles (only taught sounds)

VIEW THE CD-ROM

LEVEL K
Echo/Find Sounds

ESTIMATED ACTIVITY TIME

2-3 MINUTES

Activity Cue Echo/Find Letters

Teacher Does	Teacher Says	Response
Have a student come up to the classroom board.	/t/	
Hold up Echo.		/t/
	Point to /t/.	Students find and point to the letter. The student at the Standard Sound Card display selects the letter.
Hold up Echo.	What says /t/, (student name)?	Have the student at the front say the letter name or call on another student.
	Match it.	Students place Magnetic Letter Tiles onto their Letter Board (on the Alphabet Overlay).
Say another sound, and repeat procedure. Do approximately ten sounds, include vowels.		

Echo/Find Letters

SYNOPSIS

Students reinforce their skill of matching a letter with a given sound.

PROCEDURE

- Say a sound and hold up Echo. This is the students' cue to echo the sound. For example:

Say

/t/ (hold up Echo and students echo /t/)

Point to /t/.

Students then point to the Letter Tile that has the letter(s) representing the sound (t).

What says /t/?

Call on a student to answer ("t") by naming the letter that makes that sound.

- Students can also make the letter(s) with their index fingers on their Letter Building Boards or desks to add a tactile-kinesthetic reinforcement.

- Call on individual students to come to the front of the class to find and point to letter(s) on the Standard Sound Card display.

- Be sure they repeat the sound before answering. This **"echoing"** of the sound helps you know the students have heard it correctly, and helps them to better process the sound.

- Students need to name the letter, not just point to it.

In a Nutshell

- Dictate a sound; students repeat the sound and then find the corresponding Letter Tiles.

- There is no need to do every sound taught.

- Frequently include all vowel sounds.

- Dictate new sounds, review some previously taught sounds, and target "trouble sounds."

TEACHER MATERIALS

- Standard Sound Cards (magnetized for use on magnetic board/card display)
- Echo the Owl

STUDENT MATERIALS

- Letter Board
- Alphabet Overlay
- Magnetic Letter Tiles (only taught sounds)

VIEW THE CD-ROM

LEVEL 1
Echo/Find Sounds

ESTIMATED ACTIVITY TIME

2-3 MINUTES

Activity Cue Echo/Find Letters

Teacher Does	Teacher Says	Response
Select a sound.	/t/	
Hold up Echo.		/t/
	Point to /t/.	Students find and point to the letter.
	What says /t/, (student name)?	Have the student say the letter name or call on another student.
Say another sound, and repeat procedure. Do approximately ten sounds, include vowels.		

Echo/Letter Formation

SYNOPSIS

Students develop correct pencil grip and letter formation procedures with guidance. This activity also reinforces sound-symbol correspondence.

Students need proper "pencil grip", so when you give them markers, show them how to pinch it (with pointer and thumb) and rest it (on other 3 fingers) and place it on the table.

PROCEDURE

- As students show they are ready to write (chairs pulled in, feet on floor, hands on table), pass out Dry Erase Writing Tablets and dry erase markers.

- Use the Pencil Grip Picture (see Appendix) as a cue to consistently reinforce proper pencil grip. Assist individual students throughout the day to help them with this pencil grip. It is important to establish this grip.

Say

Get your markers ready. Pinch it, rest it, and put it on the table.

- Say a sound and hold up Echo. This is the students' cue to echo the sound. For example:

Say

/t/ (hold up Echo and students echo /t/)

What says /t/?

- Call on a student to answer ("t") by naming the letter that makes that sound.

- Next have that student come up to the classroom board to make the letter on the Writing Grid.

- Then have all students write the answer on the their Dry-Erase Writing Tablets as you direct them with the verbalization.

- Do several sounds. See the Echo Sounds Resource List in each Unit from which to select sounds.

In a Nutshell

- You dictate sounds, students write the corresponding letter.

TEACHER MATERIALS

- Letter Formation Verbalization Guide
- Echo the Owl
- Wilson Writing Grid on Classroom Board or Writing Grid Overhead
- Pencil Grip Picture
- Unit Resource (Echo Sounds)

STUDENT MATERIALS

- Dry Erase Writing Tablet
- Dry Erase Markers and Erasers

Dry erase markers and erasers are not provided with Fundations since many classrooms are already equipped with them. Old socks can be used for erasers!

VIEW THE CD-ROM

LEVEL K

Dry Erase Letters

ESTIMATED ACTIVITY TIME

5 MINUTES

Activity Cue Echo/Letter Formation

Teacher Does	Teacher Says	Response
Select a sound.	/t/	
Hold up Echo.		/t/
	What says /t/?	Students answer, **t.**
Show students proper pencil grip. Display the Pencil Grip Picture.	**Everyone pinch your marker, rest it and put it on the table.**	Have students hold marker.
Select a student or make the letter yourself on the Writing Grid.		
Demonstrate on the Writing Grid while you say the verbalization, directing all students.	**Okay. Let's make a t.** Use the verbalization for the letter. Be sure to be consistent.	Students make the letter on their Dry Erase Writing Tablets.
	What letter is it?	**t**
	Where does it start?	**On the sky line.**
.	**What says /t/?**	**t says /t/.**
	Erase your boards.	Students erase.
Dictate another letter.		

Echo/Find Words

SYNOPSIS

Students must segment sounds and identify the letter(s) that go with each segmented sound. The segmenting is done with finger tapping.

PROCEDURE

- Dictate the word, and hold up Echo. This is the students' cue to echo the word. For example:

Say

  Elbows up-tap (the word).

- Tap the word with the students.

  Make the word.

- Students then find the Magnetic Letter Tiles to make the word on their Building Boards.

- One student can come to the front of the class to find the letters at the Standard Sound Card display.

- When students have formed the word with their tiles, ask someone to spell it orally. Then say, **"clear the deck."** Students return the Letter Tiles to their places in preparation for a new word.

In a Nutshell

- You dictate words, students tap and spell with tiles.
- Practice 2-3 current words and 2-3 review words.

TEACHER MATERIALS

- Echo the Owl or Baby Echo
- Standard Sound Cards (magnetized for use on magnetic board/card display)
- Unit Resources (Review and Unit Word List)

STUDENT MATERIALS

- Magnetic Letter Tiles
- Letter and Building Boards

VIEW THE CD-ROM

LEVEL K
Unit 4 (Video)

LEVEL 1
Echo Sound/Words

ESTIMATED ACTIVITY TIME

5-7 MINUTES

Activity Cue Echo/Find Words

Teacher Does	Teacher Says	Response
Select a word from the Unit Resource List.	**mad**	
Hold up Echo.		**mad**
	Elbows up. Lets tap it /m/ /a/ /d/.	Tap the word with the students.
	Find mad.	Students find Magnetic Letter Tiles and spell word on their Building Board.
	Who can spell mad?	
Select a student to spell the word orally.		**m - a - d**
Make word with Standard Sound Cards (or call on a student to form the word on the card display board).	**Yes, m - a - d.** **Check your word.**	
	Clear the deck.	Students return Magnetic Letter Tiles to their Letter Board.
Dictate 2-3 current words and 2-3 review words.		

Letter-Keyword-Sound

SYNOPSIS

This activity introduces students to the corresponding letter names and sounds with the help of a "keyword" picture.

PROCEDURE

Large Sound Card

- Hold up the Large Sound Card with the letter you are introducing.

Ask

Does anyone know the name of this letter? (Name the letter.)

What is this picture? (Name the keyword.)

- As you say the word, emphasize the sound at the beginning of the word. Tell the students that the word begins with that sound.

- Explain that the picture is there to help them remember that the letter makes a special sound and **say the sound**.

- Tell them that Echo wants them to echo so that they can learn all about this new letter and the sound it makes.

- Say the letter-keyword-sound and have the students echo.

Standard Sound Card

- Next show students the letter on the Standard Sound Card. Tell them that the letter on this card is the same letter, but it doesn't have a picture.

- If appropriate, point out the difference in how it looks on the Large Sound Card. For example, explain that **a** is the way this letter sometimes looks in books but the students will write an **a** similar to the Large Sound Card.

- Tell the students that Echo wants them to practice this letter with both the Large Sound Card with a picture on it, and the Standard Sound Card.

- Hold up the Standard Sound Card and say the letter-keyword-sound and have the students echo.

Ask

Tell me the name of this letter. (t)

What is the sound that it makes? (/t/)

What is the word that will help us remember the sound /t/? (top)

Say

t-top-/t/ (hold up Echo and students echo **t-top-/t/**)

In a Nutshell

- Teach letter-keyword-sound.
- Students echo.

TEACHER MATERIALS

- Echo the Owl, Baby Echo
- Large Sound Cards
- Standard Sound Cards

VIEW THE CD-ROM

LEVEL K
Drill Sounds
Introduce Letter-Keyword-Sound

ESTIMATED ACTIVITY TIME

2-3 MINUTES

Note
This activity teaches new letters. The same procedures are used in Drill Sounds to practice letters that have been introduced.

Activity Cue Letter-Keyword-Sound

Teacher Does	Teacher Says	Response
Hold up a Large Sound Card (for example for the letter **t**).	**Who knows the name of this letter?**	Select a student to answer. **t**.
	What is this picture?	Select a student to answer. **top**
	Say picture name, emphasizing the initial sound. Tell students the word in the picture begins with the sound and the picture helps us remember the sound: **/t/, /t/, /t/, top** Say that Echo wants them to learn the sound by echoing it: **t - top - /t/**	
Hold up Echo.		**t - top - /t/**
Hold up a Standard Sound Card (for example the letter **t**). Hold up Echo.	**t - top - /t/. Echo.**	**t - top - /t/**
Add Standard Sound Card to your card display board and point to it.	**What is the name of this letter?**	t
	What is the word to help us learn the sound?	top
	What is the sound?	/t/
	t - top - /t/	
Hold up Echo.		**t - top - /t/**

Sky Write/Letter Formation   K-1

SYNOPSIS

Students use gross-motor memory to learn letter formation following your verbalization.

PROCEDURE

- Draw the Wilson Writing Grid on the classroom board at least 2 feet tall. Attach copies of the Wilson Writing Grid Pictures next to their respective lines on the classroom board. Or make an overhead from the Wilson Writing Grid Overhead.

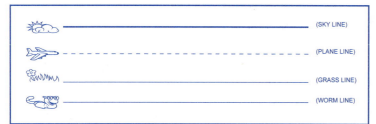

(SKY LINE)

(PLANE LINE)

(GRASS LINE)

(WORM LINE)

- Have the students stand. Always start this activity by shaking out arms and body and stretching. Tell the students to point their arm out **"straight as a pencil."** Tell them to point with 2 fingers. (Two fingers creates more of a muscle pull, and thus is felt more. A straight arm is necessary for gross motor memory.)

Say

> **Let's warm up.**
>
> **Point to the sky line.**
>
> **Point to the plane line.**
>
> **Point to the grass line.**
>
> **Point to the worm line.** (also, mix order)

- Students put their arms down. Next demonstrate how to make the letter you are going to practice. Be sure to face the board and use the verbalization. After you demonstrate, have students put their arms out **"straight as a pencil"** and point with 2 fingers.

- Do the letter again and have the students do it with you, following the verbalization. Do it together several times. At least once, make the letter while saying the letter-keyword-sound **(t-top-/t/)**. This helps to make an association between the formation and the sound. You can have students shake out their arms before teaching or practicing a new letter.

In a Nutshell

- Students follow your verbalization to sky write a letter.

TEACHER MATERIALS

- Letter Formation Guide (see Appendix)
- Wilson Writing Grid Pictures
- Wilson Writing Grid on Classroom Board or Writing Grid Overhead (see Appendix)

VIEW THE CD-ROM

LEVEL K
Sky Write Letters

LEVEL 1
Unit 1(Video)

ESTIMATED ACTIVITY TIME

2-3 MINUTES

Activity Cue Sky Write/Letter Formation

Teacher Does	Teacher Says	Response
Face the Writing Grid. Extend your arm straight out, pointing with two fingers. Point to each line.		
Demonstrate how to make a letter, facing the Writing Grid using your straight arm, pointing with two fingers.	Verbalize the letter formation as you make it. Be sure to use verbalization provided for that letter. Be consistent!	Students face Writing Grid. Using a straight arm and a two-finger pointer, they follow your verbalization to form the letter.
Practice several times. Say letter-keyword-sound at least once while forming the letter.	**t - top - /t/**	Students make letter and say letter-key-word-sound. **t - top - /t/**

Student Notebook

SYNOPSIS

Students use tactile and motor-memory to practice letter-keyword-sounds and letter formation in their Student Notebooks.

PROCEDURE

Introduce New Letter

- Direct the students to find the letter that you are working on in their Student Notebooks. When students find the letter,

Ask

What is the name of this letter?

What is the picture to help us remember the sound?

What is the sound that this letter makes?

- Say the letter-keyword-sound and have students echo.

- Next, hold up your copy of the Student Notebook and show them how to trace the letter with their finger.

- Use the letter formation verbalization to direct students while they trace the letter with their finger.

- Next, have them trace it again, saying the letter-keyword-sound. Do it with them to model.

- After you do this with a new sound, the students can then color the keyword picture.

Practice Letters

- As letters are added to their Student Notebooks, students should practice previous letters as well. To do this, students should trace the letter with their finger while naming the letter-keyword-sound.

- Sometimes do this together as a group. Other times, students can do this independently as you circle around the room to assist them.

- Any student having difficulty should do all taught letters with a specialist or assistant every day.

In a Nutshell

- Students trace letter and say letter-keyword-sound.

TEACHER MATERIALS

- Letter Formation Verbalization Guide (see Appendix)
- Student Notebook

STUDENT MATERIALS

- Student Notebook

VIEW THE CD-ROM

LEVEL K
Student Notebook

ESTIMATED ACTIVITY TIME

5 MINUTES

Activity Cue Student Notebook

Teacher Does	Teacher Says	Response
Hold up the Student Notebook opened to the current page. Walk around and assist students.	**Find the letter in your Student Notebook.**	Students find correct letter in their Student Notebooks.
Point to the letter on the page in your sample Student Notebook.	**What is the name of this letter?**	Select a student or have them answer in unison. **t**
Point to the picture.	**What picture helps us remember the sound?**	Select a student or have them answer in unison. **top**
	What sound does the letter make?	Select a student or have them answer in unison. /t/
	t - top - /t/. Echo.	Select a student or have them answer in unison. **t - top - /t/**
Trace the letter in the Student Notebook sample with your finger, holding it up for students to see.	**Now, let's practice.** **Get your tracing finger ready.** Say verbalization of letter formation while you make letter. **t - top - /t/**	Have students trace letter with their finger, following your verbalization. **t - top - /t/**
	Let's practice the sound one more time. **t - top - /t/. Echo.**	**t - top - /t/**
For practice: Select some letters taught thus far.		Students turn page to practice the letter, as directed.

Trick Words

SYNOPSIS

Certain words in the English language need to be memorized because they do not follow the "system" of the language. They are phonetically irregular. In Fundations, these words are called **trick words**. Students learn non-phonetic words using gross-motor memory.

PROCEDURE

Trick words must be presented to students as words that can't be tapped out. To teach trick words, do the following steps:

- Write the trick word in very large letters (at least a foot high) on the board or on overhead. Read the word. Have the students echo the word. Explain that this word must be memorized. You can show them the **"tricky"** part of the word.

- Demonstrate how to practice the word. Face the word and extend your arm straight, pointing to the word with 2 fingers. Say the word, and then spell the word as you make big letters with your extended arm. Then say the word again. Have the students stand up and do it with you. Tell them to keep their arms **"straight as a pencil."**

- Direct students to write the word again, this time with their eyes closed. Tell students to picture the word as they say the word and spell it while making letters in the air. The students can pretend to write the word with purple or red paint coming from their fingers.

- Have the students write the word with their finger on a surface (white building board or desk). Have them say the word, write it with fingers while spelling orally and say the word again. Have them do the word again with eyes closed.

- If the word is a new trick word, have the students add it to the Trick Word section of their Student Notebooks.

Level 1

- As trick words are introduced, students write them on the appropriate page of the Trick Word section (or dictionary), of their Student Notebooks. Students can refer to this dictionary at any time. Encourage them to use this for all of their written work done during the school day.

- Hold students accountable for words in their Trick Word Dictionary, but allow them to **"look words up"** as often as needed.

In a Nutshell

- Students sky write and finger write words that must be memorized.

- Students add these to the Trick Word section of their Student Notebook. (Level 1)

TEACHER MATERIALS

- Classroom Board

STUDENT MATERIALS

- Building Boards or desk surface

- Student Notebook if introducing a new Trick Word (Level 1)

VIEW THE CD-ROM

LEVEL 1
Trick Words

ESTIMATED ACTIVITY TIME

5 MINUTES PER NEW TRICK WORD

Note (Level 1)
Students can add the words to the Trick Word section in their Student Notebooks at a later time.

This section is arranged in columns like a dictionary, not left to right.

Activity Cue Trick Words

Teacher Does	Teacher Says	Response
Write word on classroom board in large letters (at least 1 foot tall) or on overhead.	**Does anyone know this word?**	Select a student or say the word for them.
Show students the part of the word that is tricky.	**This is a tricky word because it looks different than you expect it to look. It is tricky here.**	
Face the word and using a straight arm and pointing with 2 fingers, trace and spell the word.	**Let's write the word "was."** **was - w - a - s - was**	Have students imitate you, saying letters as they do it.
	Now close your eyes and let's do it again. Pretend to see the letters and trace them. **Make the word "was"** **w - a - s - was**	Students use straight-arm to write word as they say the letters with you, eyes closed.
Direct students to write the word with their finger, first with eyes open and again with eyes closed. Each time, be sure they name the letters while writing.	**Okay, now use your finger to write on your table.** **Pretend your finger is a marker. Let's write it really big.** **The word is "was."** **Ready. Everybody write the word "was".** **"w-a-s – was."**	Students make the letters with their fingers on the table as they say the letter names.
Level 1 If it is a new trick word, have students add it to the dictionary in their Student Notebook.	**This is a trick word.** **We have to practice it a lot so you can learn it!** **Let's put it in your dictionary."**	Students in Level 1 add the word to the appropriate Trick Word dictionary page in their Student Notebook.

Word of the Day

1

SYNOPSIS

This activity will allow students to review the word structure being taught in the current Unit and to discuss a vocabulary word from that Unit.

PROCEDURE

- Select a word from the Word of the Day list provided in each Unit. Make it with the Standard Sound Cards. Follow the same instructions you used to Introduce New Concept(s) for the Unit and re-teach the word structure using the Word of the Day. Show the students how to mark the word or have a student come "mark it" up.

- Put the word on a 5x8 blank index card. You will accumulate a Word of the Day card packet over time. These will be used for both Word Talk and some Make It Fun activities.

- Ask if anyone knows what the word means and discuss it. Use it in a sentence and also have students use it in a sentence. Select a sentence to write on the board. Later, students will copy this to the appropriate page of the Vocabulary section in their Student Notebooks. Initially, be sure to select short sentences.

- After you make the Word of the Day and discuss it, make additional Current Word examples (see Unit Resources) with the Standard Sound Cards to practice decoding. Include at least 5 words from the current Unit to practice. Students can tap words chorally or you can call on an individual student to tap a word. Ask questions as directed in the Teacher's Manual to reinforce the concepts.

- The students should add the Word of the Day to the appropriate page of the Vocabulary section in their Student Notebooks.

In a Nutshell

- Make the Word of the Day with sound cards in order to review word structure and discuss vocabulary.

TEACHER MATERIALS

- Standard Sound Cards (magnetized for use on magnetic board/card display)
- Blank 5x8 Index Cards
- Baby Echo (on a pointer or ruler)
- Unit Resources (Current Word List)

STUDENT MATERIALS

- Student Notebook

VIEW THE CD-ROM

LEVEL 1
Word of the Day

ESTIMATED ACTIVITY TIME

5 MINUTES

(If students write the word and sentence into their Student Notebook at another time of the day.)

10 MINUTES

(If students add the word and sentence to Student Notebook immediately.)

Activity Cue Word of the Day

Teacher Does	Teacher Says	Response
Make Word of the Day with Standard Sound Cards on your classroom board.	**Elbows up. Let's tap.** Explain about the word, emphasizing the current concept.	Tap and read the word together.
Show students how to **"mark up"** the word, or, if it is not a first lesson in the Unit, select a student to do it.	**We can mark this word up like this.** or **Who can remember how to mark this word?**	Student comes up to **"mark up"** word.
Write the word with black magic marker on 5x8 Blank Index Card.	**Does anyone know what this word means?**	Select a student to answer and/or explain.
	Who can give me a sentence with this word?	Select students. Help re-phrase sentences as needed.
Select a short sentence to write on the classroom board.	Say each word as you write the sentence. **This glass has a chip in it.**	
Point to words with Baby Echo.	**Let's read this sentence.**	Have students repeat.
Discuss meaning of sentence.	**What is this sentence telling us?**	Select a student to answer and/or explain.
Now or at a later time, direct students to find the appropriate page in the Vocabulary section of their Student Notebooks.	**Let's write this sentence in your Student Notebooks.**	Students add the word and sentence to their Student Notebooks. Have them **"mark up"** the word.
Make 4-5 other Current Words with Standard Sound Cards. See Unit Resources for possible words.	For each word, say: **Elbows up. Let's tap.** Then ask questions as directed in the current Unit.	Students tap and read words as well as answer questions.

Word Talk

SYNOPSIS

Word Talk activities are designed to practice decoding and review past concepts and vocabulary.

PROCEDURE

Make and Discuss Words

- Select 4-5 words from the accumulated Words of the Day index card packet. Be sure to include 1 or 2 from the current Unit as well as 2-3 from previous Units.

- First, make each word with Standard Sound Cards and have students tap and read them. Do this chorally, or call on an individual student.

- You can have a student come up to the front and "mark it." Have a student tell you what a word means. Students can give a word that means the same thing, or if appropriate, a word that means the opposite. Have the student use it in a sentence. (You can also have a student read aloud the sentence written in their Vocabulary section of their Student Notebooks.)

Read Words

- Use your Word of the Day packet of words as flashcards. Have students quickly read words (without tapping) as you flash the cards.

Word Card Packet

- Next, weave questions or instructions regarding word structure, for example:

Say

Find the word that means to throw.

Do any of these words have the sound /k/?

- You can put the index cards in a pocket chart.

- If you do not have a pocket chart, simply put masking tape on the back of the selected Word of the Day cards to do the weaving with questions, write them on the Blue Sentence Frames found in your kit, or clip them to magnetized clips.

- If you laminate the index cards, students can use dry erase markers to mark up the words.

In a Nutshell

- Students decode words made with sound cards, fluently read flashcards, and discuss word structure.

TEACHER MATERIALS

- Accumulated Word of the Day Index Card Packet

- Standard Sound Cards or Magnetic Card Display Board

- Pocket Chart

VIEW THE CD-ROM

LEVEL 1
Word Talk

ESTIMATED ACTIVITY TIME

5-10 MINUTES

Activity Cue Word Talk

Teacher Does	Teacher Says	Response
Select 4-5 previous Words of the Day from your 5x8 index card packet. Variation: Fan out cards and have students pick a word to get your cards.		
Make each word with the Standard Sound Cards.	For each word say **Elbows up. Let's tap.**	Students tap and read each word (chorally or select a student).
Have students mark 1 or 2 of the words.	**Who can mark this?** Examples: **Can you underline the digraph?** **Who can put a star over the bonus letter?**	Select a student to mark a word. Use questioning to discuss concepts.
Have students discuss the meaning of 1 or 2 of the words and use the word in a sentence.	**Who can think of a sentence for this word?**	Select a student to read the sentence in their Student Notebook or think of a new one.
Quickly flash each Word of the Day index card.		Students read words orally as they are presented.
Display index cards. Ask questions about words.	**Do any of these words have a digraph?** **Which word means to run very fast?**	Select a student to answer.

Variable Activities

Word Play (Level K)

SYNOPSIS

Word Play activities will allow students to develop their print awareness and phonological awareness skills.

Students will learn key elements of basic sentence structure.

PROCEDURE

In the beginning of the year, the emphasis is on the understanding that sentences have separate words. Then you emphasize that words have separate syllables.

In the second half of the year, the students learn that words or syllables have separate sounds. Activities for Word Play will be described in each Unit.

Materials needed for this activity vary with activity as described in each Unit.

View the Level K Word Play section on the CD-ROM.

Make it Fun (Levels K-1)

SYNOPSIS

Make It Fun Activities are designed to reinforce the unit concepts or review previously taught concepts with a game activity. These activities often focus on letter formation, letter sounds or phonemic awareness.

PROCEDURE

These activities often focus on letter formation, letter sounds or phonemic awareness. Suggestions for various reinforcing activities are provided in each Unit.

Materials needed for this activity vary with activity as described in each Unit.

Make It Fun is not on the CD-ROM since these activities are so varied throughout the program.

Storytime (Levels K-1)

SYNOPSIS

Storytime involves listening, reading and writing activities designed to develop the students' awareness of print, understanding of story structure, verbal memory and auditory comprehension.

PROCEDURE

Activities for Storytime will be described in each Unit.

Materials needed for this activity vary with activity as described in each Unit.

Storytime is not on the CD-ROM since these activities are so varied throughout the program.

Wilson Language Basics

Level K

Orientation & Units 1-5

Level K of Fundations will set a very strong foundation for reading and writing.

In addition to Fundations, provide your students with a wide variety of literature experiences, exposing them to poetry, narrative and expository text.

By The End f Level K, Students Will Be Able To:

- Segment words in an oral sentence
- Segment words into syllables
- Segment syllables into sounds (phonemes) - up to 3 sounds
- Name all letters of the alphabet
- Write all manuscript letters in lower-case and upper-case
- Sequence letters of the alphabet
- Name sounds of consonants (primary) and short vowels when given the letter
- Name corresponding letter(s) when given sounds of consonants and vowels
- Read and spell approximately 200 CVC words
- Read Trick Words or targeted high-frquency words: **the**, **a**, **and**, **is**, **was**, **of**
- Identify correct punctuation (period or question mark)
- Identify upper-case letter use for beginning of sentences and names of people
- Re-tell short narrative stories
- Echo-read a passage with correct phrasing and expression

Unit 1 (12 weeks)
- Letter formations (a-z)
- Letter name, keywords and sounds: short vowels, consonants
- Word awareness
- Print awareness
- Story re-telling
- Prosody with echo reading

Unit 2 (3 weeks)
- Letter formations (A-Z), Review (a-z)
- Alphabetical order
- Sound mastery (consonants, short vowels)
- Syllable awareness

Unit 3 (4 weeks)
- Rhyming
- Phonemic awareness skills: sound manipulation (initial, final sounds)
- Blending 3 sounds to read CVC words beginning with continuous consonant sounds
- Story Prediction
- Sample words: sip, log, mat, rug

Unit 4 (6 weeks)
- Segmenting and spelling three-sound short vowel words
- Blending and reading three-sound short vowel words
- Phonemic awareness skills: sound manipulation (medial sounds)
- Narrative story structure
- Beginning composition skills
- Story re-telling
- Prosody with echo reading
- Sample words: top, dig, fox

Unit 5 (6 weeks)

- Blending and reading three-sound short vowel words
- Segmenting and spelling three-sound short vowel words
- Phonemic awareness skills: sound manipulation (initial, final, and medial sounds)
- Trick Words: the, a, and, is, was, of
- Sentence dictation procedures: capitalization, period, word spacing
- Sentence proofreading procedures
- Narrative vs. expository test
- Beginning composition skills
- Story re-telling
- Prosody with echo reading

Introduction

Take time first to get "oriented" and to prepare both yourself and your students for your year ahead with Fundations®.

THE WILSON WRITING GRID

The Wilson Writing Grid is designed to guide students in proper letter formation. It consists of four lines that correspond to specific letter placement. The lines are named and the pictures will assist students in identifying the lines.

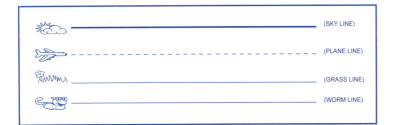

(SKY LINE)

(PLANE LINE)

(GRASS LINE)

(WORM LINE)

The bold line (or the "dark" line) helps locate the top of the grid, especially on pages with multiple grids. This bold line is also the starting point for all upper-case letters.

Lower-case letters start on this bold line or on the (dashed) plane line just beneath it. You will stress this so that students do not form letters from the bottom up.

THE WILSON FONT

The Wilson Font provides a basic manuscript form of print. Often students come to Kindergarten or Grade 1 with an ability to write upper-case letters of the alphabet. To begin reading and spelling instruction, lower-case letter knowledge is key. Rather than reinforce or teach the upper-case letters first, Fundations starts with the lower-case letters.

In Fundations, letter formation is closely connected with sound instruction. Students learn the letter name, its formation and its sound simultaneously. This creates an important link and uses motor memory learning to associate letters with their sounds. Students will succeed with consistent verbal cues, repetition, sky writing, tracing and writing practice (all described in the Lesson Activities).

In a Nutshell

NEW CONCEPTS

Echoing (Echo the Owl and Baby Echo)

The Wilson Writing Grid with the line names

Following verbalizations in making lines

Pencil grip and writing posture

The meaning of the word 'trace'

Letter-Keyword-Sound and Letter Formation for the letter t

TIME IN ORIENTATION

5 DAYS

Days 1-3 lessons will take approximately five minutes.

Days 4 and 5 will take approximately twenty minutes.

WILSON WRITING GRID

The Wilson Writing Grid will be used on your classroom board. Copy the grid pictures (see Appendix) and cut and tape them to your board. Draw a large grid (at least 2 feet tall).

As an option, if you have an overhead projector and screen in the classroom, use the Wilson Writing Grid Overhead in the Appendix and make an overhead. This will be very useful for work with students in sky writing.

STUDENT NOTEBOOK

Write the name of the student on the front of the students' notebooks. Use a thin black marker. Be sure to print the name clearly using the Wilson Font letters (see Appendix for guide). Do this for each student to provide them with a model to copy.

LETTER BOARDS AND ALPHABET OVERLAY

For each student, tape the Alphabet Overlay in the upper left hand corner of one of the magnetic boards. This will be used as the student's letter board.

BABY ECHO

To facilitate pointing with Baby Echo place it on a pointer or ruler.

PENCIL GRIP PICTURE

Copy the Pencil Grip Pictures (see Appendix). Tape the pictures in a place that can be seen by all students. These will serve as a reminder on how to properly hold a pencil or marker.

DESK STRIPS

Put a Desk Strip on each student's desk. This can be removed at the end of the year.

STUDY LESSON ACTIVITIES

Introduce Letter-Keyword-Sound

Drill Sounds

Student Notebook

Sky Write/Letter Formation

Echo/Letter Formation

VIEW THE CD-ROM

WELCOME
Introduction

LEVEL K
Unit 1
Introduction

Lesson Activities
Drill Sounds
Sky Write Letters
Dry Erase Letters
Student Notebook

TEACHER MATERIALS

Echo the Owl, Baby Echo

Wilson Writing Grid on Classroom Board or Writing Grid Overhead

Pencil Grip Picture

STUDENT MATERIALS

Student Notebooks

Dry Erase Writing Tablet

Dry Erase Markers and Erasers

Dry erase markers and erasers are not provided with Fundations since many classrooms are already equipped with them. Old socks can be used for erasers!

DAY ❶

Teach How To Echo

Hold up the large white owl and ask the students to name the kind of bird. Explain that owls have very good eyesight and hearing.

Next, tell the students its name, Echo. Ask if anyone knows what the word echo means. Explain that Echo the Owl is going to help them learn their letters and sounds and that he wants the students to "echo" him whenever you hold him up.

Say the word, "hello" and hold up Echo. The students should say "hello." Say several words or phrases to practice echoing.

You can also introduce Baby Echo and say that he is just like big Echo. He wants to help the students learn their letters and sounds and so he has them echo too.

Teach The Writing Grid

In order to learn the letters, students will need to follow basic directions. Prepare them by teaching them the names of the lines on the writing grid.

Show Students The Wilson Writing Grid On Your Classroom Board

Explain that all the lines have names. Point to the cloud and ask what it is. Point to the sun and ask what it is.

Ask

> **Where do you find the sun and clouds? (In the sky).**

Tell students the top line is called the sky line. Do the same for the other lines. Tell them that these lines will help them make their letters.

Show them that the plane flies along the plane line, tracing your finger from left to right. It reminds us to make our letters and words in that direction.

Have Students Point To The Grid Lines

Next have the students stand up and tell them to point their arms out "straight as a pencil." Don't let them bend their elbows. Tell them to point with their pointer fingers.

Face the writing grid and point with the students to model.

Say

> **Point to the sky line.**
>
> **Point to the plane line.**
>
> **Point to the worm line.**

Next ask for line names randomly:

Say

> **Listen carefully, I'll try to trick you.**
>
> **Point to the plane line.**
>
> **Point to the sky line.**
>
> **Point to the plane line.**

Repeat until students can easily point to each line.

DAY ❷

 Teach How to Follow Verbalizations

Have students shake out their hands. Demonstrate wiggling and shaking body and arms. Have them stretch (stand on toes and stretch hands up to the ceiling).

Next, tell them you are going to do something a little different. First show them and then have them do it with you. Say the verbalization each time in order to direct them.

Say

> Point to the sky line – go down to the grass line. Stop!
>
> Point to the plane line, go down to the grass line. Stop!
>
> Point to the plane line, go all the way to the worm line. Stop!
>
> Shake out your hand.

DAY ❸

 Teach Pencil Grip and Tracing

Teach the students how to hold their markers and sit for writing. Have them follow your verbalizations to make lines. Lastly, teach students how to trace. You will need to reinforce these concepts daily throughout Unit 1.

Before you give out the Dry Erase Writing Tablets, explain to the students that you will help them do what they need to do in order to get a tablet.

Say

> First, all children need to pull in their seats and put their feet on the floor. Now put your hands on the desk.
>
> This is your writing position. Whenever we write, you need to sit like this.
>
> Maria is ready for her tablet.

As students show readiness, give out the Dry Erase Writing Tablets, (but not the markers).

Say

> Next, let me show you how you will hold the markers.
>
> The first thing you do is pinch the marker between your thumb and pointer finger.
>
> Then put your other fingers together to rest your pencil and put it on the table.

Help students with their pencil grip as you give them the markers.

When all the markers are dispersed have the students do the following all together:

Say

> Pinch your marker between your thumb and your pointer finger.
>
> Put your other fingers together and rest your marker on the table.
>
> Now I think you are ready to use the special tablets.

Have students practice following your direction, simply making lines.

Say

> Point your marker to the sky line. Go down to the grass line and stop.

Hold up your Dry Erase Writing tablet and model and then do it again with them (say the same verbalization each time). After making each line, have students check to see if their line looks like your line and then erase.

Say

> Point your marker to the plane line. Go to the grass line. Stop!
>
> Point your marker to the plane line. Go to the worm line and stop!
>
> Now let's do one more thing. This is tricky.

Make a line from the sky line to the grass line and then explain what "trace" means, tracing the line back up to the sky line. Have them trace as you verbalize the directions:

Say

> Point to the plane line, go to the grass line.
> Now trace back up to the plane line and stop.

Do other variations, directing students with your verbalizations.

Example

> Point to the sky line, go to the grass line.
> Now trace back up to the plane line and stop.

DAY ④

 Introduce Letter-Keyword-Sound

Teacher Materials

- Large Sound Card (letter t)
- Standard Sound Card (letter t) with magnetic tape
- Echo Owl
- Wilson Writing Grid (at least 2 feet tall)
- Student Notebook

Student Materials

- Student Notebook

Hold Up The Large Sound Card With The Letter You Are Introducing

Ask

> Does anyone know the name of this letter?

Tell students the letter name.

Ask

> What is this picture?

Say the word, **top**, and emphasize the /t/ sound at the beginning of the word. Tell the students that the word begins with the sound /t/.

Explain that the picture is there to help them remember that the letter makes a special sound and say the sound.

Tell them that Echo the Owl wants them to echo so that they can learn all about this new letter and the sound it makes.

Say

> t-top-/t/

Hold up Echo and have students repeat.

Next show the students the letter on the Standard Sound Card. Tell them that the letter on this card is also the same letter, but it doesn't have a picture. Tell them that Echo the Owl wants them to practice this letter with both the big card with a picture on it and the small card.

Hold up the Standard Sound Card and say, the letter name-keyword-sound.

Say

> t-top-/t/.

Have the students echo.

Ask

> Tell me the name of this letter. (t)
>
> What is the sound that it makes? (/t/)

What is the word that will help us remember the sound /t/? (top)

Say

t-top-/t/

Have the students echo. Be sure that you do not add /ŭ/ to the sound of consonants. The sound of t is /t/ not /tŭ/.

 Sky Write/Letter Formation

Warm Up

Have students stand up. Start this activity by shaking out arms and body and stretching. Tell them to point their arm out "straight as a pencil." Tell them to point with 2 fingers.

Say

Let's warm up.

Point to the sky line.

Point to the plane line.

Point to the grass line.

Point to the worm line.

Students put their arms down. Next, demonstrate how to make the letter t. Be sure to face the board and use the verbalization. After you demonstrate, have students put their arms out "straight as a pencil" and point with 2 fingers. Do the letter again and have the students do it with you, following the verbalization. Do it together several times.

Letter Formation for **t**

Use the following verbalization to direct students in proper letter formation.

t is a sky line letter.

It starts on the (sky line).

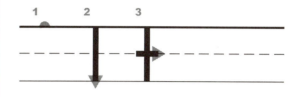

1. Point to the sky line.

2. Go down to the grass line.

3. Cross it on the plane line.

 Introduce Student Notebook

Give each student their Student Notebook and explain that they will be learning and practicing lower-case letters with this book.

Tell them that the lower case letters are very important to learn for reading and writing. Direct the students to find the letter t.

Ask

What is the name of this letter? (t)

What is the picture to help us remember the sound? (top)

What is the sound that this letter makes? (/t/)

Say the letter-keyword-sound and have the students echo.

Next, hold up your Student Notebook and show them how to trace the letter with their finger. Use the verbalization for the letter formation to direct the students while they trace it with their finger. Hold up your notebook to model. Next, have them trace it again, saying the letter-keyword-sound. Do it with them to model. After you do this, the students can then color the picture of the top.

DAY ⑤

 Drill Sounds

Say **t-top-/t/**, as you point to the Large Sound Card with the Baby Echo pointer. Hold up Echo and have students repeat. Point to the Standard Sound Card, and say **t-top-/t/** and have students repeat.

 Sky Write/Letter Formation

Practice sky writing the letter **t**. Follow the sky writing directions from Day 4.

 Echo/Letter Formation

Prepare The Students

Pass out Dry Erase Writing Tablets and dry erase markers as students show they are ready to write: chairs pulled in, feet on floor, and hands on table.

When you give the marker to each child, help them pinch it (with pointer and thumb) and rest it (on three other fingers) and place it on the table.

Say

> Get your markers ready. Pinch it, rest it, and put it on the table.

You can make a reminder poster using the Pencil Grip Picture (see Appendix). Use this cue consistently to reinforce the pencil grip throughout the year. Assist individual students to help them with this pencil grip. It is important to firmly establish this grip.

First have students follow your directions to make lines.

Say

> Point to the sky line. Go down to the grass line. Stop.

> Point to the plane line. Go down to the worm line. Trace back up to the plane line. Stop.

Dictate The Sounds

Say

> /t/

Hold up Echo and have students repeat.

Say

> What says /t/?

Have a student give you the answer, naming the letter **t**. Next have that student come up to the classroom board to make the letter on the Writing Grid.

Then have all students write the answer on their Dry Erase Tablets as you direct them with the letter formation verbalization.

Unit 1   Level K

Introduction

You are ready to begin your "routine" for letter introduction. Each week you will introduce 2 new letters, teaching the letter name-keyword-sound as well as the lower-case formation for each of the new letters. You will practice these letters all week, reviewing previous letters as well as the new letters.

THE LESSON ACTIVITY PLAN

Each week there is an outline of the Daily Schedule.

Week 2

DAY ❶	DAY ❷	DAY ❸	DAY ❹	DAY ❺
Letter-Keyword-Sound	Drill Sounds	Drill Sounds	Drill Sounds	Drill Sounds
Drill Sounds	Sky Write/Letter Formation	Make it Fun	Word Play	Storytime
Sky Write/Letter Formation	Student Notebook	Echo/Find Letters	Sky Write/Letter Formation	Echo/Find Letters
Student Notebook	Echo/Find Letters		Echo/Letter Formation	

For example, on Day 1, you will do the following activities: Letter-Keyword-Sound, Drill Sounds, Sky Write/Letter Formation, Student Notebook.

Lesson Activity Procedures (In General)

There are standard procedures for each lesson activity. To smoothly execute these activities, refer to the Lesson Activity section of this manual and view the corresponding CD-ROM. Note that the Lesson Activities are listed in alphabetical order for your quick reference. Over time, these lesson procedures will become second nature!

Lesson Activity Information (Specific To The Unit)

In each week you will also find *specific* information for Lesson Activities as it relates to that week. This guide will give you what you need to present the Unit lessons.

Unit In a Nutshell

NEW CONCEPTS

Letter-Keyword-Sound for Consonants

Letter-Keyword-Sound for Short Vowels

Letter Formation for Lower-case Letters (a-z)

Sound Recognition for Consonants and Short Vowels

Word Awareness

Print Awareness

Story Re-telling

PLANNED TIME IN UNIT

12 WEEKS

See Resource at end of Unit for Scope and Sequence.

ALPHABETICAL ORDER

Week	Letters
1	t b f
2	n m
3	c a
4	i r
5	o g
6	d s
7	e u
8	l h k
9	p j
10	v w
11	z q
12	y x

PREPARING YOUR MATERIALS

Arrange your Standard Sound Card display in the following manner

As letters are introduced, the Standard Sound Cards (a-z) are placed on display. If your classroom board is magnetic, use a magnetic strip on the back of each Standard Sound Card to adhere it to the board. If your board is not magnetic, you can use a pocket chart or masking tape to display the cards. The letter cards should be added gradually during the weeks in Unit 1.

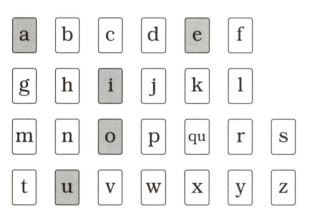

Note How The Cards Are Arranged In Four Rows

This arrangement is designed to help the students learn the alphabet in four quadrants. These four quadrants are used for beginning dictionary skills.

VOWEL EXTENSION PICTURES

Make a copy of the Keyword Pictures of the vowels **a - apple**, **e - Ed**, **i - itch**, **o - octopus**, **u - up** (see Appendix) . These will be used for the Vowel Extension activity.

LETTER BOARD AND ALPHABET OVERLAY

For each student, tape the Alphabet Overlay in the upper left hand corner of one of the magnetic boards. This will be used as the student's Letter Board.

LETTER FORMATION GUIDE

Copy the Letter Formation Guide (see Appendix). If possible, laminate for easy reference during your instruction.

STUDY LESSON ACTIVITIES

Introduce Letter-Keyword-Sound

Drill Sounds

Student Notebook

Sky Write/Letter Formation

Echo/Letter Formation

Echo/Find Letters

VIEW THE CD-ROM

Lesson Activities

Review all activities.

Unit 1 (Video)

View letters as they are introduced.

Sounds

View this section as letters are introduced.

TEACHER MATERIALS

Echo and Baby Echo

Large Sound Cards (a-z, as introduced)

Standard Sound Cards, magnetized (a-z, as introduced)

Wilson Writing Grid on Classroom Board or Writing Grid Overhead

Pencil Grip Pictures

Keyword Vowel Pictures

STUDENT MATERIALS

Student Notebook

Dry Erase Writing Tablet

Letter Board and Building Board with Magnetic Letter Tiles (letters added as introduced)

Alphabet Overlay

The Keyword Puzzle can be placed in the classroom to be used by students independently.

Week 1

DAY ❶	DAY ❷	DAY ❸	DAY ❹	DAY ❺
Letter-Keyword-Sound	Drill Sounds	Drill Sounds	Drill Sounds	Drill Sounds
Sky Write/Letter Formation	Sky Write/Letter Formation	Make it Fun	Word Play	Storytime
Student Notebook	Echo/Find Letters	Echo/Find Letters	Sky Write/Letter Formation	Echo/Find Letters
			Echo/Letter Formation	

 Letter-Keyword-Sound

Introduce Letter-Keyword-Sound with Large and Standard Sound Cards.

These letters are sky line letters.

Note

As a new letter is taught, its Standard Sound Card is added to your card display to be drilled at each lesson.

 Drill Sounds

Do All The Introduced Sounds Each Day

Practice sounds with the Large Sound Cards. Say the letter-keyword-sound and have the students echo.

Next, point to the Standard Sound Cards (in card display) with the Baby Echo pointer. You say the letter-keyword-sound and hold up Baby Echo to have the students repeat.

 Sky Write/Letter Formation

Letter Formation for b

Use the following verbalization to direct students in proper letter formation.

Say

  b is a sky line letter.

  It starts on the (sky line).

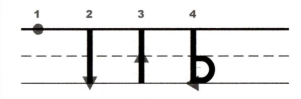

  1. **Point to the sky line.**

  2. **Go down to the grass line.**

  3. **Trace up to the plane line,**

  4. **and around to the grass line.**

Letter Formation for f

Use the following verbalization to direct students in proper letter formation.

Say

  f is a sky line letter.

It starts on the (sky line).

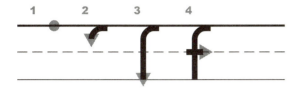

1. **Point to the sky line.**

2. **Trace back on the sky line,**

3. **and then way down to the grass line.**

4. **Cross it on the plane line.**

 Student Notebook

Direct the students to find the newly introduced letters.

Use the verbalization for the letter formation to direct the students while they trace it with their finger. Do it with them to model. After you do this, the students can then color the Keyword Picture.

 Echo/Letter Formation

Remind students of proper pencil grip and sitting position, and give them their Dry Erase Writing Tablets.

Sounds appear between //. Dictate new sounds and a selection of previously taught sounds. You select and say the sound. Students echo the sound and say the letter.

Next have a student come up to the classroom board to make the letter on the Writing Grid.

Then have all students write the answer on their Dry Erase Writing Tablets as you direct

them with the letter formation verbalization.

Sounds

/t/ - t   /b/ - b   /f/ - f

 Make It Fun

Challenge students to think of words that start with the current sounds. Repeat any answer and respond appropriately.

Say

I'm thinking of someone whose name starts with /t/ (/b/, /f/).

Yes, Tom starts with /t/.

Or if incorrect, reply

Mary starts with /m/. I want /t/.

Let's name other words that start with /t/.

Let's name other words that start with /b/.

Let's name other words that start with /f/.

Echo/Find Letters

Students match Magnetic Letter Tiles to the Alphabet Overlay on their Letter Boards. Start with tiles off the board. Dictate sounds. Students echo sound and match the tiles.

 Word Play

Teacher Materials

- Blue Sentence Frames
- Baby Echo

WORD AWARENESS

You will teach the students that sentences are made up of words. Do this by writing the words onto the word frame and adding a punctuation mark at the end. Be sure to use the high-cut frame for the first word in the sentence. Explain to them that this is for a capital or upper-case letter, which always starts a sentence.

Simply write sentences on the word frames. Use students' names and ask questions to help them generate sentences. Ask questions and then erase and change the words to answer the question.

Ask

  Who is here today?

Write

Explain that this is a sentence.

Say

  Every sentence puts together words to say something.

  When we write sentences, we always start the first word with an upper-case or capital letter.

We also end sentences with a period.

Tell students that Baby Echo will help them read the sentence. Point to each word and read it. Then use Baby Echo to point again and have the students repeat.

Ask the students, **"Who else is here today?"** Erase the first student name and put another name. Read again pointing to each word. Each time, be sure to have students echo to read the sentence. Be sure to discuss capital letter and period.

After doing several examples, ask:

  Who was here yesterday?

Erase and write the answer:

 Storytime

Teacher Materials

- Echo the Owl

Read through and practice the story prior to the lesson with your students.

ECHO FINDS DINNER

Perform the Story

  One day Echo was deep in the forest. She sat on a branch of a very tall tree.

Extend your arm out and sit Echo on it.

  Echo had a problem. She was very hungry!

Rub Echo's stomach with her wing.

  Echo had to find food so she searched and searched, looking all around the forest.

Have Echo look down and all around.

Echo saw something move! It was a mouse.

Have Echo pause and look in one spot.

Echo was fast. She flew down and scooped it up.

Fly Echo down and back to her branch... your arm!

Echo ate the mouse and was happy.

Move her wings.

Ask the Following Questions

Who was in this story?

Where did it take place?

What was Echo's problem?

What did she do about it?

How did things turn out? What happened in the end?

How did Echo feel at the beginning of the story?

How did Echo feel at the end of the story?

Week 2

DAY ❶	DAY ❷	DAY ❸	DAY ❹	DAY ❺
Letter-Keyword-Sound	Drill Sounds	Drill Sounds	Drill Sounds	Drill Sounds
Drill Sounds	Sky Write/Letter Formation	Make it Fun	Word Play	Storytime
Sky Write/Letter Formation	Student Notebook	Echo/Find Letters	Sky Write/Letter Formation	Echo/Find Letters
Student Notebook	Echo/Find Letters		Echo/Letter Formation	

 Letter-Keyword-Sound

Introduce Letter-Keyword-Sound with Large and Standard Sound Cards.

These letters are plane line letters. Have the students look at your mouth position when saying /m/ and /n/. They sound alike but your mouth is closed when you say /m/.

Note

As a new letter is taught, its Standard Sound Card is added to your card display to be drilled at each lesson.

 Drill Sounds

Do All The Introduced Sounds Each Day

Practice sounds with the Large Sound Cards. Say the letter-keyword-sound and have the students echo.

Next, point to the Standard Sound Cards (in card display) with the Baby Echo pointer. You say the letter-keyword-sound and hold up Baby Echo to have the students repeat.

 Sky Write/Letter Formation

Letter Formation for n

Use the following verbalization to direct students in proper letter formation.

Say

n is a plane line letter.

It starts on the (plane line).

1. **Point to the plane line.**

2. **Go down to the grass line.**

3. **Trace back up to the plane line,**

4. **and make a hump.**

Letter Formation for m

Use the following verbalization to direct students in proper letter formation.

Say

m is a plane line letter.

It starts on the (plane line).

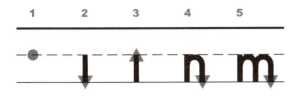

1. **Point to the plane line.**

2. **Go down to the grass line.**

3. **Trace back up to the plane line,**

4. **and make a hump,**

5. **and then back up to the plane line and make another hump.**

 Student Notebook

DAY ❶

Direct the students to find the newly introduced letters.

Use the verbalization for the letter formation to direct the students while they trace it with their finger. Do it with them to model. After you do this, the students can then color the Keyword Picture.

DAY ❷

Trace and say the letter-keyword-sound for the previous letters introduced.

 Echo/Letter Formation

Remind students of proper pencil grip and sitting position, and give them their Dry Erase Writing Tablets.

Sounds appear between //. Dictate new sounds and a selection of previously taught sounds. You select and say the sound. Students echo

the sound and say the letter.

Next have a student come up to the classroom board to make the letter on the Writing Grid.

Then have all students write the answer on their Dry Erase Writing Tablets as you direct them with the letter formation verbalization.

Sounds

/t/ - t	/b/ - b	/f/ - f
/n/ - n	/m/ - m	

 Make It Fun

Pass out the Standard Sound Cards (only those taught thus far). Have one student at a time come up and hold up their card and say the letter-keyword-sound.

You hold up Echo so the other students repeat. Select a student by saying:

Who is holding the card that says /t/?

Echo/Find Letters

Students match Magnetic Letter Tiles to the Alphabet Overlay on their Letter Boards. Start with tiles off the board. Dictate sounds. Students echo sound and match the tiles. Include previous sounds and new sounds.

 Word Play

Teacher Materials

• Blue Sentence Frames

• Baby Echo

WORD AWARENESS

Use the frame to write sentences. Discuss capital (upper-case) letter at the beginning of the sentence and the period at the end. Use Baby Echo to point to each word to read. Have the students echo and read the sentence as you point to the words again.

Ask

What does Peter like?

Write the answer on the word frames.

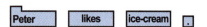

Ask several students this question. Each time, erase the words and replace with the new words. Read the sentence, pointing with Baby Echo and have the students read with you as you point to the words again.

Next ask, **"What do you dislike?"** Write the answer on the frames and follow the procedure above.

 Storytime

Teacher Materials

• Echo the Owl

ECHO FINDS DINNER

This week you will say and act out the same story, "Echo Finds Dinner." Then you will perform it again, without words, and have the children re-tell the story as you "play it out."

Re-perform the Story

Tell and act out "Echo Finds Dinner." (See Week 1, Day 5).

Perform the Story Without Words

Perform the story again, without words, (see below) and have children tell you what happened.

After a student tells you in his/her own words, restate the words from the story to clarify as needed.

Be sure to provide students positive feedback for re-telling in their own words.

Extend your arm out and sit Echo on it.

One day Echo was deep in the forest. She sat on a branch of a very tall tree.

Rub Echo's stomach with her wing.

Echo had a problem. She was very hungry!

Have Echo look down and all around.

Echo had to find food so she searched and searched, looking all around the forest.

Have Echo pause and look in one spot.

Echo saw something move! It was a mouse.

Fly Echo down and back to her branch... your arm!

Echo was fast. She flew down and scooped it up.

Move her wings.

Echo ate the mouse and was happy.

Week 3

DAY ❶	DAY ❷	DAY ❸	DAY ❹	DAY ❺
Letter-Keyword-Sound	Drill Sounds	Drill Sounds	Drill Sounds	Drill Sounds
Drill Sounds	Sky Write/Letter Formation	Make it Fun	Word Play	Storytime
Sky Write/Letter Formation	Student Notebook	Echo/Find Letters	Sky Write/Letter Formation	Echo/Find Letters
Student Notebook	Echo/Find Letters		Echo/Letter Formation	

Letter-Keyword-Sound

Introduce Letter-Keyword-Sound with Large and Standard Sound Cards.

Explain that **a** is a vowel and that it is special. Tell the students that the vowels will be on the orange-colored cards. Demonstrate how to hold the vowel sound /ă/ until you run out of breath. Also show the students that the letter **a** on the Standard Sound Card looks different, similar to the way it looks in books. Tell them that they do not need to write it that way, but that they can write it like the one on the Large Sound Card.

Note

As a new letter is taught, its Standard Sound Card is added to your card display to be drilled at each lesson.

Drill Sounds

Do All The Introduced Sounds Each Day

Practice sounds with the Large Sound Cards. Say the letter-keyword-sound and have the students echo.

Next, point to the Standard Sound Cards (in card display) with the Baby Echo pointer. You say the letter-keyword-sound and hold up Baby Echo to have the students repeat.

Sky Write/Letter Formation

Letter Formation for **C**

Use the following verbalization to direct students in proper letter formation.

Say

c is a plane line round letter.

It starts on the (plane line).

1. **Point to the plane line.**

2. **Start to fly backwards,**

3. **and then go down and around to the grass line.**

Letter Formation for *a*

Use the following verbalization to direct students in proper letter formation.

Say

a is a plane line round letter.

It starts on the (plane line).

1. Point to the plane line.

2. Go back on the plane line then down and around on the grass line,

3. and up to the plane line.

4. Trace back down to the grass line.

 Student Notebook

DAY ❶

Direct the students to find the newly introduced letters.

Use the verbalization for the letter formation to direct the students while they trace it with their finger. Do it with them to model. After you do this, the students can then color the Keyword Picture.

DAY ❷

Trace and say the letter-keyword-sound for the previous letters introduced.

 Echo/Letter Formation

Remind students of proper pencil grip and sitting position, and give them their Dry Erase Writing Tablets.

Sounds appear between //. Dictate new sounds and a selection of previously taught sounds. You select and say the sound. Students echo the sound and say the letter.

Next have a student come up to the classroom board to make the letter on the Writing Grid.

Then have all students write the answer on their Dry Erase Writing Tablets as you direct them with the letter formation verbalization.

Sounds

/t/ - t	/b/ - b	/f/ - f
/n/ - n	/m/ - m	/k/ - c
/ă/ - a		

Make It Fun

Teacher Materials
- Standard Sound Cards
- Echo the Owl

Say a sound /t/ and have students repeat. Call on a student to come get the Standard Sound Card from your card display.

Ask

Who can come find /t/?

When they find it, have them say the letter-key-word-sound.

Hold up Echo the Owl so all the students can repeat. Have the student sit down with the card.

When all cards are taken, tell the children with the cards to hand their card to someone who doesn't have a card. Next, have the students bring back each card.

Ask

I'm looking for /b/. Who has /b/?

 Echo/Find Letters

Students match Magnetic Letter Tiles to the Alphabet Overlay on their Letter Boards. Start with tiles off the board. Dictate sounds. Students echo sound and match the tiles. Include previous sounds and new sounds.

 Word Play

Teacher Materials
- Blue Sentence Frames
- Baby Echo

WORD AWARENESS

Use the following idea for a sentence:

Ask

Why did I use this frame to begin the sentence?

Point to the tall frame.

What does this tell me?

Point to the period.

Explain to the students that this time you are going to do the word game a little different to make it trickier!

Ask

Who else has a pet dog?

This time, rather than you erase the words to write the replacement words, ask for a student's help.

Say

Today I am going to have someone be my helper to erase the words we need to change.

We don't want to erase all the words, just the ones that change.

Point to cards and say the new sentence. Then ask, pointing to each word:

Does this word change?

If it does, let the student erase it and you write the new word. When the sentence is done, let the student use Baby Echo and point to words while everyone reads the new sentence.

Next select another student who has a pet. Say the sentence, such as:

Mike has a pet hamster.

Have the student erase the words to be changed with your guidance.

 Storytime

Teacher Materials

- Echo the Owl
- 4 Sheets of Large Chart Paper

ECHO FINDS DINNER

This week you will say and act out the same story, "Echo Finds Dinner." Then, as the students re-tell the story, you will illustrate the story with four simple pictures. Leave space at the bottom of each page. You will need this space next week to write the words of the story. Keep these illustrations for next week's lesson. Remember that these illustrations can be simple. Do not worry about your artistic ability.

Perform the Story

Tell and act out "Echo Finds Dinner." (See Week 1, Day 5).

Draw the Story

Next have children re-tell it to you as you draw it on chart paper. To assist them in re-telling the story, ask:

Who was in the story? Where did the story begin?

1. Draw Echo on a branch.

What was Echo's problem?

2. Draw Echo looking down.

What did she do to solve the problem?

3. Draw Echo flying.

How did it end?

4. Draw Echo smiling or rubbing stomach.

After the pictures are drawn, model re-telling the story. It is very important to do this in your own words. Then select a student to come tell the story, pointing to the pictures. (You can have several students do this or have them do it at another time during the day or throughout the week.)

Week 4

DAY ❶	DAY ❷	DAY ❸	DAY ❹	DAY ❺
Letter-Keyword-Sound	Drill Sounds	Drill Sounds	Drill Sounds	Drill Sounds
Drill Sounds	Sky Write/Letter Formation	Make it Fun	Word Play	Storytime
Sky Write/Letter Formation	Student Notebook	Echo/Find Letters	Sky Write/Letter Formation	Echo/Find Letters
Student Notebook	Echo/Find Letters		Echo/Letter Formation	

 Letter-Keyword-Sound

Introduce Letter-Keyword-Sound with Large and Standard Sound Cards.

These letters are plane line letters.

Note

As a new letter is taught, its Standard Sound Card is added to your card display to be drilled at each lesson.

 Drill Sounds

Do All The Introduced Sounds Each Day

Practice sounds with the Large Sound Cards. Say the letter-keyword-sound and have the students echo.

Next, point to the Standard Sound Cards (in card display) with the Baby Echo pointer. You say the letter-keyword-sound and hold up Baby Echo to have the students repeat.

 Sky Write/Letter Formation

Letter Formation for *i*

Use the following verbalization to direct students in proper letter formation.

Say

i is a plane line letter.

It starts on the (plane line).

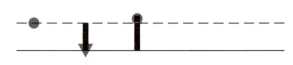

1. Point to the plane line.

2. Go down to the grass line.

3. Add a dot.

Letter Formation for *r*

Use the following verbalization to direct students in proper letter formation.

Say

r is a plane line letter.

It starts on the (plane line).

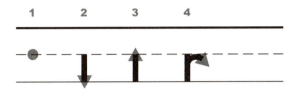

1   2   3   4

1. **Point to the plane line.**

2. **Go down to the grass line.**

3. **Trace back up to the plane line,**

4. **and make a little curve.**

 Student Notebook

DAY ❶

Direct the students to find the newly intro-duced letters.

Use the verbalization for the letter formation to direct the students while they trace it with their finger. Do it with them to model. After you do this, the students can then color the Keyword Picture.

DAY ❷

Trace and say the letter-keyword-sound for the previous letters introduced.

 Echo/Letter Formation

Remind students of proper pencil grip and sit-ting position, and give them their Dry Erase Writing Tablets.

Sounds appear between //. Dictate new sounds and a selection of previously taught sounds. You select and say the sound. Students echo the sound and say the letter.

Next have a student come up to the classroom board to make the letter on the Writing Grid.

Then have all students write the answer on their Dry Erase Writing Tablets as you direct them with the letter formation verbalization.

Sounds

/t/ - t	/b/ - b	/f/ - f
/n/ - n	/m/ - m	/k/ - c
/ă/ - a	/ĭ/ - i	/r/ - r

 Make It Fun

Collect objects that start with the letters taught so far. Put them in a big shopping bag. Call on a student to pick something out of the bag. Ask what it is (truck) and then have the student find the letter which starts the word (t).

They should then say the letter-keyword-sound. Hold up Echo to have the other stu-dents repeat.

 Echo/Find Letters

Students match Magnetic Letter Tiles to the Alphabet Overlay on their Letter Boards. Start with tiles off the board. Dictate sounds. Stu-dents echo sound and match the tiles. Include previous sounds and new sounds.

 **Word Play**

Teacher Materials
- Blue Sentence Frames
- Baby Echo

WORD AWARENESS

Again this week, students will help you erase the words for you to then write the replacement words.

Write the sentence:

Call on someone in the class and orally change the sentence, using that student's name. Change the name and gender as appropriate.

Have that student be your helper to erase the word(s) that need to change. Have the student erase the words to be changed with your guidance.

 Storytime

Teacher Materials
- Baby Echo (on a pointer or ruler)
- Echo Story Illustrations on Large Chart Paper

ECHO FINDS DINNER

This week, use your pictures on the chart paper for "Echo Finds Dinner." Have the students re-tell the story. Write the words of the story to correspond with each picture.

Use the Baby Echo pointer to read the story one sentence at a time and have the students echo. Be sure to scoop and read sentences in phrases. (Choral read with them again while they echo.)

1. **One day Echo was deep in the forest. She sat on a branch of a very tall tree.**

2. **Echo had a problem. She was very hungry!**

3. **Echo had to find food so she searched and searched, looking all around the forest.**

4. **Echo saw something move! It was a mouse. Echo was fast. She flew down and scooped it up. Echo ate the mouse and was happy.**

Note

Be sure to write it so that you can scoop phrases. Use a different color marker to scoop the sentence into phrases.

Example

One day Echo was deep in the forest.

Week 5

DAY ❶	DAY ❷	DAY ❸	DAY ❹	DAY ❺
Letter-Keyword-Sound	Drill Sounds	Drill Sounds	Drill Sounds	Drill Sounds
Drill Sounds	Sky Write/Letter Formation	Make it Fun	Word Play	Storytime
Sky Write/Letter Formation	Student Notebook	Echo/Find Letters	Sky Write/Letter Formation	Echo/Find Letters
Student Notebook	Echo/Find Letters		Echo/Letter Formation	

 ### Letter-Keyword-Sound

Introduce Letter-Keyword-Sound with Large and Standard Sound Cards.

These letters are plane line round letters. Show students that the letter **g** also looks different on the Standard Sound Card, similar to the way it looks in books.

Note

As a new letter is taught, its Standard Sound Card is added to your card display to be drilled at each lesson.

 ### Drill Sounds

Do All The Introduced Sounds Each Day

Practice sounds with the Large Sound Cards. Say the letter-keyword-sound and have the students echo.

Next, point to the Standard Sound Cards (in card display) with the Baby Echo pointer. You say the letter-keyword-sound and hold up Baby Echo to have the students repeat.

 ### Sky Write/Letter Formation

Letter Formation for **O**

Use the following verbalization to direct students in proper letter formation.

Say

o is a plane line round letter.

It starts on the (plane line) just like a c.

1. Point to the plane line.

2. Trace back, then down to the grass line,

3. and around back up to the plane line.

Letter Formation for **g**

Use the following verbalization to direct students in proper letter formation.

Say

g is a plane line round letter.

It starts on the (plane line) just like a c.

1 2 3 4

1. **Point to the plane line.**

2. **Trace back on the plane line,**

3. **down and around all the way back to the plane line.**

4. **Trace back down all the way to the worm line and make a curve.**

 Student Notebook

DAY ❶

Direct the students to find the newly introduced letters.

Use the verbalization for the letter formation to direct the students while they trace it with their finger. Do it with them to model. After you do this, the students can then color the Keyword Picture.

DAY ❷

Trace and say the letter-keyword-sound for the previous letters introduced.

 Echo/Letter Formation

Remind students of proper pencil grip and sitting position, and give them their Dry Erase Writing Tablets.

Sounds appear between //. Dictate new sounds and a selection of previously taught sounds. You select and say the sound. Students echo the sound and say the letter.

Next have a student come up to the classroom board to make the letter on the Writing Grid.

Then have all students write the answer on their Dry Erase Writing Tablets as you direct them with the letter formation verbalization.

Sounds

/t/ - t	/b/ - b	/f/ - f
/n/ - n	/m/ - m	/k/ - c
/ă/ - a	/ĭ/ - i	/r/ - r
/ŏ/ - o	/g/ - g	

 Make It Fun

Pass out the Standard Sound Cards. Have one student at a time come up and hold up their card and say the letter-keyword-sound.

You hold up Echo so the other students repeat. Select a student by saying:

Who is holding the card that says /t/?

Echo/Find Letters

Students match Magnetic Letter Tiles to the Alphabet Overlay on their Letter Boards. Start with tiles off the board. Dictate sounds. Students echo sound and match the tiles. Include previous sounds and new sounds.

 **Word Play**

Teacher Materials

- Blue Sentence Frames
- Baby Echo

WORD AWARENESS

Use the following idea for a sentence:

Erase the sentence.

Ask

Who else has a bike?

Get the other tall word frame in order to write the sentence:

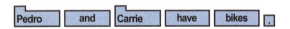

Point to the words with Baby Echo, read the sentence and have the students echo. Explain that a person's name always starts with a capital (upper-case) letter so you need to write it on a tall word frame.

Do several sentences with two names.

Examples

Fernando and Tony have brown hair.

Cathy and Maria have blonde hair.

Each time, ask why you selected the tall frame.

Ask this for both the first word in the sentence and for the student's name. Be sure to echo read each sentence.

 Storytime

Teacher Materials

- Echo the Owl (on the floor behind you)
- Baby Echo

Read through and practice the story prior to the lesson with your students.

BABY ECHO FINDS ECHO AT LAST

Perform the Story

One day Baby Echo was looking for his mother.

Put Echo on the floor behind you. Put Baby Echo on your finger and stretch out your other arm. 'Sit' Baby Echo up at your shoulder of your outstretched arm.

He looked and looked but he couldn't see her.

Bend him to look down at the floor.

So he hopped over to the middle of the big branch.

Hop Baby Echo to your elbow.

He looked and looked there, but he still couldn't see her.

Bend him to look at the floor.

So he hopped over to the very edge of the big long branch.

Hop him down to your fingertips.

He looked and looked there, but he still couldn't see her.

Bend him down to the floor.

He sat up and thought, "Where is my mother?"

Face him up.

Just then he heard a noise behind him. He turned around and looked down.

Turn Baby Echo around and look down.

Baby Echo saw his mother. At last he was happy.

Ask the Following Questions

Who was in this story?

Where did it take place?

What was Baby Echo's problem?

What did he do about it?

How did things turn out? What happened in the end?

How did Baby Echo feel at the beginning of the story?

How did Baby Echo feel at the end of the story?

Week 6

DAY ❶	DAY ❷	DAY ❸	DAY ❹	DAY ❺
Letter-Keyword-Sound	Drill Sounds	Drill Sounds	Drill Sounds	Drill Sounds
Drill Sounds	Sky Write/Letter Formation	Make it Fun	Word Play	Storytime
Sky Write/Letter Formation	Student Notebook	Echo/Find Letters	Sky Write/Letter Formation	Echo/Find Letters
Student Notebook	Echo/Find Letters		Echo/Letter Formation	

Letter-Keyword-Sound

Introduce Letter-Keyword-Sound with Large and Standard Sound Cards.

These letters are plane line round letters.

Note

As a new letter is taught, its Standard Sound Card is added to your card display to be drilled at each lesson.

Drill Sounds

Do All The Introduced Sounds Each Day

Practice sounds with the Large Sound Cards. Say the letter-keyword-sound and have the students echo.

Next, point to the Standard Sound Cards (in card display) with the Baby Echo pointer. You say the letter-keyword-sound and hold up Baby Echo to have the students repeat.

Sky Write/Letter Formation

Letter Formation for d

Use the following verbalization to direct students in proper letter formation.

Say

d is a plane line round letter.

It starts on the (plane line) **just like a c.**

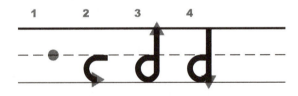

1. **Point to the plane line.**
2. **Go back, down and around to the grass line,**
3. **all the way back up to the sky line.**
4. **Trace back down to the grass line.**

Letter Formation for s

Use the following verbalization to direct students in proper letter formation.

Say

s is a plane line round letter.

It starts on the (plane line) **just like a c.**

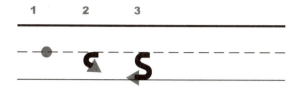

1. **Point to the plane line.**

2. **Trace back and it curves in,**

3. **and goes back again and lands on the grass.**

 Student Notebook

DAY ❶

Direct the students to find the newly introduced letters.

Use the verbalization for the letter formation to direct the students while they trace it with their finger. Do it with them to model. After you do this, the students can then color the Keyword Picture.

DAY ❷

Trace and say the letter-keyword-sound for the previous letters introduced.

 Echo/Letter Formation

Remind students of proper pencil grip and sitting position, and give them their Dry Erase Writing Tablets.

Sounds appear between //. Dictate new sounds and a selection of previously taught sounds. You select and say the sound. Students echo the sound and say the letter.

Next have a student come up to the classroom board to make the letter on the Writing Grid.

Then have all students write the answer on their Dry Erase Writing Tablets as you direct them with the letter formation verbalization.

Sounds

/t/ - t	/b/ - b	/f/ - f
/n/ - n	/m/ - m	/k/ - c
/ă/ - a	/ĭ/ - i	/r/ - r
/ŏ/ - o	/g/ - g	**/d/ - d**
/s/ - s		

 Make It Fun

Student Materials

• Keyword Puzzle

Use the puzzle pieces for the letters taught thus far. Pass out the letters (one per child) and the pictures (one per child) until they are all disseminated. Then direct the students:

Stand up if you have the letter b. Stand up if you have the picture that goes with b.

Make a match!

Have the children come up front and put the cards together, then have everyone say the letter-keyword-sound.

b-bat-/b/

 Echo/Find Letters

Students match Magnetic Letter Tiles to the Alphabet Overlay on their Letter Boards. Start with tiles off the board. Dictate sounds. Students echo sound and match the tiles. Include previous sounds and new sounds.

 **Word Play**

Teacher Materials

- Blue Sentence Frames
- Baby Echo

WORD AWARENESS

Reinforce the capitalization of names, following the same procedures from Week 5.

Write sentences with two names.

Examples:

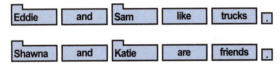

Each time, ask why you selected the tall frames. Ask this for both the first word in the sentence and for the student's name. Be sure to echo read each sentence.

 **Storytime**

Teacher Materials

- Echo the Owl (on the floor behind you)
- Baby Echo

BABY ECHO FINDS ECHO AT LAST

This week you will say and act out the same story, "Baby Echo Finds Echo At Last." Then you will perform it again, without words, and have the children re-tell the story as you "play it out."

Re-perform the Story

Tell and act out "Baby Echo Finds Echo At Last." (See Week 5, Day 5).

Perform the Story Without Words

Perform the story again, without words, and have children tell you what happened.

After a student tells you in his/her own words, restate the words from the story to clarify as needed.

Be sure to provide students positive feedback for re-telling in their own words.

Put Echo on the floor behind you. Put Baby Echo on your finger and stretch out your other arm. 'Sit' Baby Echo up at your shoulder of your out-stretched arm.

One day Baby Echo was looking for his mother.

Bend him to look down at the floor.

He looked and looked but he couldn't see her.

Hop Baby Echo to your elbow.

So he hopped over to the middle of the big branch.

Bend him to look at the floor.

He looked and looked there, but he still couldn't see her.

Hop him down to your fingertips.

So he hopped over to the very edge of the big long branch.

Bend him down to the floor.

He looked and looked there, but he still couldn't see her.

He sat up and thought, "Where is my mother?"

Face him up.

Just then he heard a noise behind him. He turned around and looked down.

Turn Baby Echo around and look down.

Baby Echo saw his mother. At last he was happy.

Week 7

DAY ❶	DAY ❷	DAY ❸	DAY ❹	DAY ❺
Letter-Keyword-Sound	Drill Sounds	Drill Sounds	Drill Sounds	Drill Sounds
Drill Sounds	Sky Write/Letter Formation	Make it Fun	Word Play	Storytime
Sky Write/Letter Formation	Student Notebook	Echo/Find Letters	Sky Write/Letter Formation	Echo/Find Letters
Student Notebook	Echo/Find Letters		Echo/Letter Formation	

 ### Letter-Keyword-Sound

Introduce Letter-Keyword-Sound with Large and Standard Sound Cards.

These letters are the last two vowels. The letter **e** is a plane line round letter that is different because it starts between the plane line and the grass line. The letter **u** is a plane line letter. Do the Vowel Extension activity with all the vowels.

Note

As a new letter is taught, its Standard Sound Card is added to your card display to be drilled at each lesson.

 ### Vowel Extension

Use the Keyword Pictures (see Appendix) to make a Vowel Extension activity on chart paper on your classroom board.

Vowels are open-mouth sounds and therefore they can be held. This activity helps the students extend the vowel sound. Model 'reading' the Keyword Picture: /ă/...**pple**. Extend the /ă/ sound while you trace the line and finish the

word when you get to the picture.

Have a student come trace the line while everyone extends the /ă/ sound.

 ### Drill Sounds

Do All The Introduced Sounds Each Day

Practice sounds with the Large Sound Cards. Say the letter-keyword-sound and have the students echo.

Next, point to the Standard Sound Cards (in card display) with the Baby Echo pointer. You say the letter-keyword-sound and hold up Baby Echo to have the students repeat.

Sky Write/Letter Formation

Letter Formation for **e**

Use the following verbalization to direct students in proper letter formation.

Say

e is a plane line round letter, but it is special.

e starts below the plane line.

1. **Point between the plane line and the grass line.**

2. **Fly under the plane line.**

3. **Then go up to the plane line,**

4. **and around to the grass.**

Letter Formation for **u**

Use the following verbalization to direct students in proper letter formation.

Say

u is a plane line round letter.

It starts on the (plane line).

1. **Point to the plane line.**

2. **Go down to the grass line.**

3. **Curve up to the plane line,**

4. **and trace straight down to the grass line.**

 Student Notebook

DAY ❶

Direct the students to find the newly introduced letters.

Use the verbalization for the letter formation to direct the students while they trace it with their finger. Do it with them to model. After you do this, the students can then color the Keyword Picture.

DAY ❷

Trace and say the letter-keyword-sound for the previous letters introduced.

 Echo/Letter Formation

Remind students of proper pencil grip and sitting position, and give them their Dry Erase Writing Tablets.

Sounds appear between //. Dictate new sounds and a selection of previously taught sounds. You select and say the sound. Students echo the sound and say the letter.

Next have a student come up to the classroom board to make the letter on the Writing Grid.

Then have all students write the answer on their Dry Erase Writing Tablets as you direct them with the letter formation verbalization.

Sounds

/t/ - t	/b/ - b	/f/ - f
/n/ - n	/m/ - m	/k/ - c
/ă/ - a	/ĭ/ - i	/r/ - r
/ŏ/ - o	/g/ - g	/d/ - d
/s/ - s	/ĕ/ - e	/ŭ/ - u

Make It Fun

Teacher Materials

- Standard Sound Cards
- Baby Echo (on a pointer or ruler)

Call a student to the front of the room. Have the student close his (her) eyes and point to a letter with the Baby Echo pointer. Then have the student open eyes and see the selected letter.

Ask

> **What is the name of the letter?**
>
> **What is the sound of the letter?**
>
> **Name three words that start with /__/.**

Other students can help. Then allow the student to select the next student to come up and do the same.

Echo/Find Letters

Students match Magnetic Letter Tiles to the Alphabet Overlay on their Letter Boards. Start with tiles off the board. Dictate sounds. Students echo sound and match the tiles. Include previous sounds and new sounds.

Word Play

Teacher Materials

- Blue Sentence Frames
- Baby Echo

WORD AWARENESS

During word play, you will further develop the students' word awareness by adding a new step.

The students will now have to get you the frames needed so that you can write the sentence.

Display Sentence Frames in a Column

Display the word frames and period frame in a column rather than across the board. Tell the students that you are going to have them help you get the pieces you need to write your sentence.

Demonstrate

Say a sentence orally such as:

> **Maria is here today.**

Tell them that you need the high-cut frame first because every sentence must start with a capital letter.

Say the words as you place the frames. Then tell them that at the end you need to put a period because all sentences today end with a period because they tell something.

Write the words on the frames and read it again, pointing to each word.

Erase and put the frames back in a column and ask for a student volunteer. Give them the same sentence, but replace "Maria" with the student's name.

Ask them to put the pieces in order for you to write the sentence. Remind them,

> **Don't forget which one you need to begin the sentence.**

Say the sentence with them as they place the pieces. Be sure they add the period.

> **Let's see if Wanda** (the student's name) **is correct.**

Write the sentence and ask the students,

Did Wanda get all the pieces I needed?

Do several sentences. Each time, erase frames and put them in a column for students to select from.

Note

This is demonstrated in the CD-ROM: Level K, Lesson Activities, Word Play, Advanced.

 Storytime

Teacher Materials

- Echo the Owl
- 4 Sheets of Large Chart Paper

BABY ECHO FINDS ECHO AT LAST

This week you will say and act out the same story, "Baby Echo Finds Echo At Last." Then, as the students re-tell the story, you will illustrate the story with four simple pictures. Leave space at the bottom of each page. You will need this space next week to write the words of the story. Keep these illustrations for next week's lesson. Remember that these illustrations can be simple. Do not worry about your artistic ability.

Perform the Story

Tell and act out "Baby Echo Finds Echo At Last." (See Week 6, Day 5).

Draw the Story

Next have children re-tell it to you as you draw it on chart paper. To assist them in re-telling the story, ask:

Who was in the story? Where did the story begin? What was Echo's problem?

1. Draw Baby Echo at one end of the branch. Draw Echo on the ground.

What did she do about it next?

2. Draw Baby Echo in the middle of the branch looking down.

Then what did he do?

3. Draw Baby Echo at the other end of the branch, looking down.

How did it end?

4. Draw Baby Echo looking at Echo with a smile.

After the pictures are drawn, model re-telling the story. It is very important to do this in your own words. Then select a student to come tell the story, pointing to the pictures. (You can have several students do this or have them do it at another time during the day or throughout the week.)

Week 8

DAY ❶	DAY ❷	DAY ❸	DAY ❹	DAY ❺
Letter-Keyword-Sound	Drill Sounds	Drill Sounds	Drill Sounds	Drill Sounds
Drill Sounds	Sky Write/Letter Formation	Make it Fun	Word Play	Storytime
Sky Write/Letter Formation	Student Notebook	Echo/Find Letters	Sky Write/Letter Formation	Echo/Find Letters
Student Notebook	Echo/Find Letters		Echo/Letter Formation	

 Letter-Keyword-Sound

Introduce Letter-Keyword-Sound with Large and Standard Sound Cards.

These letters are sky line letters.

Note

As a new letter is taught, its Standard Sound Card is added to your card display to be drilled at each lesson.

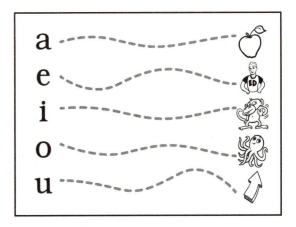

 Vowel Extension

Model 'reading' the Keyword Picture: /ă/... **pple**. Extend the /ă/ sound while you trace the line and finish the word when you get to the picture.

Have a student come trace the line while everyone extends the /ă/ sound.

 Drill Sounds

Do All The Introduced Sounds Each Day

Practice sounds with the Large Sound Cards. Say the letter-keyword-sound and have the students echo.

Select Some Sounds

Next, point to the Standard Sound Cards (in card display) with the Baby Echo pointer. You say the letter-keyword-sound and hold up Baby Echo to have the students repeat.

Sky Write/Letter Formation

Letter Formation for **l**

Use the following verbalization to direct students in proper letter formation.

Say

l is a sky line letter.

It starts on the (sky line).

1. Point to the sky line.

2. Go down to the grass and stop.

Letter Formation for **h**

Use the following verbalization to direct students in proper letter formation.

Say

h is a sky line letter.

It starts on the (sky line).

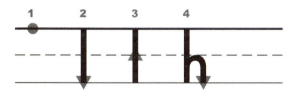

1. Point to the sky line.

2. Go down to the grass line.

3. Trace back up to the plane line,

4. and make a hump.

Letter Formation for **k**

Use the following verbalization to direct students in proper letter formation.

Say

k is a sky line letter.

It starts on the (sky line).

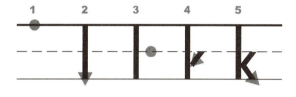

1. Point to the sky line.

2. Go all the way down to the grass line.

3. Point to the plane line and leave a space.

4. Slide over and touch your tall line,

5. and slide back to the grass line.

 Student Notebook

DAY ❶

Direct the students to find the newly introduced letters.

Use the verbalization for the letter formation to direct the students while they trace it with their finger. Do it with them to model. After you do this, the students can then color the Keyword Picture.

DAY ❷

Trace and say the letter-keyword-sound for the previous letters introduced.

Echo/Letter Formation

Remind students of proper pencil grip and sitting position, and give them their Dry Erase Writing Tablets.

Sounds appear between //. Dictate new sounds and a selection of previously taught sounds. You select and say the sound. Students echo the sound and say the letter.

Next have a student come up to the classroom board to make the letter on the Writing Grid.

Then have all students write the answer on their Dry Erase Writing Tablets as you direct them with the letter formation verbalization.

Sounds

/t/ - t	/b/ - b	/f/ - f
/n/ - n	/m/ - m	/k/ - c
/ă/ - a	/ĭ/ - i	/r/ - r
/ŏ/ - o	/g/ - g	/d/ - d
/s/ - s	/ĕ/ - e	/ŭ/ - u
/l/ - l	/h/ - h	/k/ - k

 Make It Fun

Teacher Materials

• Wilson Writing Grid (on the board at least 2 feet tall)

Have a student come up to the front of the room. Whisper a letter name to him/her. Next have the student form the letter with their finger (not write it) on the Writing Grid. (Do this on the overhead screen if possible or on the class room board).

The other students need to watch and decide which letter was formed. When they guess,

they should say the letter-keyword sound (h-hat-/h/,etc). Whoever guesses correctly gets to do the next one.

 Echo/Find Letters

Students match Magnetic Letter Tiles to the Alphabet Overlay on their Letter Boards. Start with tiles off the board. Dictate sounds. Students echo sound and match the tiles. Include previous sounds and new sounds.

 Word Play

Teacher Materials

• Blue Sentence Frames
• Baby Echo

WORD AWARENESS

During word play, you will further develop the students' word awareness by adding a new step.

Again this week, have the students get you the frames needed so that you can write out the sentence. (See Week 7).

Display Sentence Frames in a Column

Display the word frames and period frame in a column rather than across the board. Tell the students that you are going to have them help you get the pieces you need to write your sentence.

Do Several Sentences

Ask a student to put the pieces in order for you to write the sentence. Say the sentence with them as they place the pieces. Be sure the student adds the period.

Write the sentence (saying each word as you write it). Next, have the student use Baby Echo to read the sentence. Have the other students echo.

Each time, erase frames and put them in a column for another student to select. Include some sentences with two names so that the student will need to get two tall frames in constructing the sentence.

 Storytime

Teacher Materials

- Baby Echo (on a pointer or ruler)
- Echo Story Illustrations on Large Chart Paper

BABY ECHO FINDS ECHO AT LAST

This week, use your pictures on the chart paper for "Baby Echo Finds Echo At Last." Have the students re-tell the story. Write the words of the story to correspond with each picture.

Use the Baby Echo pointer to read the story one sentence at a time and have the students echo. Be sure to scoop and read sentences in phrases. (Choral read with them again while they echo.)

1. One day Baby Echo was looking for his mother. He looked and looked but he couldn't see her.

2. So he hopped over to the middle of the big branch. He looked and looked there, but he still couldn't see her.

3. So he hopped over to the very edge of the big long branch. He looked and looked there, but he still couldn't see her. He sat up and thought, "Where is my mother?".

4. Just then he heard a noise behind him. He turned around and looked down. Baby Echo saw his mother. At last he was happy.

Note

Be sure to write it so that you can scoop phrases. Use a different color marker to scoop the sentence into phrases.

Example

One day Baby Echo was looking for his mother.

Week 9

DAY ❶	DAY ❷	DAY ❸	DAY ❹	DAY ❺
Letter-Keyword-Sound	Drill Sounds	Drill Sounds	Drill Sounds	Drill Sounds
Drill Sounds	Sky Write/Letter Formation	Make it Fun	Word Play	Storytime
Sky Write/Letter Formation	Student Notebook	Echo/Find Letters	Sky Write/Letter Formation	Echo/Find Letters
Student Notebook	Echo/Find Letters		Echo/Letter Formation	

 Letter-Keyword-Sound

Introduce Letter-Keyword-Sound with Large and Standard Sound Cards.

These letters are plane line letters that go all the way down to the worm line.

Note

As a new letter is taught, its Standard Sound Card is added to your card display to be drilled at each lesson.

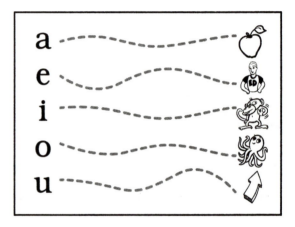

 Vowel Extension

Model 'reading' the Keyword Picture: /ă/... **pple**. Extend the /ă/ sound while you trace the line and finish the word when you get to the picture.

Have a student come trace the line while everyone extends the /ă/ sound.

 **Drill Sounds**

Do All The Introduced Sounds Each Day

Practice sounds with the Large Sound Cards. Say the letter-keyword-sound and have the students echo.

Select Some Sounds

Next, point to the Standard Sound Cards (in card display) with the Baby Echo pointer. You say the letter-keyword-sound and hold up Baby Echo to have the students repeat.

Sky Write/Letter Formation

Letter Formation for p

Use the following verbalization to direct students in proper letter formation.

Say

> p is a plane line round letter.
>
> It starts on the (plane line).

1. Point to the plane line.

2. Go down to the worm line.

3. Trace back up to the plane line,

4. and curve all the way around to the grass line.

Letter Formation for j

Use the following verbalization to direct students in proper letter formation.

Say

> j is a plane line letter.
>
> It starts on the (plane line).

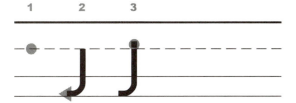

1. Point to the plane line.

2. Go all the way down to the worm line, and make a curve.

3. Add a dot.

 Student Notebook

DAY ❶

Direct the students to find the newly introduced letters.

Use the verbalization for the letter formation to direct the students while they trace it with their finger. Do it with them to model. After you do this, the students can then color the Keyword Picture.

DAY ❷

Trace and say the letter-keyword-sound for the previous letters introduced.

 Echo/Letter Formation

Remind students of proper pencil grip and sitting position, and give them their Dry Erase Writing Tablets.

Sounds appear between //. Dictate new sounds and a selection of previously taught sounds. You select and say the sound. Students echo the sound and say the letter.

Next have a student come up to the classroom board to make the letter on the Writing Grid.

Then have all students write the answer on their Dry Erase Writing Tablets as you direct them with the letter formation verbalization.

Sounds

/t/ - t	/b/ - b	/f/ - f
/n/ - n	/m/ - m	/k/ - c
/ă/ - a	/ĭ/ - i	/r/ - r

/ŏ/ - o	/g/ - g	/d/ - d
/s/ - s	/ĕ/ - e	/ŭ/ - u
/l/ - l	/h/ - h	/k/ - k
/p/ - p	**/j/ - j**	

 Make It Fun

Teacher Materials

• Standard Sound Cards
• Echo the Owl

Ask the students to listen to the end of a word. Emphasize the last sound when you say the word. For example, with **/p/** emphasized, say:

map

Select a student to come get the Standard Sound Card that *ends* with the last sound in the word. If they select the correct letter, have them take it and sit down. If they select the wrong letter, say:

map

/p/ ends the word map.

Find me the letter that says /p/.

Help them locate the correct letter.

Do several words. Then have the students with cards give their card to a student without a card. Say other words and have the students return cards with the correct final sound.

 Echo/Find Letters

Students match Magnetic Letter Tiles to the Alphabet Overlay on their Letter Boards. Start with tiles off the board. Dictate sounds. Students echo sound and match the tiles. Include previous sounds and new sounds.

 Word Play

Teacher Materials

• Blue Sentence Frames
• Baby Echo

WORD AWARENESS

Say

I'm going to ask you a question.

Does Tyler have a bike?

Write the sentence on the word frames. Show the students how to write a question mark. Make one on the tall blue punctuation frame and add it to the sentence.

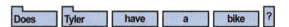

Explain that the question mark shows that this is a question. It asks something. Model reading this (be sure to raise your voice for a question). Have students echo.

The period is used when we tell something.

The question mark is used when we ask something.

Read and have students echo. Make other question sentences.

Examples

What is your name?

What is your favorite color?

Each time, read with proper expression, emphasizing the question with your voice. Have students echo, pointing to the words. Erase the frames, and write an answer to the question. Have students echo read the answer and discuss the period.

 **Storytime**

Teacher Materials

- Echo the Owl and Baby Echo

Read through and practice the story prior to the lesson with your students.

BABY ECHO FLIES

Perform the Story

Baby Echo sat on a branch snuggled in the shelter of his mother's wings.

Put Baby Echo on your finger and tuck him into Echo's wings.

It was warm and safe there. Baby Echo was happy. Then Echo looked down at Baby Echo and said, "It is time for you to fly."

Move Echo's head to look at Baby Echo.

Baby Echo snuggled closer to his mother and said, "But I don't know how to fly!"

Move Baby Echo closer to Echo.

Echo said, "Watch me, I will teach you," and she flapped her wings.

Fly Echo to the floor.

Baby Echo was brave. He followed his mother and landed next to her.

Fly Baby Echo to the floor.

"I did it!" cried Baby Echo. "Yes you did and I am proud," said Echo. "Hooray for you."

Ask the Following Questions

Who was in this story?

Where did it take place?

What was Baby Echo's problem?

What did he do about it?

How did things turn out? What happened in the end?

How did Baby Echo feel at the beginning of the story?

How did Baby Echo feel at the end of the story?

Week 10

DAY ❶	DAY ❷	DAY ❸	DAY ❹	DAY ❺
Letter-Keyword-Sound	Drill Sounds	Drill Sounds	Drill Sounds	Drill Sounds
Drill Sounds	Sky Write/Letter Formation	Make it Fun	Word Play	Storytime
Sky Write/Letter Formation	Student Notebook	Echo/Find Letters	Sky Write/Letter Formation	Echo/Find Letters
Student Notebook	Echo/Find Letters		Echo/Letter Formation	

 Letter-Keyword-Sound

Introduce Letter-Keyword-Sound with Large and Standard Sound Cards.

These letters are plane line slide letters.

Note

As a new letter is taught, its Standard Sound Card is added to your card display to be drilled at each lesson.

 Vowel Extension

Model 'reading' the Keyword Picture: /ă/...**pple**. Extend the /ă/ sound while you trace the line and finish the word when you get to the picture.

Have a student come trace the line while everyone extends the /ă/ sound.

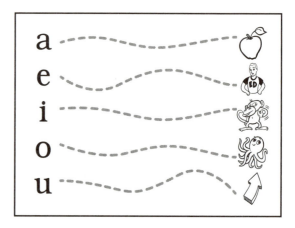

 **Drill Sounds**

Do All The Introduced Sounds Each Day

Practice sounds with the Large Sound Cards. Say the letter-keyword-sound and have the students echo.

Select Some Sounds

Next, point to the Standard Sound Cards (in card display) with the Baby Echo pointer. You say the letter-keyword-sound and hold up Baby Echo to have the students repeat.

Sky Write/Letter Formation

Letter Formation for V

Use the following verbalization to direct students in proper letter formation.

Say

v is a plane line slide letter.

It starts on the (plane line) **and** (slides).

1. **Point to the plane line.**
2. **Slide down to the grass line.**
3. **Slide up to the plane line.**

Letter Formation for W

Use the following verbalization to direct students in proper letter formation.

Say

w is a plane line slide letter.

It starts on the (plane line) **and** (slides).

1. **Point to the plane line.**
2. **Slide down to the grass line.**
3. **Slide up to the plane line.**
4. **Slide down to the grass line.**
5. **Slide up to the plane line.**

 Student Notebook

DAY ❶

Direct the students to find the newly introduced letters.

Use the verbalization for the letter formation to direct the students while they trace it with their finger. Do it with them to model. After you do this, the students can then color the Keyword Picture.

DAY ❷

Trace and say the letter-keyword-sound for the previous letters introduced.

 Echo/Letter Formation

Remind students of proper pencil grip and sitting position, and give them their Dry Erase Writing Tablets.

Sounds appear between //. Dictate new sounds and a selection of previously taught sounds. You select and say the sound. Students echo the sound and say the letter.

Next have a student come up to the classroom board to make the letter on the Writing Grid.

Then have all students write the answer on their Dry Erase Writing Tablets as you direct them with the letter formation verbalization.

Sounds

/t/ - t	/b/ - b	/f/ - f
/n/ - n	/m/ - m	/k/ - c
/ă/ - a	/ĭ/ - i	/r/ - r
/ŏ/ - o	/g/ - g	/d/ - d
/s/ - s	/ĕ/ - e	/ŭ/ - u

/l/ - l /h/ - h /k/ - k

/p/ - p /j/ - j /v/ - v

/w/ - w

Make It Fun

Collect objects that *end* with the letters taught so far. Put them in a big shopping bag. Call on a student to pick something out of the bag. Ask what it is (**pen**) and then have the student find the letter which *ends* the word (**n**).

Echo/Find Letters

Students match Magnetic Letter Tiles to the Alphabet Overlay on their Letter Boards. Start with tiles off the board. Dictate sounds. Students echo sound and match the tiles. Include previous sounds and new sounds.

Word Play

Teacher Materials

- Blue Sentence Frames
- Baby Echo

WORD AWARENESS

The students will again get you the frames needed so that you can write the sentence. Now they will need to get the question mark to complete asking sentences.

Display Sentence Frames in a Column

Display the word and punctuation frames in a column rather than across the board. Tell the students that you are going to have them help you get the pieces you need to write your sentence.

Demonstrate

Ask

Is it hot today?

Tell students that you need the high-cut frame first because every sentence must start with a capital letter. Say the words as you place the frames. Then tell them that at the end, you need to put a question mark, because it asks a question.

Write the words on the frames and read it again, pointing to each word, be sure to raise your voice in a question and be dramatic (for example, put your finger on the side of your face in a questioning look). Have students echo.

Erase and put the frames back in a column and ask for a student volunteer. Give them a sentence.

Do you like candy?

Select a student to put the frames in order for you to write the sentence. Remind the student:

Think about what you need at the end of your sentence.

Say the sentence with them as they place the pieces. Be sure they add the question mark.

Write the sentence and ask the students if the frames are correctly placed.

Erase the frames and return them to the column. Dictate other questions, emphasizing the question with your voice:

Examples

Is Jimmy here today?

Where is Juan?

Can we eat lunch?

 Storytime

Teacher Materials

• Echo the Owl and Baby Echo

BABY ECHO FLIES

This week you will say and act out the same story, "Baby Echo Flies." Then you will perform it again, without words, and have the children re-tell the story as you "play it out."

Re-perform the Story

Tell and act out "Baby Echo Flies." (See Week 9, Day 5).

Perform the Story Without Words

Perform the story again, without words, and have children tell you what happened.

After a student tells you in his/her own words, restate the words from the story to clarify as needed.

Be sure to provide students positive feedback for re-telling in their own words.

Put Baby Echo on your finger and tuck him into Echo's wings.

Baby Echo sat on a branch snuggled in the shelter of his mother's wings.

Move Echo's head to look at Baby Echo.

It was warm and safe there. Baby Echo was happy. Then Echo looked down at Baby Echo and said, "It is time for you to fly."

Move Baby Echo closer to Echo.

Baby Echo snuggled closer to his mother and said, "But I don't know how to fly!"

Fly Echo to the floor.

Echo said, "Watch me, I will teach you," and she flapped her wings.

Fly Baby Echo to the floor.

Baby Echo was brave. He followed his mother and landed next to her.

"I did it!" cried Baby Echo. "Yes you did and I am proud," said Echo. "Hooray for you."

Week 11

DAY ❶	DAY ❷	DAY ❸	DAY ❹	DAY ❺
Letter-Keyword-Sound	Drill Sounds	Drill Sounds	Drill Sounds	Drill Sounds
Drill Sounds	Sky Write/Letter Formation	Make it Fun	Word Play	Storytime
Sky Write/Letter Formation	Student Notebook	Echo/Find Letters	Sky Write/Letter Formation	Echo/Find Letters
Student Notebook	Echo/Find Letters		Echo/Letter Formation	

 Letter-Keyword-Sound

Introduce Letter-Keyword-Sound with Large and Standard Sound Cards.

The letter **z** is a plane line slide letter. The letter **q** is a plane line round letter. We call it the "chicken letter" because it will never ever go anywhere without his best buddy, **u**. Tell the students that **u** does not count as a vowel when it is with the letter **q**. It just sits there to keep **q** company.

Note

As a new letter is taught, its Standard Sound Card is added to your card display to be drilled at each lesson.

 Vowel Extension

Model 'reading' the Keyword Picture: /ă/... **pple**. Extend the /ă/ sound while you trace the line and finish the word when you get to the picture.

Have a student come trace the line while everyone extends the /ă/ sound.

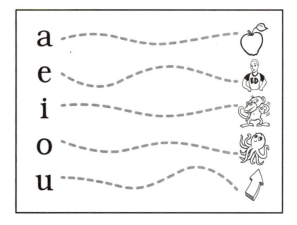

 Drill Sounds

Do All The Introduced Sounds Each Day

Practice sounds with the Large Sound Cards. Say the letter-keyword-sound and have the students echo.

Select Some Sounds

Next, point to the Standard Sound Cards (in card display) with the Baby Echo pointer. You say the letter-keyword-sound and hold up Baby Echo to have the students repeat.

Sky Write/Letter Formation

Letter Formation for **Z**

Use the following verbalization to direct students in proper letter formation.

Say

z is a plane line slide letter, but it doesn't slide right away.

Where does it start? (On the plane line).

Before it slides, the z goes on the plane line.

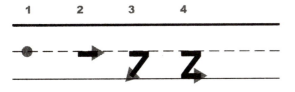

1. Point to the plane line.

2. Go on the plane line.

3. Slide back to the grass line.

4. Then go on the grass line.

Letter Formation for **q**

Use the following verbalization to direct students in proper letter formation.

Say

q is a plane line round letter.

It starts on the (plane line).

Remember that q is the chicken letter so in the end it wants to point up to its buddy, u.

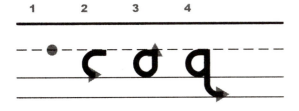

1. Point to the plane line.

2. Trace back and go down to the grass line around, back to the plane line.

3. Trace back down to the worm line,

4. and point up to his "buddy" u.

Student Notebook

DAY ❶

Direct the students to find the newly introduced letters.

Use the verbalization for the letter formation to direct the students while they trace it with their finger. Do it with them to model. After you do this, the students can then color the Keyword Picture.

DAY ❷

Trace and say the letter-keyword-sound for the previous letters introduced.

Echo/Letter Formation

Remind students of proper pencil grip and sitting position, and give them their Dry Erase Writing Tablets.

Sounds appear between //. Dictate new sounds and a selection of previously taught sounds. You select and say the sound. Students echo the sound and say the letter.

Next have a student come up to the classroom board to make the letter on the Writing Grid.

Then have all students write the answer on their Dry Erase Writing Tablets as you direct them with the letter formation verbalization.

Sounds

/t/ - t	/b/ - b	/f/ - f
/n/ - n	/m/ - m	/k/ - c
/ă/ - a	/ĭ/ - i	/r/ - r
/ŏ/ - o	/g/ - g	/d/ - d
/s/ - s	/ĕ/ - e	/ŭ/ - u
/l/ - l	/h/ - h	/k/ - k
/p/ - p	/j/ - j	/v/ - v
/w/ - w	/z/- z	/kw/ - qu

 Make It Fun

Student Materials

• Keyword Puzzle

Use the puzzle pieces for the letters taught thus far. Pass out the letters (one per child) and the pictures (one per child) until they are disseminated. Then direct the students:

Stand up if you have the letter b. Stand up if you have the picture that goes with b.

Make a match!

Have the children come up front and put the cards together, then have everyone say the letter-keyword-sound.

b - bat - /b/

 Echo/Find Letters

Students match Magnetic Letter Tiles to the Alphabet Overlay on their Letter Boards. Start with tiles off the board. Dictate sounds. Students echo sound and match the tiles. Include previous sounds and new sounds.

 Word Play

Teacher Materials

• Blue Sentence Frames
• Baby Echo

WORD AWARENESS

The students will again get you the frames needed so that you can write the sentence. Now they will need to get the question mark or period to complete the sentences. This is just the beginning of understanding. Do not expect the students to easily do this. Provide lots of guidance and cue them by over-emphasizing questions with your voice.

Display Sentence Frames in a Column

Display the word and punctuation frames in a column rather than across the board. Tell the students that you are going to have them help you get the pieces you need to write your sentence.

Demonstrate

Say

Mike and Amanda have freckles.

As you place the frames, discuss your selection. Tell them that you need the tall frame first because every sentence must start with a capital letter. Tell them you need the tall frame for the name because all names begin with a capital letter. Tell them you need a small punctuation frame because this is a sentence which tells us something. It needs a period.

Write the words on the frames and read it again, pointing to each word. Have students echo.

Erase and put the frames back in a column and ask for a student volunteer. Give them a sentence.

Do you like gum?

Ask a student to put the pieces in order for you to write the sentence. Remind the student,

Don't forget which one you need to begin the sentence.

What do you need at the end?

Say the sentence as the student places the frames. Write the sentence and ask the students if the frames are correctly placed.

Echo read the sentence.

Examples

Where is the ball?

Juan has an apple.

Can we watch tv?

 **Storytime**

Teacher Materials

• Echo the Owl and Baby Echo
• 4 Sheets of Large Chart Paper

BABY ECHO FLIES

This week you will say and act out the same story, "Baby Echo Flies." Then, as the students re-tell the story, you will illustrate the story with four simple pictures. Leave space at the bottom of each page. You will need this space next week to write the words of the story. Keep these illustrations for next week's lesson. Remember that these illustrations can be simple. Do not worry about your artistic ability.

Perform the Story

Tell and act out "Baby Echo Flies." (See Week 9, Day 5).

Draw the Story

Next have children re-tell it to you as you draw it on chart paper. To assist them in re-telling the story, ask:

Who was in the story? Where did the story begin?

1. Draw Baby Echo with Echo on a branch. Put a smile on Baby Echo's face.

What did Echo say to Baby Echo? How did Baby Echo feel?

2. Draw Baby Echo with Echo on a branch. Make Baby Echo look frightened.

What happened next?

3. Draw Echo on the ground.

How did it end?

4. Show Baby Echo flying, or draw Echo and Baby Echo on the ground, smiling.

After the pictures are drawn model re-telling the story. It is very important to do this in your own words. Then select a student to come tell the story, pointing to the pictures. (You can have several students do this or have them do it at another time during the day or throughout the week.)

Week 12

DAY ❶	DAY ❷	DAY ❸	DAY ❹	DAY ❺
Letter-Keyword-Sound	Drill Sounds	Drill Sounds	Drill Sounds	Drill Sounds
Drill Sounds	Sky Write/Letter Formation	Make it Fun	Word Play	Storytime
Sky Write/Letter Formation	Student Notebook	Echo/Find Letters	Sky Write/Letter Formation	Echo/Find Letters
Student Notebook	Echo/Find Letters		Echo/Letter Formation	

Letter-Keyword-Sound

Introduce Letter-Keyword-Sound with Large and Standard Sound Cards.

These letters are plane line slide letters.

Note

As a new letter is taught, its Standard Sound Card is added to your card display to be drilled at each lesson.

Vowel Extension

Model 'reading' the Keyword Picture: /ă̆/...**pple**. Extend the /ă̆/ sound while you trace the line and finish the word when you get to the picture.

Have a student come trace the line while everyone extends the /ă̆/ sound.

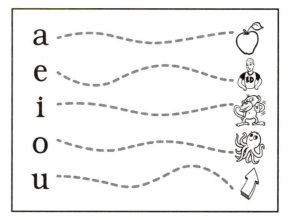

Drill Sounds

Do All The Introduced Sounds Each Day

Practice sounds with the Large Sound Cards. Say the letter-keyword-sound and have the students echo.

Select Some Sounds

Next, point to the Standard Sound Cards (in card display) with the Baby Echo pointer. You say the letter-keyword-sound and hold up Baby Echo to have the students repeat.

Sky Write/Letter Formation

Letter Formation for **y**

Use the following verbalization to direct students in proper letter formation.

Say

y is a plane line slide letter.

It starts on the (plane line) and (slides).

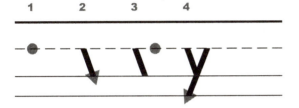

1. **Point to the plane line.**

2. **Slide down to the grass line.**

3. **Pick up your pencil (finger) and leave a space and point to the plane line.**

4. **Slide back - all the way to the worm line.**

Letter Formation for **x**

Use the following verbalization to direct students in proper letter formation.

Say

x is a plane line slide letter.

It starts on the (plane line) and (slides).

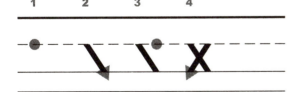

1. **Point to the plane line.**

2. **Slide down to the grass line.**

3. **Leave a space and point to the plane line.**

4. **Slide back to the grass line.**

 Student Notebook

DAY ❶

Direct the students to find the newly introduced letters.

Use the verbalization for the letter formation to direct the students while they trace it with their finger. Do it with them to model. After you do this, the students can then color the Keyword Picture.

DAY ❷

Trace and say the letter-keyword-sound for the previous letters introduced.

 Echo/Letter Formation

Remind students of proper pencil grip and sitting position, and give them their Dry Erase Writing Tablets.

Sounds appear between //. Dictate new sounds and a selection of previously taught sounds. You select and say the sound. Students echo the sound and say the letter.

Next have a student come up to the classroom board to make the letter on the Writing Grid.

Then have all students write the answer on their Dry Erase Writing Tablets as you direct them with the letter formation verbalization.

Sounds

/t/ - t	/b/ - b	/f/ - f
/n/ - n	/m/ - m	/k/ - c
/ă/ - a	/ĭ/ - i	/r/ - r

/ŏ/ - o	/g/ - g	/d/ - d
/s/ - s	/ĕ/ - e	/ŭ/ - u
/l/ - l	/h/ - h	/k/ - k
/p/ - p	/j/ - j	/v/ - v
/w/ - w	/z/- z	/kw/ - qu
/y/ - y	/ks/ - x	

 Make It Fun

Teacher Materials

• Wilson Writing Grid (on the board at least 2 feet tall)

Have a student come up to the front of the room. Whisper a letter name to him/her. Next have the student form the letter with their finger (not write it) on the Writing Grid. (Do this on the overhead screen if possible).

The other students need to watch and decide which letter was formed. When they guess, they should say the letter-keyword sound (h-hat-/h/,etc). Whoever guesses gets to do the next one.

 Echo/Find Letters

Students match Magnetic Letter Tiles to the Alphabet Overlay on their Letter Boards. Start with tiles off the board. Dictate sounds. Students echo sound and match the tiles. Include previous sounds and new sounds.

 Word Play

Teacher Materials

• Blue Sentence Frames
• Baby Echo

WORD AWARENESS

The students will again get you the frames needed so that you can write the sentence. Now they will need to get the question mark or period to complete the sentences. This is just the beginning of understanding. Do not expect the students to easily do this. Provide lots of guidance and cue them by over-emphasizing questions with your voice.

Display Sentence Frames in a Column

Display the word and punctuation frames in a column rather than across the board. Tell the students that you are going to have them help you get the pieces you need to write your sentence.

Demonstrate

Say

Sondra and Shana had fun.

As you place the frames, discuss your selection. Tell them that you need the tall frame first because every sentence must start with a capital letter. Tell them you need the tall frame for the name because all names begin with a capital letter. Tell them you need the square punctuation frame because this is a telling sentence.

Write the words on the frames and read it again, pointing to each word. Have students echo.

Erase and put the frames back in a column and ask for a student volunteer. Give them a sentence.

Bert and Maria came to school.

Ask a student to put the pieces in order for you to write the sentence. Remind the student,

Don't forget which one you need to begin the sentence.

What do you need at the end?

Say the sentence as the student places the frames. Write the sentence and ask the students:

Did Bert get all the pieces I needed? Does this sentence tell us something or ask us something?

Examples

Eileen has red hair.

Ed and Tom like to sing.

What did you eat for breakfast?

 **Storytime**

Teacher Materials

• Baby Echo (on a pointer or ruler)

• Echo Story Illustrations on Large Chart Paper

BABY ECHO FLIES

This week, use your pictures on the chart paper for "Baby Echo Flies." Have the students re-tell the story. Write the words of the story to correspond with each picture.

Use the Baby Echo pointer to read the story one sentence at a time and have the students echo. Be sure to scoop and read sentences in phrases. (Choral read with them again while they echo.)

1. **Baby Echo sat on a branch snuggled in the shelter of his mother's wings. It was warm and safe there. Baby Echo was happy.**

2. **Then Echo looked down at Baby Echo and said, "It is time for you to fly." Baby Echo snuggled closer to his mother and said, "But I don't know how to fly!"**

3. **Echo said, "Watch me, I will teach you," and she flapped her wings.**

4. **Baby Echo was brave. He followed his mother and landed next to her.**

Note

Be sure to write it so that you can scoop phrases. Use a different color marker to scoop the sentence into phrases.

Example

Baby Echo sat on a branch

snuggled in the shelter of his mother's wings.

Unit 1 Resources

Scope and Sequence

The following is the scope and sequence for letter introductions in Unit 1.

Week	Letter	Keyword	Sound
Orientation	t	top	/t/
1	b	bat	/b/
	f	fun	/f/
2	n	nut	/n/
	m	man	/m/
3	c	cat	/k/
	a	apple	/ă/
4	i	itch	/ĭ/
	r	rat	/r/
5	o	octopus	/ŏ/
	g	game	/g/
6	d	dog	/d/
	s	snake	/s/
7	e	Ed	/ĕ/
	u	up	/ŭ/
8	l	lamp	/l/
	h	hat	/h/
	k	kite	/k/
9	p	pan	/p/
	j	jug	/j/
10	v	van	/v/
	w	wind	/w/
11	z	zebra	/z/
	qu	queen	/kw/
12	y	yellow	/y/
	x	fox	/ks/

Drill Sounds

a - apple - /ă/   b - bat - /b/

c - cat - /k/   d - dog - /d/

e - Ed - /ĕ/   f - fun - /f/

g - game - /g/   h - hat - /h/

i - itch - /ĭ/   j - jug - /j/

k - kite - /k/   l - lamp - /l/

m - man - /m/   n - nut - /n/

o - octopus - /ŏ/   p - pan - /p/

qu - queen - /kw/   r - rat - /r/

s - snake - /s/   t - top - /t/

u - up - /ŭ/   v - van - /v/

w - wind - /w/   x - fox - /ks/

y - yellow - /y/   z - zebra - /z/

Echo Sounds

Sounds appear between / /. You say the sound. Students echo the sound and say the letter. Depending on the activity, students then either find or make the letter corresponding to that sound.

CONSONANTS

/b/ - b	/d/ - d	/f/ - f
/g/ - g	/h/ - h	/j/ - j
/k/ - c, k	/l/ - l	/m/ - m
/n/ - n	/p/ - p	/kw/ - qu
/r/ - r	/s/ - s	/t/ - t
/v/ - v	/w/ - w	/ks/ - x
/y/ - y	/z/ - z	

VOWELS

/ă/ - a	/ĕ/ - e	/ĭ/ - i
/ŏ/ - o	/ŭ/ - u	

Each student must be assessed individually. This will take approximately 20 minutes per student and can be done by a paraprofessional or volunteer if one is available to assist you.

Copy the **Unit Test Recording Form** for each student (see Appendix). Use the student's durable materials, e.g., Dry Erase Board, Letter Board and Letter Tiles, as needed.

If a student does not score at least **8 / 10** on any given item, this student will need additional assistance with the assessed skill. (See Supplemental Activities for guidance.)

Have Student Identify Lower-Case Letters

*Using the student's Letter Board and Letter Tiles, point to letters and have student name each letter. Ask , "What letter is this?" If student is unable to **name** the letters, have student **find** letters. Say, "Find the letter **a**." Note if student can find letters but not yet name them.*

a   r   z   b   g

j   k   e   o   v

Have Student Identify Letters Corresponding to Sounds

*Using the student's Letter Board and Letter Tiles, say sound and have student point to corresponding letters. Ask, "What says /**s**/?"*

/s/   /n/   /ĭ/   /kw/   /f/

/z/   /h/   /l/   /p/   /v/

Have Student Form Lower-Case Letters

*Using the student's Dry Erase Board, dictate letters and have student write the lower-case letter on the Writing Grid. Say, "Write the letter **t**."*

t   c   g   m   x

p   e   d   h   f

Answer Key

LOWER-CASE LETTERS

a   r   z   b   g

j   k   e   o   v

LETTERS & SOUNDS

s   n   i   q   f

z   h   l   p   v

LETTER FORMATION

t   c   g   m   x

p   e   d   h   f

Note

Allow students to independently reference their Student Notebooks. Count responses checked in their Notebooks as correct, but make a notation that the book was used.

Unit 2   Level K

Introduction

In Unit 2, you will teach children how to form capital or upper-case letters A-Z. For many students, this will be a review. Students will practice alphabetical order with their Letter Tiles.

You will also move from word awareness to syllable awareness. Now you will tune the students into the separate syllables in a word.

Note

Left-handed students can cross their letters from left to right as opposed to right to left. You will need to show this to them and work with students individually.

In a Nutshell

NEW CONCEPTS

- Upper-Case Letter Formation
- Syllable Awareness
- Alphabetical Order

PLANNED TIME IN UNIT

3 WEEKS

Note
Extend the time in this Unit if students do not demonstrate mastery.

PREPARING YOUR MATERIALS

See Storytime. You will need ABC Books for this activity.

You will need your White Syllable Frames for the Word Play activity.

Arrange your Standard Sound Card display in the following manner

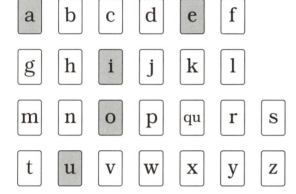

PREPARING YOUR STUDENTS

Students should have the **Magnetic Letter Tiles** (a-z) on their **Building Boards** and the **Alphabet Overlay** on their **Letter Boards**.

PREPARING FOR HOME SUPPORT

Copy and send home the **Unit 2 Letter and Activity Packet**.

Unit 2 **Lesson Activity Plan**

Weeks 1

DAY ❶	DAY ❷	DAY ❸	DAY ❹	DAY ❺
Drill Sounds	Drill Sounds	Drill Sounds	Drill Sounds	Drill Sounds
Sky Write/Letter Formation	Sky Write/Letter Formation	Sky Write/Letter Formation	Sky Write/Letter Formation	Alphabetical Order
Student Notebook	Student Notebook	Student Notebook	Student Notebook	Echo/Find Sounds
		Word Play	Make It Fun	Storytime

Weeks 2

DAY ❶	DAY ❷	DAY ❸	DAY ❹	DAY ❺
Drill Sounds	Drill Sounds	Drill Sounds	Drill Sounds	Drill Sounds
Sky Write/Letter Formation	Sky Write/Letter Formation	Sky Write/Letter Formation	Sky Write/Letter Formation	Alphabetical Order
Student Notebook	Student Notebook	Student Notebook	Student Notebook	Echo/Find Sounds
		Word Play	Make It Fun	Storytime

Weeks 3

DAY ❶	DAY ❷	DAY ❸	DAY ❹	DAY ❺
Drill Sounds	Drill Sounds	Drill Sounds	Drill Sounds	Drill Sounds
Sky Write/Letter Formation	Sky Write/Letter Formation	Sky Write/Letter Formation	Sky Write/Letter Formation	Alphabetical Order
Student Notebook	Student Notebook	Student Notebook	Student Notebook	Echo/Find Sounds
		Word Play	Make It Fun	Storytime

Sky Write/Letter Formation

Use the following verbalizations to direct students in proper letter formation.

WEEK 1 DAY ❶

Letter Formation for **A**

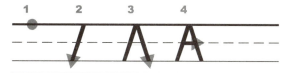

1. **Point to the sky line.**

2. **Slide back to the grass line.**

3. **Start back at the sky line and slide down to the grass line.**

4. **Cross on the plane line.**

Letter Formation for **B**

1. **Point to the skyline.**

2. **Go down to the grass line.**

3. **Start back at the skyline and go around to the plane line,**

4. **and around again to the grass line**

WEEK 1 DAY ❷

Letter Formation for **C**

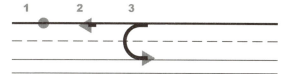

1. **Point to the sky line.**

2. **Fly back on the sky line,**

3. **and down around to the grass line.**

Letter Formation for **D**

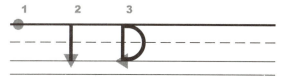

1. **Point to the sky line.**

2. **Go down to the grass line.**

3. **Start back on the sky line and go all the way around to the grass line.**

WEEK 1 DAY ❸

Letter Formation for **E**

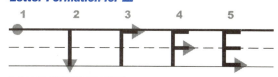

1. **Point to the sky line.**

2. **Go down to the grass line.**

3. **Make a line on the sky line.**

4. **Make a line on the plane line,**

5. **and make a line on the grass line.**

Letter Formation for *F*

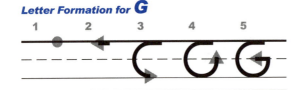

1. Point to the sky line.

2. Go down to the grass line.

3. Make a line on the sky line.

4. Make a line on the plane line.

Letter Formation for *G*

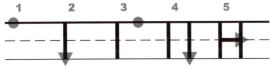

1. Point to the sky line.

2. Fly back on the sky line.

3. Around to the grass line.

4. Up to the plane line,

5. and back straight on the plane line.

Letter Formation for *H*

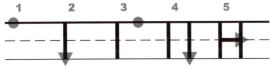

1. Point to the sky line.

2. Go down to the grass line.

3. Leave a space and point to the sky line.

4. Go down to the grass line.

5. Cross straight on the plane line.

Letter Formation for *I*

1. Point to the sky line.

2. Go down to the grass line

3. Cross in the sky line,

4. and cross in the grass line.

Letter Formation for *J*

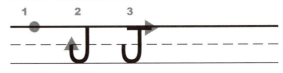

1. Point to the sky line.

2. Go down to the grass line and curve back.

3. Cross it on the sky line.

Letter Formation for *K*

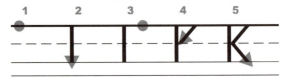

1. Point to the sky line.

2. Go down to the grass line.

3. Leave a space and point to the sky line.

4. Slide back to the plane line.

5. Slide over to the grass line.

Letter Formation for **L**

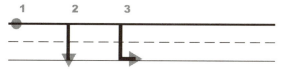

1. Point to the sky line.

2. Go down to the grass line.

3. Make a line across the grass line.

WEEK 2 DAY ❸

Letter Formation for **M**

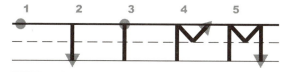

1. Point to the sky line.

2. Go down to the grass line.

3. Point to the sky line.

4. Slide down to the plane line, and slide back up to the sky line.

5. Go down to the grass line.

Letter Formation for **N**

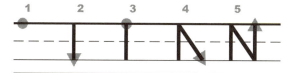

1. Point to the sky line.

2. Go down to the grass line.

3. Point to the sky line.

4. Slide down to the grass line.

5. Go straight up to the sky line.

WEEK 2 DAY ❹

Letter Formation for **O**

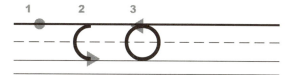

1. Point to the sky line.

2. Trace back, then down around to the grass line,

3. and around back up to the sky line.

Letter Formation for **P**

1. Point to the sky line.

2. Go down to the grass line.

3. Point to the sky line and go around to the plane line.

WEEK 3 DAY ❶

Letter Formation for **Q**

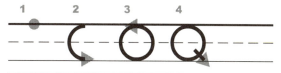

1. Point to the sky line.

2. Trace back, then down around to the grass line,

3. and around back up to the sky line.

4. Make a tail.

Letter Formation for **R**

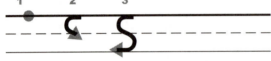

1. Point to the sky line.

2. Go down to the grass line.

3. Point to the sky line and go around to the plane line,

4. and slide down to the grass line.

WEEK 3 DAY ❷

Letter Formation for **S**

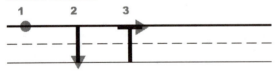

1. Point to the sky line.

2. Trace back and curve in to the plane line,

3. and curve back to the grass line.

Letter Formation for **T**

1. Point to the sky line.

2. Go down to the grass line.

3. Cross on the sky line.

Letter Formation for **U**

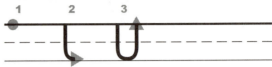

1. Point to the sky line.

2. Go to the grass line,

3. and curve up to the sky line.

WEEK 3 DAY ❸

Letter Formation for **V**

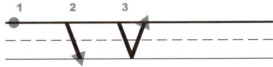

1. Point to the sky line.

2. Slide down to the grass line,

3. and slide back up to the sky line.

Letter Formation for **W**

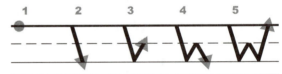

1. Point to the sky line.

2. Slide down to the grass line.

3. Slide up to the plane line.

4. Back down to the grass line,

5. and slide all the way back to the sky line.

WEEK 3 DAY ❹

Letter Formation for **X**

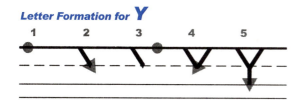

1. Point to the sky line.

2. Slide down to the grass line.

3. Leave a space and point to the sky line.

4. Slide back down to the grass line.

Letter Formation for **Y**

1. Point to the sky line.

2. Slide down to the plane line.

3. Leave a space and point to the sky line,

4. and slide way back to plane line.

5. Go straight down to grass line.

Letter Formation for **Z**

1. Point to the sky line.

2. Make a line.

3. Slide back to the grass line,

4. and make a line.

Drill Sounds

Large Sound Cards

First practice sounds with the Large Sound Cards. Say the letter-keyword-sound and have students echo. Be selective.

Standard Sound Cards

Next, point to the Standard Sound Cards (on display) with the Baby Echo pointer. You say the letter-keyword-sound and hold up Baby Echo to have students repeat. You can have a student be the drill leader for some of the sounds.

Student Notebook

Direct students to find the letters corresponding to the letters introduced with sky writing.

Have students trace the large upper-case letter, then lower case letter with their index finger while you direct them with the verbalization.

Next, have students hold their pencil. Remind them of the correct grip and be sure they are sitting with their chairs pulled in and their feet on the floor. The elbow of their writing arm should be on the desk. They should hold their Student Notebooks with their other hand. Say the verbalization to have students make the letters on their writing grids.

Circulate the room and assist students with the correct position and the proper pencil grip.

 **Word Play**

WEEK 1

Preparation

- White Syllable Frames

SYLLABLE COUNT

This activity will help students segment words into syllables.

Instruct Students

Say a word (see Resources). Have students echo the word. Have them put their hands under their chin to "feel" the syllables. Then have them clap out the syllables. Ask them, how many syllables in the word? After they answer, write the word on the syllable frames, one syllable per frame. Read the word, pointing to each syllable. Count the frames and tell the student whether or not their count was correct. Do 8-10 words.

base	ball

WEEKS 2 • 3

Do the activity from Week 1, but add the following step after you do each two-syllable word.

Instruct Students

base	ball

Point to each syllable as you say it.

Ask

What would it be if I took away ball ?

Remove the | **ball** | *frame. After students answer, put it back.*

Ask

The word is baseball.

- **What would it be if I took away base?**

Again, point to each syllable as you say it. Remove the | **base** | frame. After students answer, erase the frames.

Word Resources

Use Students' names interwoven with a selection of words below.

baseball	basketball	book
jelly	dog	spotlight
picnic	candy	gingerbread
hat	cupcake	kitten
trophy	kite	molasses
king	marketplace	airplane

 Alphabetical Order

Students start with their Magnetic Letter Tiles randomly placed on their Building Boards. Have them sequentially match Letter Tiles onto the Alphabet Overlay.

After students have the Tiles placed, chorally say the alphabet. Students should point to each letter as they say its name.

 Echo/Find Sounds

Echo/Find Sounds

Say a sound. Have students echo and find the letter on their magnetic Letter Board.

Ask

What says /b/? (b)

(See Echo Sounds in Unit Resources for expected student responses.)

Make It Fun

WEEK 1

Preparation

- Your sample set of student Magnetic Letter Tiles (put in paper bag)
- Magnetic Letter Tiles (Each student selects 9)
- Copy the Bingo Square Sheet for each student (See Appendix)
- Chips or paper scraps to cover bingo squares

SOUND BINGO

This activity will reinforce letter-sound correspondence.

Instruct Students

Students should select any 9 Magnetic Letter Tiles from their Letter Boards and randomly place them onto their Bingo sheets.

Pull a letter out of your paper bag. Say the sound and have students echo. If any students have the corresponding letter, they should then place a chip (or paper scrap) over it. The first student to cover all squares wins.

Keep the selected letters to check the winner's accuracy. To check the winner, the student should read their tiles, saying the letter-key-word-sound.

Variation

Hold the bag out for a student to select a letter. Have that student name its sound.

WEEKS 2 • 3

Preparation

- Your sample set of student Magnetic Letter Tiles (put into paper bag)
- Dry Erase Writing Tablets
- Student Notebooks (as needed for reference)

PICK-A-LETTER

This activity will enable students to practice letter formation of upper-case letters and to reinforce alphabetical order and letter-sound correspondence.

Instruct Students

Walk around and have each student select a letter from your paper bag. Have them make the upper-case letter corresponding to the selected letter tile on their Dry Erase Writing Tablets.

Tell them to look in their Student Notebooks or on their Desk Strip if needed. Walk around to assist students and help them with pencil grip and formation. When all students have their letter made, do the next part of the activity.

1. Have them arrange themselves in alphabetical order, circling around the room.
2. If there is not a student for each letter, they should leave a space.
3. When students are arranged, say the alphabet altogether.
4. The student holding the spoken letter can hold it up when it is said.

Storytime

Preparation

During Storytime in Unit 2, select an ABC Book to read to your students. There are many different ABC Books and the following list provides a small selection.

Aylesworth, J. 1992. *Old Black Fly*. New York: Holt

Lobel, Arnold. 1981. *On Market Street.* New York: Greenwillow.

MacDonald, S. 1986. *Alphabatics.* New York: Aladdin.

Micklethwait, L. 1992. *I spy: An Alphabet in Art.* New York: Greenwillow.

Instruct Students

Read the book. Pause on each letter page:

Point out the letter (It is helpful to show students various letter fonts).

Have a student tell you the corresponding keyword and sound.

Have students find and name words that begin with the letter sound.

Note

The book can be one that you have previously read to students. Young children love the repetition, and repeated exposure to text is beneficial.

Drill Sounds

a - apple - /ă/	b - bat - /b/
c - cat - /k/	d - dog - /d/
e - Ed - /ĕ/	f - fun - /f/
g - game - /g/	h - hat - /h/
i - itch - /ĭ/	j - jug - /j/
k - kite - /k/	l - lamp - /l/
m - man - /m/	n - nut - /n/
o - octopus - /ŏ/	p - pan - /p/
qu - queen - /kw/	r - rat - /r/
s - snake - /s/	t - top - /t/
u - up - /ŭ/	v - van - /v/
w - wind - /w/	x - fox - /ks/
y - yellow - /y/	z - zebra - /z/

Echo Sounds

Sounds appear between / /. You say the sound. Students echo the sound and say the letter. Depending on the activity, students then either find or make the letter corresponding to that sound.

CONSONANTS

/b/ - b	/d/ - d	/f/ - f
/g/ - g	/h/ - h	/j/ - j
/k/ - c, k	/l/ - l	/m/ - m
/n/ - n	/p/ - p	/kw/ - qu
/r/ - r	/s/ - s	/t/ - t
/v/ - v	/w/ - w	/ks/ - x
/y/ - y	/z/ - z	

VOWELS

/ă/ - a	/ĕ/ - e	/ĭ/ - i
/ŏ/ - o	/ŭ/ - u	

Each student must be assessed individually. This will take approximately 20 minutes per student and can be done by a paraprofessional or volunteer if one is available to assist you.

Copy the **Unit Test Recording Form** for each student (see Appendix). Use the student's durable materials, e.g., Dry Erase Board, Letter Board and Letter Tiles, as needed.

If a student does not score at least **8/10** on any given item, this student will need additional assistance with the assessed skill. (See Supplemental Activities for guidance.)

Have Student Identify Beginning Sounds

Say a word and ask student to tell you the sound at the beginning of the word. Provide an example: "What is the first sound in the word **sink***?" Student responds: /s/*

meat	talk	sip	door	clap
bang	face	zebra	lion	wagon

Have Student Identify Upper-Case Letters

Point to upper-case letters (see Unit 2 Test in Teacher's Manual) and have student name each letter. Ask , "What letter is this?" If student is unable to name the letters, have student find letters. Say, "Find the letter A." Note if student can find letters but not yet name them.

A	E	W	B	D
Q	G	M	N	R

Have Student Form Upper-Case Letters

Using the student's Dry Erase Board, dictate letters and have student write the upper-case letter on a Writing Grid. Say, "Write the upper-case letter **G***."*

G	N	Z	P	H
T	F	X	B	V

Answer Key

BEGINNING SOUNDS

/m/	/t/	/s/	/d/	/k/
/b/	/f/	/z/	/l/	/w/

UPPER-CASE LETTERS

A	E	W	B	D
Q	G	M	N	R

LETTER FORMATION

G	N	Z	P	H
T	F	X	B	V

Note
Allow students to independently reference their Student Notebooks. Count responses checked in their Notebooks as correct, but make a notation that the book was used.

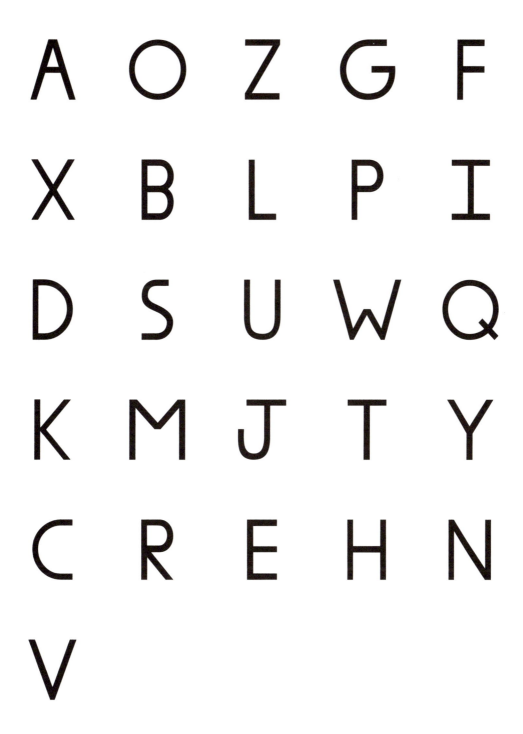

A O Z G F
X B L P I
D S U W Q
K M J T Y
C R E H N
V

Use this page when asking student to name upper-case letters.

Unit 3   Level K

Introduction

In Unit 3, you will move from syllable awareness to phoneme awareness. You will start to tune the students into the separate sounds (or phonemes) in a word.

You will work with students with rhyming words. You will also progress to blending sounds to form words.

In this unit, you will teach children how to blend and read three-sound short vowel words. These words are often called CVC words.

You will see that the words begin with the consonants **f**, **l**, **m**, **n**, **r** and **s**. These consonants have sounds that can be 'held' into the vowel sound and thus are easier to blend.

In a Nutshell

NEW CONCEPTS

- Phonemic awareness skills
- Blending and reading three-sound short vowel words
- Story prediction

SAMPLE WORDS

map   sad   rat

PLANNED TIME IN UNIT

4 WEEKS

Note
Extend the time in this Unit if students do not demonstrate mastery.

PREPARING YOUR MATERIALS

See Storytime. You will need to find appropriate story books with rhymes.

Arrange your Standard Sound Card display in the following manner

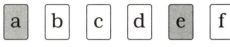

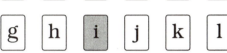

PREPARING YOUR STUDENTS

Students should have the **Magnetic Letter Tiles** (a-z) on their **Building Boards** and the **Alphabet Overlay** on their **Letter Boards**.

PREPARING FOR HOME SUPPORT

Copy and send home the **Unit 3 Letter and Activity Packet**.

Getting Ready

VIEW THE CD-ROM

LEVEL K
- Unit 3
  Lesson Activities (see below)

STUDY LESSON ACTIVITIES

Review the following activities in your manual's Lesson Activity Overview and on CD-ROM:

- The Segment Sounds video on the CD-ROM relates to the Echo/Find Words Activity in the manual.

Weeks 1

DAY ❶	DAY ❷	DAY ❸	DAY ❹	DAY ❺
Drill Sounds	Drill Sounds	Drill Sounds	Drill Sounds	Drill Sounds
Introduce New Concepts	Word Play	Word Play	Word Play	Make it Fun
Sky Write/Letter Formation	Echo/Letter Formation	Alphabetical Order	Echo/Letter Formation	Storytime
		Echo/Find Sounds		

Weeks 2 • 4

DAY ❶	DAY ❷	DAY ❸	DAY ❹	DAY ❺
Drill Sounds	Drill Sounds	Drill Sounds	Drill Sounds	Drill Sounds
Word Play	Word Play	Word Play	Word Play	Make it Fun
Sky Write/Letter Formation	Echo/Letter Formation	Alphabetical Order	Echo/Letter Formation	Storytime
		Echo/Find Sounds		

Introduce New Concepts

WEEK 1 DAY ❶

TEACH TAPPING TO READ WORDS

Teach students how to blend words with three sounds.

If students have trouble with any sound, point to the corresponding Large Sound Card (or poster) and ask them to say the letter-keyword-sound. Then tap out the word, using the sounds.

Use your Standard Sound Card display to make the words.

Example

Say

> Say each sound separately, then blend the sounds together.
>
> Tap a finger to your thumb over each sound card while saying the sound.
>
> Tap your index finger to thumb while saying /m/,
>
> middle finger to thumb while saying /a/
>
> and ring finger to thumb while saying /t/.
>
> Then blend the sounds and say the word as you drag your thumb across your fingers beginning with the index finger.

Have the students do this. Explain that they can say sounds while tapping and blending them together to make words.

Continue with 8-10 other word examples. (See Unit Resources.) Each time, make the words with the Standard Sound Cards. Tap and blend sounds with your students.

 Drill Sounds

Large Sound Cards

First practice sounds with the Large Sound Cards. Say the letter-keyword-sound and have students echo. Be selective.

Standard Sound Cards

Next, point to the Standard Sound Cards (on display) with the Baby Echo pointer. You say the letter-keyword-sound and hold up Baby Echo to have students repeat. You can have a student be the drill leader for some of the sounds.

 Sky Write/Letter Formation

Choose 3-4 letters to review. You can select a student to trace the letter on the Writing Grid at the front of the class. The other students can stand and sky write as you verbalize the directions.

 Echo/Letter Formation

Remind students of proper pencil grip and sitting position, and give them their Dry Erase Tablets.

Dictate 5-6 previously taught sounds. You select and say the sound. Students echo the sound and say the letter.

Next have a student come up to the classroom board to make the letter on the Writing Grid.

Then have all students write the answer on their Dry Erase Tablets as you direct them with the letter formation verbalization.

(See Unit Resources.)

 **Word Play**

RETEACH TAPPING TO READ WORDS

Use your Standard Sound Card display to make Unit words. (See below.)

Make each word then say and tap each sound. Have students tap with you. Then blend the sounds as you drag your thumb across your fingers. Say the word.

Next, point under each card as you say each sound, then drag your finger under all three cards as you blend the sounds to read the word.

Word Resources

WEEK 1

DAY ❷

| sad | sat | sap | map | mad | mat |

DAY ❸

| rag | rap | rat | nag | nap | nab |

DAY ❹

| lad | lag | lap | sip | sit | lit |

WEEK 2

DAY ❶

| rig | rip | lip | lit | fit | fig |

DAY ❷

| rot | not | nod | rug | rut | rub |

DAY ❸

| mud | mug | lug | set | met | net |

DAY ❹

| sap | sad | sag | nag | nap | lap |

WEEK 3

DAY ❶

| sip | lip | lid | lit | fit | fig |

DAY ❷

| red | led | let | met | mat | fat |

DAY ❸

| mop | map | mad | lad | lap | nap |

DAY ❹

| lit | lot | log | fog | fig | fit |

 **Echo/Find Sounds**

Echo/Find Sounds

Say a sound. Have students echo and find the letter on their magnetic Letter Board.

Ask

   What says /b/? (b)

(See Echo Sounds in Unit Resources for expected student responses.)

 Alphabetical Order

Students start with their Magnetic Letter Tiles randomly placed on their Building Boards. Have them sequentially match Letter Tiles onto the Alphabet Overlay.

After students have the Tiles placed, chorally say the alphabet. Students should point to each letter as they say its name.

Make It Fun

WEEKS 1 • 2

Preparation

- Your Standard Sound Card Display

LET'S RHYME

This activity will help students begin to manipulate sounds with rhyming patterns.

Instruct Students

Make the word **cat** with your Sound Cards.

c	a	t

Say

> This word is cat. If this says cat, what is this?

Remove the **c** card and replace it with the **b**.

Continue rhyming words, each time changing the first letter.

Word Resources

bat	fat	sat	rat	mat
wig	big	pig		
hop	top	mop	cop	
sap	tap	rap	lap	
kit	pit	fit	bit	sit
lug	tug	bug	rug	mug
wet	let	set	bet	pet
lap	tap	map	sap	cap
wag	bag	sag	tag	rag

WEEKS 3 • 4

Preparation

- Unit Word Resources

GUESS MY WORD

This activity will help students develop blending skills.

Instruct Students

Say

> I am going to say three sounds. Listen and see if you can guess the word.

Tap words to assist blending. Do some altogether and then call on individual students.

Word Resources

WEEK 3

/m/	/ă/	/p/	(map)
/m/	/ŏ/	/p/	(mop)
/f/	/ĭ/	/t/	(fit)
/r/	/ĕ/	/d/	(red)
/r/	/ă/	/g/	(rag)
/l/	/ă/	/p/	(lap)
/s/	/ĕ/	/t/	(set)
/l/	/ŏ/	/g/	(log)
/n/	/ĕ/	/t/	(net)
/n/	/ă/	/p/	(nap)

WEEK 4

/p/	/ĕ/	/t/	(pet)
/c/	/ă/	/t/	(cat)
/b/	/ŭ/	/g/	(bug)
/d/	/ŏ/	/t/	(dot)
/t/	/ŭ/	/g/	(tug)
/d/	/ŏ/	/g/	(dog)

/t/	/ŭ/	/b/	(tub)
/d/	/ĭ/	/p/	(dip)
/w/	/ă/	/g/	(wag)
/g/	/ŭ/	/m/	(gum)

Note

The Week 4 words are more challenging since the initial consonant does not have a continuous sound. This activity will help prepare students for word blending in the next Unit. You might need to do all these together with the students.

 **Storytime**

Preparation

During Storytime in Unit 3, select a rhyming picture book to read to your students. Be sure that the story has no more than 4-5 sentences per page. It should have predictable rhyming patterns. The following list provides some suggestions.

Domanska, J. 1974. **What Do You See?** New York: Macmillan.

Galdone, P. 1986. **Three Little Kittens.** New York: Clarion.

Guarino, D. 1989. **Is Your Mama a Llama?** New York: Scholastic.

Hawkins, C., and J. Hawkins. 1987. **I Know an Old Lady Who Swallowed a Fly.** New York: Putnam.

Hayes, S. 1986. **This Is the Bear.** Philadelphia, PA: Lippincott.

Prater, J. 1991. **No! Said Joe.** Cambridge, MA: Candlewick.

Shaw, N. 1989. **Sheep On a Ship.** Boston: Houghton Mifflin.

Weiss, N. 1992. **On a Hot, Hot Day.** New York: G. P. Putnam's Sons.

Instruct Students

Read the book once moving your finger under the words and emphasizing the rhymes. Pause 2-3 times and ask students to predict what will happen.

Say

> Now let's do it again but this time you can help me read.

Read the book again, moving your finger under the words. This time, do not say the rhyming words and let the students say it for you.

Lastly, write the rhyming words from the story on chart paper or the board. Put rhyming words on the same line.

Example

bat   cat   sat   down   clown

Tell the students that these are the words they read in the story. Explain that they rhyme. Read a set of rhyming words with Baby Echo and have the students repeat. Ask them to think of other words that rhyme with each set. Add them to the list and read.

Drill Sounds

a - apple - /ă/	b - bat - /b/
c - cat - /k/	d - dog - /d/
e - Ed - /ĕ/	f - fun - /f/
g - game - /g/	h - hat - /h/
i - itch - /ĭ/	j - jug - /j/
k - kite - /k/	l - lamp - /l/
m - man - /m/	n - nut - /n/
o - octopus - /ŏ/	p - pan - /p/
qu - queen - /kw/	r - rat - /r/
s - snake - /s/	t - top - /t/
u - up - /ŭ/	v - van - /v/
w - wind - /w/	x - fox - /ks/
y - yellow - /y/	z - zebra - /z/

Echo Sounds

Sounds appear between / /. You say the sound. Students echo the sound and say the letter. Depending on the activity, students then either find or make the letter corresponding to that sound.

CONSONANTS

/b/ - b	/d/ - d	/f/ - f
/g/ - g	/h/ - h	/j/ - j
/k/ - c, k	/l/ - l	/m/ - m
/n/ - n	/p/ - p	/kw/ - qu
/r/ - r	/s/ - s	/t/ - t
/v/ - v	/w/ - w	/ks/ - x
/y/ - y	/z/ - z	

VOWELS

/ă/ - a	/ĕ/ - e	/ĭ/ - i
/ŏ/ - o	/ŭ/ - u	

Each student must be assessed individually. This will take approximately 20 minutes per student and can be done by a paraprofessional or volunteer if one is available to assist you.

Copy the **Unit Test Recording Form** for each student (see Appendix). Use the student's durable materials, e.g., Dry Erase Board, Letter Board and Letter Tiles, as needed.

If a student does not score at least **8 / 10** on any given item, this student will need additional assistance with the assessed skill. (See Supplemental Activities for guidance.)

Have Student Identify Ending Sounds

*Say a word and ask student to tell you the sound at the end of the word. Provide an example: "What is the last sound in the word **bat**?" Student responds: /t/*

sharp	lick	stuff	phone	bag
lend	fuzz	drum	sheet	talk

Have Student Blend Sounds to Form Words

Say sounds one at a time and have student blend to form word. Say, "I will say sounds slowly. Blend them together and tell me the word."

/s/ /ă/ /t/   /f/ /ĭ/ /t/   /l/ /ŏ/ /g/   /m/ /ă/ /t/   /n/ /ă/ /p/

Have Student Read C-V-C Words

Form words using the student's Letter Board and Letter Tiles and have student tap and read the words. Say, "Tap these sounds and tell me the word that I made."

nap	sit	rob	mud	net

Have Student Name Letters in Alphabetical Order

Ask student to place Letter Tiles onto Letter Board and to recite the alphabet in order.

Answer Key

ENDING SOUNDS

/p/	/k/	/f/	/n/	/g/
/d/	/z/	/m/	/t/	/k/

WORDS

sat   fit   log   mat   nap

C-V-C WORDS

nap   sit   rob   mud   net

Note
Allow students to independently reference their Student Notebooks. Count responses checked in their Notebooks as correct, but make a notation that the book was used.

Unit 4 Level K

Introduction

In Unit 4, you will teach children how to blend and read additional three-sound words. These words are still CVC words but they will begin with any consonant. You will change the initial, final and medial sounds to create new words.

You will also teach children how to segment and spell these words. Students will learn how to tap out the sounds in a word and find the letters corresponding to each tap in order to spell the word.

You will continue to work with students to re-tell stories. You will introduce narrative story structure and help students re-write a short narrative story. You will also practice reading with echo and choral reading.

In a Nutshell

NEW CONCEPTS

- Phonemic awareness skills
- Segmenting and spelling three-sound short vowel words
- Narrative story structure
- Fluency and phrasing with echo and choral reading
- Beginning composition skills

SAMPLE WORDS

cut   tap   wet

PLANNED TIME IN UNIT

6 WEEKS

Note
Extend the time in this Unit if students do not demonstrate mastery.

PREPARING YOUR MATERIALS

See Storytime. You will need to find short narrative stories to use for this activity.

Arrange your Standard Sound Card display in the following manner

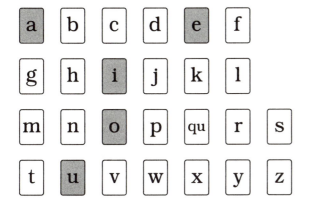

PREPARING YOUR STUDENTS

Students should have the **Magnetic Letter Tiles** (a-z) on their **Letter Boards**. Students place the **Alphabet Overlay** on their boards and then match the tiles to the corresponding square on the overlay.

PREPARING FOR HOME SUPPORT

Copy and send home the **Unit 4 Letter and Activity Packet**.

Getting Ready

VIEW THE CD-ROM

LEVEL K
• Unit 4
  Lesson Activities (see below)

STUDY LESSON ACTIVITIES

Review the following activities in your manual's Lesson Activity Overview and on CD-ROM:

CD-ROM LEVEL 1 Activities:

• Echo Sounds/Words

• Dictation (Dry-Erase)

Note
The students in the video have a Level 1 Dry Erase Writing Tablet.

Do the same activity using the Level K Unit words and the Level K Writing Tablet.

Week 1

DAY ❶	DAY ❷	DAY ❸	DAY ❹	DAY ❺
Drill Sounds	Drill Sounds	Drill Sounds	Drill Sounds	Drill Sounds
Introduce New Concepts	Word Play	Word Play	Word Play	Word Play
Echo/Find Sounds & Words	Echo/Find Sounds & Words	Echo/Letter Formation	Make it Fun	Storytime
	Echo/Letter Formation	Introduce New Concepts	Dictation (Dry-Erase)	

Weeks 2 • 6

DAY ❶	DAY ❷	DAY ❸	DAY ❹	DAY ❺
Drill Sounds	Drill Sounds	Drill Sounds	Drill Sounds	Drill Sounds
Word Play	Word Play	Word Play	Word Play	Word Play
Echo/Find Sounds & Words	Echo/Find Sounds & Words	Echo/Letter Formation	Make it Fun	Storytime
	Echo/Letter Formation	Dictation (Dry Erase)	Dictation (Dry Erase)	

Introduce New Concepts

WEEK 1 DAY ❶

TEACH TAPPING TO READ WORDS

In Unit 4 move on to form words beginning with other consonants.

You can now change the initial consonant to any consonant to make words. Also, change the vowel and final consonants to form new words. Make 8-10 words. Each time, tap and blend the word with your students.

Example

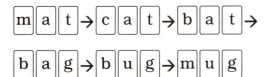

TEACH TAPPING TO SPELL

Use your Standard Sound Card display to teach sound tapping for segmentation and spelling skills.

Say

> Now we are going to do something a little bit different.
>
> I'm going to say a word and we are going to tap it without seeing the letters.
>
> Are you ready to try?

Say the word **map**, and tap out the three separate sounds without the cards. Tell the students to try to picture the three cards in their mind.

Now re-tap with fingers, but this time select the Standard Sound Cards with each tap to form the word **map**.

Repeat this procedure dictating the word **lip**, then **mat**. Tap out sounds and have students repeat. Then find the corresponding cards and place them together to form the word.

Next, dictate the words **nap**, **mud** and **sat**. Have a student come to the front and try tapping out the sounds and finding the corresponding cards.

WEEK 1 DAY ❸

TEACH WORD DICTATION

Tell students that they are now ready to write words. They will need their Dry Erase Writing tablets. Dictate a word. (See Unit Resources.) Have the students echo. Next, tap the word with the students.

Say

> Name the letters that go with each tap.

Tap the word again, this time naming the letters. Then direct student to write the word. Have a student come find the Sound Cards to form the word. Tap the word again and have students check to see if they spelled the word correctly.

Dictate 4-5 words.

 Drill Sounds

Large Sound Cards

First practice sounds with the Large Sound Cards. Say the letter-keyword-sound and have students echo. Be selective.

Standard Sound Cards

Next, point to the Standard Sound Cards (on display) with the Baby Echo pointer. You say the letter-keyword-sound and hold up Baby Echo to have students repeat. You can have a student be the drill leader for some of the sounds.

Unit 4 Lesson Activity Plan

 Echo/Letter Formation

Remind students of proper pencil grip and sitting position, and give them their Dry Erase Tablets.

Dictate 5-6 previously taught sounds. You select and say the sound. Students echo the sound and say the letter.

Next have a student come up to the classroom board to make the letter on the Writing Grid.

Then have all students write the answer on their Dry Erase Tablets as you direct them with the letter formation verbalization.

(See Unit Resources.)

 Word Play

RETEACH TAPPING TO READ WORDS

Use your Standard Sound Card display to make 5-6 Unit words. (See Unit Resources.)

Make each word then say and tap each sound. Have students tap with you. Then blend the sounds as you drag your thumb across your fingers.

Next, point under each card as you say each sound, then drag your finger under all three cards as you blend the sounds to read the word.

 Dictation

Refer to this Unit's Resource List of Echo Sounds and Words.

Proper Dictation Activity procedures are very important. Be sure to follow their demonstration on the CD-ROM.

DRY ERASE

Dictate 3 sounds, 3 current words

This is a teaching time, not a testing time. Be sure students repeat each dictation. They should tap and orally spell the Unit words before writing.

 Echo/Find Sounds & Words

Echo/Find Sounds

Say a sound. Have students echo and find the letter on their magnetic Letter Board.

Ask

   What says /b/? (b)

(See Echo Sounds in Unit Resources for expected student responses.)

Echo/Find Words

Dictate a unit word. Have one student come find your corresponding cards.

(See Current Unit Words in Unit Resources.)

Have students find Letter Tiles needed to make words on their Magnetic Letter Boards. After finding a word, have a student spell it orally.

 **Make It Fun**

WEEKS 1, 3 and 5

Preparation

- Word Resource List
- Copy the Bingo Square Sheet for each student (See Appendix)
- Magnetic Letter Tiles (each student selects 9 consonants)
- Chips or paper scraps to cover Bingo Squares

SOUND BINGO 2

This activity helps students to learn to listen for the last sound in a word.

Instruct Students

Students should select any 9 consonants from the Magnetic Letter Tiles and randomly place them onto their Bingo sheets.

Say

> I am going to say a word.
>
> Everyone will echo it and then listen for the last sound.
>
> If I say the word bug, you echo (bug) and tell me the last sound that you hear (/g/).
>
> If you have the letter that says /g/, put a chip on it.

Continue to dictate words orally and direct the students to listen for the last sound and place a chip on the corresponding consonant if they have it on their Bingo Sheet.

If no student gets Bingo after you say one-syllable words ending in different letters (**b**, **d**, **g**, **f**, **l**, **m**, **n**, **p**, **s**, **t**, **x**, **z**), have students listen for the first sound in dictated words. Dictate words beginning with the other letters (such as **h**, **j**, **r**, **w** and **y**).

WEEKS 2, 4 and 6

Preparation

- Standard Sound Cards
- Word Resource List

KID SPELLING

This activity helps students to spell.

Instruct Students

Disseminate your Standard Sound Cards, giving one card per student. Avoid uncommon letters (such as **y**) unless you plan to dictate words with that sound to practice them.

Tell the students that you need them to help you spell and that they will come up to the front if they have a letter that will help to spell a word.

Dictate a word such as **map**. Have students echo and tap it out.

Say

> What is the first sound in map?
>
> *(Hold your index finger to your thumb.)*
>
> I need that letter.

Have the student come up to the front of the room. Proceed with the other sounds until the word is spelled with the three children holding the cards. Have the children spell the word before they sit down. Dictate several words.

 **Storytime**

WEEKS 1 • 2

Preparation

During Storytime, select a picture book that tells a narrative story. Be sure that there are no more than 5-6 sentences per page.

The story can include predictable language patterns. It is important that it presents sequential events. The following list provides some suggestions.

> Allard, Harry. 1977. *Miss Nelson Is Missing.* Houghton Mifflin.
>
> Hoban, Russell. 1964,1992. *A Baby Sister for Frances.* Harper Trophy.
>
> Hutchins, P. 1972. *Good-Night Owl.* New York: Macmillan.
>
> McCloskey, Robert. 1941, 1969. *Make Way for Ducklings.* Viking Press, Penguin.
>
> Rey, H. A. 1941, 1969. *Curious George.* Houghton Mifflin.
>
> Rice, E. 1977. *Sam Who Never Forgets.* New York: Greenwillow.
>
> Rosen, M. 1989. *We're Going On a Bear Hunt.* New York: McElderry.

Instruct Students

Read the title, look at the cover and discuss what the story might be about. Read the book to the students. Pause to have students predict what might happen next.

After you read the book,

Ask

Who was in this story?

What happened first?

Then what happened?

What happened next?

What happened at the end?

Note

The book can be one that you have previously read to students. Young children love the repetition, and repeated exposure to text is beneficial.

WEEKS 3 • 4

Preparation

Use one of the storybooks selected in Weeks 1 or 2. You will use this book to help develop the student's re-telling ability.

Instruct Students

Last week I read this story to you.

Today, I am going to see if you can tell it to me.

Let's see if you remember the story.

Tell the students the story's title. Next go through the book, page by page and show the students the pictures. Have them tell you what happened on each page. Go through the whole book, without reading.

Instruct Students

Let's see if you remember it.

I'll read it to see if you were right.

(Read the story.)

Who was in the story?

What happened first?

Then what happened?

What happened next?

What happened in the end?

WEEKS 5 • 6

Preparation

Use one of the storybooks selected in previous weeks. You will use this to develop re-telling, beginning composition skills and prosody.

Have some large chart paper on hand.

Instruct Students

> **Last week you told me this story.**
>
> **Today you will help me write the story.**
>
> **Who was in the story?**
>
> **What happened first?**
>
> **Then what happened?**
>
> **What happened next?**
>
> **What happened in the end?**

As the students tell you the story, write corresponding sentences on chart paper. Help direct students with your questions.

Read the story on the chart paper, scooping the sentences into phrases with Baby Echo. Be sure to model good phrasing. Have the students repeat, doing one sentence at a time.

Lastly, read it altogether. Point with Baby Echo, scooping phrases, and chorally reading with your students.

Unit 4 **Resources**

Drill Sounds

a - apple - /ă/	b - bat - /b/
c - cat - /k/	d - dog - /d/
e - Ed - /ĕ/	f - fun - /f/
g - game - /g/	h - hat - /h/
i - itch - /ĭ/	j - jug - /j/
k - kite - /k/	l - lamp - /l/
m - man - /m/	n - nut - /n/
o - octopus - /ŏ/	p - pan - /p/
qu - queen - /kw/	r - rat - /r/
s - snake - /s/	t - top - /t/
u - up - /ŭ/	v - van - /v/
w - wind - /w/	x - fox - /ks/
y - yellow - /y/	z - zebra - /z/

Echo Sounds

Sounds appear between / /. You say the sound. Students echo the sound and say the letter. Depending on the activity, students then either find or make the letter corresponding to that sound.

CONSONANTS

/b/ - b	/d/ - d	/f/ - f
/g/ - g	/h/ - h	/j/ - j
/k/ - c, k	/l/ - l	/m/ - m
/n/ - n	/p/ - p	/kw/ - qu
/r/ - r	/s/ - s	/t/ - t
/v/ - v	/w/ - w	/ks/ - x
/y/ - y	/z/ - z	

VOWELS

/ă/ - a	/ĕ/ - e	/ĭ/ - i
/ŏ/ - o	/ŭ/ - u	

Current Unit Words

mop	map	tap	tab	tub	rub
led	lad	bad	bud	bug	rug
dig	dip	zip	zap	tax	wet
bet	bit	fit	fig	fog	rib
sob	job	cop	dot	lid	mud
Ted	fix	lap	web	not	ten
bed	at	hip	peg	had	pen
bat	hit	pet	bus	bun	bib
red	jab	kid	nod	but	cup
mix	pot	Ben	pat	tab	Jim
tin	cob	rat	big	tip	cot
mad	den	gum	mug	sub	wig
yes	fun	cub	pup	lot	hut
sit	let	gap	sip	dug	cab
Sid	vet	wax	mat	lit	pig
nap	kit	did	pal	fox	nut
gas	him	tug	yet		

Each student must be assessed individually. This will take approximately 20 minutes per student and can be done by a paraprofessional or volunteer if one is available to assist you.

Copy the **Unit Test Recording Form** for each student (see Appendix). Use the student's durable materials, e.g., Dry Erase Board, Letter Board and Letter Tiles, as needed.

If a student does not score at least **8 / 10** or **4 / 5** on any given item, this student will need additional assistance with the assessed skill. (See Supplemental Activities for guidance.)

Have Student Identify Vowel Sounds

*Say a word and have student say the vowel sound. Provide an example: "What vowel sound is in the word **pat**?" Student responds: /ă/*

tag   pit   log   pen   mud

Have Student Tap and Read Words

Form words using the student's Letter Board and Letter Tiles and have student tap and read the words. Say, "Tap these sounds and tell me the word that I made."

top   gum   dip   bet   wax

Have Student Segment a Word into Its Sounds

*Say a word and have student say its sounds. Provide an example: "Tell me each sound in the word **cup**." Student responds: /k/ /ŭ/ /p/*

tap   rug   job   dig   nut

bat   bib   pet   cot   led

Have Student Tap and Spell Words

Say a word and have student repeat the word, tap it and then find corresponding Letter Tiles to spell the word on the student's Letter Board.

sit   job   pet   mad   bug

Have Student Retell a Story

Using one of the stories from a Storytime activity, see if student can retell the story with the pictures as a guide.

Answer Key

VOWEL SOUNDS

/ă/   /ĭ/   /ŏ/   /ĕ/   /ŭ/

SEGMENTED WORDS

/t/ /ă/ /p/	/r/ /ŭ/ /g/
/j/ /ŏ/ /b/	/d/ /ĭ/ /g/
/n/ /ŭ/ /t/	/b/ /ă/ /t/
/b/ /ĭ/ /b/	/p/ /ĕ/ /t/
/k/ /ŏ/ /t/	/l/ /ĕ/ /d

Note
Allow students to independently reference their Student Notebooks. Count responses checked in their Notebooks as correct but make a notation that the book was used.

Unit 5 Level K

Introduction

In this Unit, you will introduce the students to sentence structure. The students will read short sentences and begin to write sentences.

You will also teach students some high frequency non-phonetic sight words. In Fundations®, these are called Trick Words.

Lastly, you will discuss the differences between narrative and expository text.

In a Nutshell

NEW CONCEPTS

- Sentence structure
- Sentence dictation
- Narrative vs. expository text

TRICK WORDS

the	is	was
a	and	of

PLANNED TIME IN UNIT

6 WEEKS

Note
Extend the time in this Unit if students do not demonstrate mastery.

PREPARING YOUR MATERIALS

- You will need the Blue Word Frames for Word Play.

- You will need narrative and non-fiction animal books for Storytime.

Arrange your Standard Sound Card display in the following manner

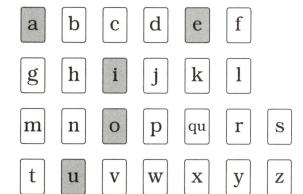

PREPARING YOUR STUDENTS

Students should have the **Magnetic Letter Tiles** (a-z) on their **Letter Boards**. Students place the **Alphabet Overlay** on their boards and then match the tiles to the corresponding square on the overlay.

PREPARING FOR HOME SUPPORT

Copy and send home the **Unit 5 Letter and Activity Packet**.

Getting Ready

VIEW THE CD-ROM

LEVEL K
- Unit 5
  Lesson Activities (see below)

STUDY LESSON ACTIVITIES

Review the following activities in your manual's Lesson Activity Overview and on CD-ROM:

CD-ROM LEVEL 1 Activities:

- Trick Words

The students will sky write and finger spell these words, as well as write them on their Dry Erase Writing Tablet.

Note
In Level 1, the students add trick words to their Student Notebooks, but not in Level K

Week 1

DAY ❶	DAY ❷	DAY ❸	DAY ❹	DAY ❺
Drill Sounds	Drill Sounds	Drill Sounds	Drill Sounds	Drill Sounds
Introduce New Concepts	Introduce New Concepts	Word Play	Trick Words	Storytime
Echo/Find Sounds & Words	Echo/Find Sounds & Words	Dictation (Dry Erase)	Make It Fun	
	Word Play	Echo/Letter Formation	Dictation (Dry Erase)	

Weeks 2 • 6

DAY ❶	DAY ❷	DAY ❸	DAY ❹	DAY ❺
Drill Sounds	Drill Sounds	Drill Sounds	Drill Sounds	Drill Sounds
Trick Words	Trick Words	Word Play	Trick Words	Storytime
Word Play	Word Play	Dictation (Dry Erase)	Make It Fun	
Echo/Find Sounds & Words	Echo/Find Sounds & Words	Echo/Letter Formation	Dictation (Dry Erase)	

 **Introduce New Concepts**

TEACH SENTENCE READING

Write the following sentence on the board:

Meg is sad.

Help students tap out the words **Meg** and **sad**. Tell them the word **is** (do not tap it out).

Use Baby Echo to point to the words and read the sentence. Have students echo. Discuss the capital letter at the beginning of the sentence and the period at the end.

Do the same with the following sentences. (Explain the word **the** if it is unknown to the students.)

Rob sat in the sun.

The rat sat in the mud.

Next, demonstrate how to read these sentences with fluency. Draw the scoops under the sentences. Read it in phrases as you scoop with Baby Echo.

Rob sat in the sun.

The rat sat in the mud.

TEACH SENTENCE DICTATION

Teach sentence dictation using the Blue Word Frames on your magnetic board.

Say the sentence and have students echo. Then write the sentence on the Blue Word Frames.

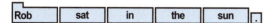

| Rob | sat | in | the | sun | . |

Explain that at the beginning of a sentence, the word must begin with a capital letter. That is why the frame at the beginning is tall.

Discuss period used to end the sentence.

Erase the Word Frames and place them in a column. Next dictate another sentence.

Say

> Tom had a dog.

Have the students echo. Select a student to come forward and find the Blue Word Frames needed for the sentence. Next, tap out the first word and have a student come up and write the word on the Blue Word Frame. Continue with each word, calling on a different student. Tap each word before the student writes it. Write the word **a** for the student. (Do not tap it - it is a Trick Word.) Be sure to discuss capital letter and punctuation.

Proofread the sentence with students, tapping each word to check the spelling. Do not tap the word **a**.

TRICK WORDS

Tell the students that some words cannot be tapped out. They are important and they need to be memorized.

Say

> We call these words trick words because they are very tricky.

Write the word **the** on the classroom board in large (2 foot) letters. Follow the Lesson Activity procedure to teach trick words.

Next, teach the word **is**, following the same procedure.

Unit 5 Lesson Activity Plan

 Drill Sounds

Large Sound Cards

First practice sounds with the Large Sound Cards. Say the letter-keyword-sound and have students echo. Be selective.

Standard Sound Cards

Next, point to the Standard Sound Cards (on display) with the Baby Echo pointer. You say the letter-keyword-sound and hold up Baby Echo to have students repeat. You can have a student be the drill leader for some of the sounds.

 Echo/Letter Formation

Remind students of proper pencil grip and sitting position, and give them their Dry Erase Tablets.

Dictate 5-6 previously taught sounds. You select and say the sound. Students echo the sound and say the letter.

Next have a student come up to the classroom board to make the letter on the Writing Grid.

Then have all students write the answer on their Dry Erase Tablets as you direct them with the letter formation verbalization.

(See Unit Resources.)

 Word Play

RETEACH TAPPING TO READ WORDS

Use your Standard Sound Card display to make 3-5 Unit words. (See Unit Resources.)

Make each word then say and tap each sound.

Have students tap with you. Then blend the sounds as you drag your thumb across your fingers.

Next, point under each card as you say each sound, then drag your finger under all three cards as you blend the sounds to read the word.

READ SENTENCES

Write a sentence on the board and scoop it into phrases. Have the students try to read each word to themselves and then call on a student. Tell them untaught Trick Words. After each word is decoded, chorally read the sentence with fluency. Do 3-5 sentences. (See Unit Resources.)

WRITE SENTENCES

Use the Blue Word Frames and dictate 2-3 sentences. (See Unit Resources.) Follow the procedure for sentence dictation described in Introduce New Concepts.

 Trick Words

Trick words require lots of practice. Sky write and finger write Trick Words, but **do not** tap them out or make them with the Magnetic Letter Tiles.

Word Resource

WEEK 1	
the	is

WEEK 2	
was	a

WEEK 3	
and	of

Echo/Find Sounds & Words

Echo/Find Sounds

Say a sound. Have students echo and find the letter on their magnetic Letter Board.

Ask

  What says /b/? (b)

(See Echo Sounds in Unit Resources for expected student responses.)

Echo/Find Words

Dictate a unit word. Have one student come find your corresponding cards.

(See Current Unit Words in Unit Resources.)

Have students find Letter Tiles needed to make words on their Magnetic Letter Boards. After finding a word, have a student spell it orally.

Dictation

Refer to this Unit's Resource List of Echo Sounds and Words.

Proper Dictation Activity procedures are very important. Be sure to follow their demonstration on the CD-ROM.

DRY ERASE

Dictate 3 sounds, 3 words and 3 trick words.

Make It Fun

Preparation
• Blue Word Frames

CHANGE THE SENTENCE

The purpose of this activity is to reinforce sentence structure and spelling.

Instruct Students

Say a sentence and have students repeat. Have a student place the Word Frames as needed. Write the sentence on the Frames.

Say

  Let's change this sentence to: Pat had the red hat.

Have a student erase **Meg** and change the word to **Pat**.

Tap out the word to check the student's spelling.

Continue dictating changes, reading the entire sentence and have a student make the necessary change. If you change a trick word do not tap it out.

Sentence Resource

WEEK 1

Meg had the red hat.

Pat had the red hat.

Pat had the red mug.

Jim had the red mug.

WEEK 2

Jim had the pup.

Jim had the map.

Tom had the map.

Tom <u>hid</u> the map.

WEEK 3

Sid is a dog.

Sid is a <u>cat</u>.

<u>Tab</u> is a cat.

Tab is a <u>rat</u>.

WEEK 4

The bug is in a pot.

The bug is in <u>the</u> pot.

The bug is in the <u>mud</u>.

The <u>fox</u> is in the mud.

WEEK 5

The gum is in the bag.

The gum <u>was</u> in the bag.

The gum was in the <u>box</u>.

The <u>nut</u> was in the box.

WEEK 6

Mom sat on the log.

<u>Deb</u> sat on the log.

Deb sat on the <u>cot</u>.

<u>Ted</u> sat on the cot.

 Storytime

WEEKS 1 • 6

Preparation

You will select books to demonstrate narrative versus non-fiction text. Do this by finding a narrative story with an animal in it and a corresponding non-fiction book about that animal. For example, you can select a story with an owl in it and then a book about owls.

Narrative

Yolen, Jane. 1987. ***Owl Moon***. New York: Philonel Books

Non-fiction (expository) text

Amosky, Jim. 1995. ***All About Owls.*** New York, New York: Scholastic Inc.

Jarvis, Kila and Holt, Denver. 1996. ***Owls: Whoo Are They?*** Missoula, MT: Mountain Press Publishing Company.

Instruct Students

Show the students the two books. Tell them that some books tell make-believe stories and other books tell us facts that are true. Read the narrative story.

Ask

Who was in the story?

What happened first?

Then what happened?

What happened next?

What happened in the end?

Tell the students that stories which are make-believe have something happen in them, and they have an ending like the one you just read.

Then show them the non-fiction book and explain that this book has true facts. You do not need to do the entire non-fiction book but select different facts to share.*

After you finish, have the students tell you 5 facts about the animal. Write these in full sentences on chart paper. Read each fact and have the students echo. Lastly, chorally read the facts together.

* In weeks 2-6 read both the narrative and part of the non-fiction book. Ask the students to decide which book is make-believe and which one presents true facts.

Drill Sounds

a - apple - /ă/	b - bat - /b/
c - cat - /k/	d - dog - /d/
e - Ed - /ĕ/	f - fun - /f/
g - game - /g/	h - hat - /h/
i - itch - /ĭ/	j - jug - /j/
k - kite - /k/	l - lamp - /l/
m - man - /m/	n - nut - /n/
o - octopus - /ŏ/	p - pan - /p/
qu - queen - /kw/	r - rat - /r/
s - snake - /s/	t - top - /t/
u - up - /ŭ/	v - van - /v/
w - wind - /w/	x - fox - /ks/
y - yellow - /y/	z - zebra - /z/

Echo Sounds

Sounds appear between / /. You say the sound. Students echo the sound and say the letter. Depending on the activity, students then either find or make the letter corresponding to that sound.

CONSONANTS

/b/ - b	/d/ - d	/f/ - f
/g/ - g	/h/ - h	/j/ - j
/k/ - c, k	/l/ - l	/m/ - m
/n/ - n	/p/ - p	/kw/ - qu
/r/ - r	/s/ - s	/t/ - t
/v/ - v	/w/ - w	/ks/ - x
/y/ - y	/z/ - z	

VOWELS

/ă/ - a	/ĕ/ - e	/ĭ/ - i
/ŏ/ - o	/ŭ/ - u	

Current Unit Trick Words

the	is	was
a	and	of

Current Unit Words

mop	map	tap	tab	tub	rub
led	lad	bad	bud	bug	rug
dig	dip	zip	zap	wet	bet
bit	fit	fig	fog	rib	sob
job	cop	dot	lid	mud	Ted
fix	lap	web	not	ten	bed
at	hip	peg	had	pen	bat
hit	pet	bus	bun	bib	red
jab	kid	nod	but	cup	mix
pot	Ben	pat	Jim	tin	cob
rat	big	tip	cot	mad	den
gum	mug	sub	wig	yes	fun
cub	pup	lot	hut	sit	let
gap	sip	dug	cab	Sid	vet
wax	mat	lit	pig	nap	kit
did	pal	fox	nut	gas	him
tug	yet				

Sentences

*Words in **bold** are trick words. Write untaught trick words from this Unit on Blue Words Frames for students. After you have taught a trick word, students should write it in a sentence.*

Nat **is** sad.

The rag **is** on the mat.

The rat **had a** nap.

Mom **had a** map.

Rob **is** on **the** mat.

The rat sat in **the** mud.

Rob sat in **the** sun.

Meg **is** not sad.

Mom sat on **the** log.

The bug **is** in **the** pot.

The gum **is** in **the** bag.

Rob bit **the** fig.

Mom had **a** sip **of** pop.

Deb met Tom.

Deb had **a** bad cut.

Meg had **a** red hat.

The cat hid in **the** box.

The wax **is** hot.

The pup had fun.

Max had **a** dog.

The wig **is** on Viv.

The fox **is** in the pen.

Tom had **a** quiz.

Each student must be assessed individually. This will take approximately 20 minutes per student and can be done by a paraprofessional or volunteer if one is available to assist you.

Copy the **Unit Test Recording Form** for each student (see Appendix). Use the student's durable materials, e.g., Dry Erase Board, Letter Board and Letter Tiles, as needed.

If a student does not score at least **4** correct on any given item, this student will need additional assistance with the assessed skill. (See Supplemental Activities for guidance.)

Have Student Identify Trick Words

Present trick words on flashcards and have student read them. (Do not tap trick words.)

the   is   was   of   and   a

Have Student Read a Sentence

Using your Blue Sentence Frames, write the following sentence and have student read it: **The rat had a nap.** *Note which words student reads correctly.*

The   rat   had   a   nap

Have Student Complete a Sentence

Using your Blue Sentence Frames, write the following sentence, omitting Deb, mat, and the period. **Deb is on the mat.** *Have student complete the sentence and note which items are completed successfully. Say, "I will say a sentence. Repeat the sentence and finish making it for me."*

Have Student Relate Events in a Narrative

Using a fiction and a non-fiction book from Storytime, ask the following questions:

Which of these books tells a make-believe story?

What happened first?

What happened next?

What happened at the end?

Which of these books tells true facts?

Can you tell me two true facts?

Answer Key

TRICK WORDS

the   is   was   of   and   a

SENTENCE COMPLETION

student correctly spells *Deb*

student uses capital *D*

student correctly spells *mat*

student adds the period

Note
Allow students to independently reference their Student Notebooks. Count responses checked in their Notebooks as correct but make a notation that the book was used.

Level 1

Orientation & Units 1-14

Level 1 **Fundations® Program Overview**

Level 1 of Fundations reinforces the basic skills that were learned in Kindergarten and progresses further into the study of word structure.

In addition to Fundations, provide your students with a wide variety of literature experiences, exposing them to poetry, narrative and expository text.

By The End Of Level 1, Students Will Be Able To

- Segment words into syllables
- Segment syllables into sounds (phonemes) – up to 5 sounds
- Name sounds of consonants (primary) and short and long vowels when given letters
- Name corresponding letter(s) when given sounds of consonants and vowels
- Identify word structures such as blends, digraphs, basewords, suffixes, syllable types (closed and vowel-consonant-e syllables)
- Read and spell CVC, CCVC, CVCC, CCVCC, CVCe words
- Read and spell compound words and other words with two syllables
- Read and spell words with s , es, ed, ing suffixes
- Read and spell Trick Words or targeted high-frequency words:
- Construct sentences using vocabulary words
- Read controlled stories with fluency, expression and understanding
- Apply beginning dictionary skills
- Apply correct punctuation (period, question mark, exclamation point)
- Apply capitalization rules for beginning of sentences and names of people
- Re-tell short narrative stories
- Re-tell facts from expository text

Unit 1 (2-3 weeks)
- Letter formations (a-z)
- Alphabetical order
- Letter names, keywords and sounds: short vowels, consonants

Unit 2 (2 weeks)
- Blending and reading three-sound short vowel words
- Segmenting and spelling three-sound short vowel words
- Phonemic awareness skills: sound manipulation (initial, final, medial)
- Sentence dictation procedures: capitalization, period, word spacing
- Sentence proofreading procedures
- Trick words: the, of, and
- Sample words: cat, sip, log, fox

Unit 3 (3 weeks)
- Concept of consonant digraph, keywords and sounds: sh, ch , th, wh, ck
- Spelling of ck at the end of words
- Sentence dictation procedures: question mark
- Narrative vs. expository text
- Prosody with echo reading
- Trick words: to, a, was, is, he, for, as, his, has
- Sample words: wish, chop, sock

Unit 4 (2 weeks)
- "Bonus" Letter spelling rule – ff, ll, ss and sometimes z
- Glued sounds – all
- Story re-telling
- Prosody with echo reading
- Trick words: I, you, we, they, one, said
- Sample words: hill, puff, bill, miss, call

Unit 5 (1 week)
- Glued sounds: am, an
- Story re-telling
- Prosody with echo reading
- Trick words: from, or, have
- Sample words: ham, can, fan

Unit 6 (3 weeks)
- Baseword and suffix with the suffix, s

- Plural nouns
- Story re-telling
- Prosody with echo reading
- Narrative story structure
- Beginning composition skills
- Trick words: were, her, put, there, what, she, been, by, who

Unit 7 (3 weeks)

- Glued sounds: ang, ing, ong, ung, ank, ink, onk, unk
- Blending and reading words with ng and nk
- Segmenting and spelling words with ng and nk
- Story re-telling
- Prosody with echo reading
- Narrative story structure
- Beginning composition skills
- Trick words: out, so, are, two, about, into, only, other, new
- Sample words: bang, bank, pink

Unit 8 (3 weeks)

- Blending and reading words with 4 sounds (+ suffix, s)
- Segmenting and spelling words with 4 sounds (+ suffix, s)
- Story re-telling
- Prosody with echo reading
- Narrative story structure
- Paragraph structure
- Trick words: some, could, want, say, do, first, any, my, now
- Sample words: bump, stash, bled, past, steps

Unit 9 (2 weeks)

- Teach the concept of closed syllable
- Story re-telling
- Prosody with echo reading
- Trick words: our, over, come, would, after, also
- Sample words: kit, slip, stash

Unit 10 (3 weeks)

- Blending and reading words with 5 sounds (+ suffix, s)
- Segmenting and spelling words with 5 sounds (+ suffix, s)
- Words with suffix s used as action words vs. plurals
- Story re-telling
- Prosody with echo reading

- Narrative story structure
- Beginning composition skills
- Trick words: many, before, called, how, your, down, should, because, each
- Sample words: stump, clasp, strap

Unit 11 (3 weeks)

- Concept of syllable
- Compound words
- Syllable division rules for closed syllables: compound words between 2 vowels
- Story re-telling
- Prosody with echo reading
- Expository text
- Beginning composition skills
- Trick words: people, Mr., Mrs., years, says, little, good, very, own
- Sample words: catnip, publish

Unit 12 (2 weeks)

- Adding s and es suffix to unchanging basewords with closed syllables
- Story re-telling
- Prosody with echo reading
- Trick words: see, work, between, both, being, under
- Sample words: bumps, steps, wishes, lunches

Unit 13 (2 weeks)

- Adding ed, ing suffixes added to unchanging basewords with closed syllables
- Story re-telling
- Prosody with echo reading
- Trick words: never, another, day, words, look, through
- Sample words: wishing, rented, slashing, blended

Unit 14 (2 weeks)

- Long vowel sounds for vowel-consonant-e
- Vowel-consonant-e syllable type (one-syllable words)
- Expository text
- Prosody with echo reading
- Trick words: friend, around, circle, does, nothing, write, none, color, month
- Sample words: stove, hope, caves

Orientation   Level 1

Introduction

Take time first to get "oriented" and to prepare both yourself and your students for your year ahead with Fundations®.

THE WILSON WRITING GRID

The Wilson Writing Grid is designed to guide students in proper letter formation. It consists of four lines that correspond to specific letter placement. The lines are named and the pictures will assist students in identifying the lines.

The bold line (or the "dark" line) helps locate the top of the grid, especially on pages with multiple grids. This bold line is also the starting point for all upper-case letters.

Lower-case letters start on this bold line or on the (dashed) plane line just beneath it. You will stress this so that students do not form letters from the bottom up.

THE WILSON FONT

The Wilson Font provides a basic manuscript form of print. Often students come to Kindergarten or Grade 1 with an ability to write upper-case letters of the alphabet. To begin reading and spelling instruction, lower-case letter knowledge is key. Rather than reinforce or teach the upper-case letters first, Fundations starts with the lower-case letters.

In Fundations, letter formation is closely connected with sound instruction. Students learn the letter name, its formation and its sound simultaneously. This creates an important link and uses motor memory learning to associate letters with their sounds. Students will succeed with consistent verbal cues, repetition, sky writing, tracing and writing practice (all described in the lesson activities).

In a Nutshell

NEW CONCEPTS

- Echoing (Echo the Owl and Baby Echo)
- The Wilson Writing Grid with the line names
- Sky Write/Letter Formation
- Following verbalizations in making lines
- Pencil grip and writing posture
- The meaning of the word 'trace'

PLANNED TIME IN ORIENTATION

1 DAY (30 MINUTE LESSON)

Do this Orientation Lesson the week preceding the start of Unit 1.

WILSON WRITING GRID

The Wilson Writing Grid will be used on your classroom board. Copy the grid pictures (see Appendix) and cut them and tape to your board. Draw a large grid (at least 2 feet tall).

As an option, if you have an overhead projector and screen in the classroom, use the Wilson Writing Grid Overhead in the Appendix and make an overhead. This will be very useful for work with students in sky writing.

PENCIL GRIP PICTURE

Copy the Pencil Grip Picture (see Appendix). Tape the picture in a place that can be seen by all students. It will serve as a reminder to them on how to properly hold a pencil or marker.

DESK STRIPS

Put a Desk Strip on each student's desk. This can be removed at the end of the year.

STUDENT NOTEBOOK AND COMPOSITION BOOKS

Write the student names on the front of the students' Composition Books and Notebooks. Use a thin black marker. Be sure to print the name clearly using the Wilson Font letters (see Appendix). Do this for each student to provide them with a model to copy.

BABY ECHO

To facilitate pointing with Baby Echo place it on a pointer or ruler.

Dry Erase Markers and Erasers

Dry erase markers and erasers are not provided with Fundations since many classrooms are already equipped with them. Old socks can be used for erasers!

Getting Ready

VIEW THE CD-ROM

LEVEL 1
- Introduction
- Unit 1

STUDY LESSON ACTIVITIES

Review the following activities in you manual's Lesson Activity Overview and on CD-ROM:

Drill Sounds
  Introduce Echo the Owl
  Introduce Baby Echo

Sky Write Letters
  Teach Wilson Writing Grid

Teach How To Echo

Hold up the large white owl and ask the students to name the kind of bird. Explain that owls have very good eyesight and hearing.

Next, tell the students its name, Echo. Ask if anyone knows what the word echo means. Explain that Echo the Owl is going to help them learn their letters and sounds and that he wants the students to "echo" him whenever you hold him up.

Say the word, "hello" and hold up Echo. The students should say "hello." Say several words or phrases to practice echoing.

You can also introduce Baby Echo and say that he is just like big Echo. He wants to help the students learn their letters and sounds and so he has them echo too.

 Teach The Writing Grid

In order to learn the letters, students will need to follow basic directions. Prepare them by teaching them the names of the lines on the writing grid.

Show Students The Wilson Writing Grid On Your Classroom Board

Explain that all the lines have names. Point to the cloud and ask what it is. Point to the sun and ask what it is.

Ask

Where do you find the sun and clouds?
(In the sky)

Tell students the top line is called the sky line. Do the same for the other lines. Tell them that these lines will help them make their letters.

Show them that the plane flies along the plane line, tracing your finger from left to right. It reminds us to make our letters and words in that direction.

Have Students Point To The Grid Lines

Next have the students stand up and tell them to point their arms out "straight as a pencil." Don't let them bend their elbows. Tell them to point with their pointer fingers.

Face the writing grid and point with the students to model.

Say

Point to the sky line.

Point to the plane line.

Point to the worm line.

Next ask for line names randomly:

Say

Listen carefully, I'll try to trick you.

Point to the plane line.

Point to the sky line.

Point to the plane line.

Repeat until students can easily point to each line.

 Teach How to Follow Verbalizations

Have students shake out their hands. Demonstrate wiggling and shaking body and arms. Have them stretch (stand on toes and stretch hands up to the ceiling).

Next, tell them you are going to do something a little different. First show them and then have them do it with you. Say the verbalization each time in order to direct them.

Say

> Point to the sky line – go down to the grass line. Stop!
>
> Point to the plane line, go down to the grass line. Stop!
>
> Point to the plane line, go all the way to the worm line. Stop!
>
> Shake out your hand.

 Teach Pencil Grip and Tracing

Teach the students how to hold their markers and sit for writing. Have them follow your verbalizations to make lines. Lastly, teach students how to trace. You will need to reinforce these concepts daily throughout Unit 1.

Before you give out the Dry Erase Writing Tablets, explain to the students that you will help them do what they need to do in order to get a tablet.

Say

> First, all children need to pull in their seats and put their feet on the floor. Now put your hands on the desk.
>
> This is your writing position. Whenever we write, you need to sit like this.
>
> Maria is ready for her tablet.

As students show readiness, give out the Dry Erase Writing Tablets, (but not the markers).

Say

> Next, let me show you how you will hold the markers.
>
> The first thing you do is pinch the marker between your thumb and pointer finger.
>
> Then put your other fingers together to rest your pencil and put it on the table.

Help students with their pencil grip as you give them the markers.

When all the markers are dispersed have the students do the following all together:

Say

> Pinch your marker between your thumb and your pointer finger.
>
> Put your other fingers together and rest your marker on the table.
>
> Now I think you are ready to use the special tablets.

Have students practice following your directions, simply making lines.

Say

> Point your marker to the sky line next to number 1. Go down to the grass line and stop.

Hold up your Dry Erase Writing Tablet and model and then do it again with them (say the same verbalization each time). After making each line, have students check to see if their line looks like your line and then erase.

Say

> Point your marker to the plane line. Go to the grass line. Stop!
>
> Point your marker to the plane line. Go to worm line and stop!
>
> Now let's do one more thing. This is tricky.

Make a line from the sky line to the grass line and then explain what "trace" means, tracing the line back up to the sky line. Have them trace as you verbalize the directions:

Say

> Point to the plane line, go to the grass line. Now trace back up to the plane line and stop.

Do other variations, directing students with your verbalization.

Example

> Point to the sky line, go to the grass line. Now trace back up to the plane line and stop.

Unit 1 Level 1

Introduction

Unit 1 varies from all other units in Level 1. Unit 1 will set the stage for the other units, reviewing or teaching the letter names, keywords, sounds and lower-case letter formations of the letters a-z.

The Sky Write/Letter Formation activity, combined with the Letter-Keyword-Sound activity helps to form and solidify an association between the letter and its corresponding sound.

THE LESSON ACTIVITY PLAN

Each Unit provides an outline of the Daily Schedule of activities.

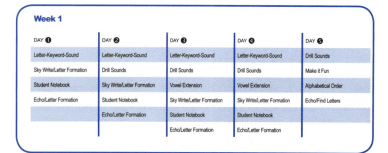

Week 1				
DAY ❶	**DAY ❷**	**DAY ❸**	**DAY ❹**	**DAY ❺**
Letter-Keyword-Sound	Letter-Keyword-Sound	Letter-Keyword-Sound	Letter-Keyword-Sound	Drill Sounds
Sky Write/Letter Formation	Drill Sounds	Drill Sounds	Drill Sounds	Make it Fun
Student Notebook	Sky Write/Letter Formation	Vowel Extension	Vowel Extension	Alphabetical Order
Echo/Letter Formation	Student Notebook	Sky Write/Letter Formation	Sky Write/Letter Formation	Echo/Find Letters
	Echo/Letter Formation	Student Notebook	Student Notebook	
		Echo/Letter Formation	Echo/Letter Formation	

For example, on Day 1, Week 1, you will do the following activities: Letter-Keyword-Sound, Sky Write/Letter Formation, Student Notebook and Echo/Letter Formation.

Lesson Activity Procedures (In General)

There are standard procedures for each lesson activity. To smoothly execute these activities, refer to the Lesson Activity Section of this Manual and view the corresponding CD-ROM. Note that the Lesson Activities are listed in alphabetical order for your quick reference. Over time, these lesson procedures will become second nature!

Lesson Activity Information (Specific To The Unit)

In the Unit, you will find *specific* information for Lesson Activities as it relates to that Unit. This guide will give you what you need to present the Unit lessons.

In a Nutshell

NEW CONCEPTS

- Letter-Keyword-Sound for consonants
- Letter-Keyword-Sound for short vowels
- Letter Formation for lower-case letters a-z
- Alphabetical Order
- Sound recognition for consonants and short vowels

PLANNED TIME IN UNIT

2 WEEKS

If students had Fundations in Kindergarten

3 WEEKS

If students did not have Fundations in Kindergarten

Note
Extend the time in this Unit if student mastery is not demonstrated on the Unit Test.

For the additional week(s) do Drill Sounds, Sky Write/Letter Formation, Alphabetic Order, Echo/Find Sounds, and Dictation.

ALPHABETICAL ORDER

Week 1
| Day 1 | t b f | Day 3 | c a |
| Day 2 | n m | Day 4 | i r |

Week 2
| Day 1 | o g | Day 3 | e u |
| Day 2 | d s | Day 4 | l h k |

Week 3
| Day 1 | p j | Day 3 | z q |
| Day 2 | v w | Day 4 | y x |

PREPARING YOUR MATERIALS

Arrange your Standard Sound Card display in the following manner

As letters are introduced, the Standard Sound Cards (a-z) should be placed on display. If your classroom board is magnetic, use the Magnetic Tape on the back of each Standard Sound Card to adhere it to the board. If your board is not magnetic, you can use a pocket chart or masking tape to display the cards. The letter cards should be added gradually during the weeks in Unit 1.

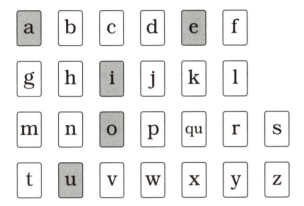

Note How The Cards Are Arranged In Four Rows

This arrangement is designed to help the students learn the alphabet in four quadrants. These four quadrants are used for beginning dictionary skills. You will see that the Vocabulary and Trick Word sections in the Student Notebook are also delineated into these four quadrants.

VOWEL EXTENSION PICTURES

Make a copy of the Keyword Pictures of the vowels **a - apple**, **e - Ed**, **i - itch**, **o - octopus**, **u - up** (see Appendix). These will be used for the Vowel Extension Activity.

LETTER BOARD AND ALPHABET OVERLAY

For each student, tape the Alphabet Overlay in the upper left hand corner of one of the magnetic boards. This will be used as the student's Letter Board. (The Syllable Overlay can be stored away until it is needed in Unit 11.)

LETTER FORMATION GUIDE

Copy the Letter Formation Guide (see Appendix). If possible, laminate for easy reference during your instruction.

Getting Ready

VIEW THE CD-ROM

LEVEL 1
- Unit 1 (Video)
  Lesson Activities (see below)

LEVEL K
- Unit 2 (Video)
  Lesson Activities (see below)

STUDY LESSON ACTIVITIES

Review the following activities in your manual's Lesson Activity Overview and on CD-ROM:

Drill Sounds
  Large Sound Cards
  Standard Sound Cards (Teacher Drill Leader)
Echo Sounds/Words
  Echo/Find Sounds

Unit 1 Lesson Activity Plan

Week 1

DAY ❶	DAY ❷	DAY ❸	DAY ❹	DAY ❺
Letter-Keyword-Sound	Letter-Keyword-Sound	Letter-Keyword-Sound	Letter-Keyword-Sound	Drill Sounds
Sky Write/Letter Formation	Drill Sounds	Drill Sounds	Drill Sounds	Make it Fun
Student Notebook	Sky Write/Letter Formation	Vowel Extension	Vowel Extension	Alphabetical Order
Echo/Letter Formation	Student Notebook	Sky Write/Letter Formation	Sky Write/Letter Formation	Echo/Find Letters
	Echo/Letter Formation	Student Notebook	Student Notebook	
		Echo/Letter Formation	Echo/Letter Formation	

Week 2

DAY ❶	DAY ❷	DAY ❸	DAY ❹	DAY ❺
Letter-Keyword-Sound	Letter-Keyword-Sound	Letter-Keyword-Sound	Letter-Keyword-Sound	Drill Sounds
Drill Sounds	Drill Sounds	Drill Sounds	Drill Sounds	Make it Fun
Vowel Extension	Vowel Extension	Vowel Extension	Vowel Extension	Alphabetical Order
Sky Write/Letter Formation	Sky Write/Letter Formation	Sky Write/Letter Formation	Sky Write/Letter Formation	Echo/Find Letters
Student Notebook	Student Notebook	Student Notebook	Student Notebook	
Echo/Letter Formation	Echo/Letter Formation	Echo/Letter Formation	Echo/Letter Formation	

Week 3

DAY ❶	DAY ❷	DAY ❸	DAY ❹	DAY ❺
Letter-Keyword-Sound	Letter-Keyword-Sound	Letter-Keyword-Sound	Letter-Keyword-Sound	Make it Fun
Drill Sounds	Drill Sounds	Drill Sounds	Drill Sounds	Alphabetical Order
Vowel Extension	Vowel Extension	Vowel Extension	Vowel Extension	Echo/Find Letters
Sky Write/Letter Formation	Sky Write/Letter Formation	Sky Write/Letter Formation	Sky Write/Letter Formation	Unit Test
Student Notebook	Student Notebook	Student Notebook	Student Notebook	
Echo/Letter Formation	Echo/Letter Formation	Echo/Letter Formation	Echo/Letter Formation	

Letter-Keyword-Sound

WEEK 1 DAY ❶

Introduce Letter-Keyword-Sound with Large and Standard Sound Cards: **t**, **b**, **f**. These letters are sky line letters.

WEEK 1 DAY ❷

Introduce Letter-Keyword-Sound with Large and Standard Sound Cards: **n**, **m**. These letters are plane line letters. Have the students look at your mouth position when saying /**m**/ and /**n**/. They sound alike but your mouth is closed when you say /**m**/.

WEEK 1 DAY ❸

Introduce Letter-Keyword-Sound with Large and Standard Sound Cards: **c**, **a**. Explain that **a** is a vowel and that it is special. Tell the students that the vowels will be on the orange colored cards. Demonstrate how to hold the vowel sound /**ā**/ until you run out of breath. Also show the students that the letter **a** on the Standard Sound Card looks different, similar to the way it looks in books. Tell them that they do not need to write it that way, but that they can write it like the one on the Large Sound Card.

WEEK 1 DAY ❹

Introduce Letter-Keyword-Sound with Large and Standard Sound Cards: **i**, **r**. These letters are plane line letters.

WEEK 2 DAY ❶

Introduce Letter-Keyword-Sound with Large and Standard Sound Cards: **o**, **g**. These letters are plane line round letters. Show them that letter **g** also looks different on the Standard Sound Card, similar to the way it looks in books.

WEEK 2 DAY ❷

Introduce Letter-Keyword-Sound with Large and Standard Sound Cards: **d**, **s**. These letters are plane line round letters.

WEEK 2 DAY ❸

Introduce Letter-Keyword-Sound with Large and Standard Sound Cards: **e**, **u**. These letters are the last two vowels. The letter **e** is a plane line round letter that is different because it starts between the plane line and the grass line. The letter **u** is a plane line letter. Do the Vowel Extension activity with all the vowels.

WEEK 2 DAY ❹

Introduce Letter-Keyword-Sound with Large and Standard Sound Cards: **l**, **h**, **k**. These letters are sky line letters.

WEEK 3 DAY ❶

Introduce Letter-Keyword-Sound with Large and Standard Sound Cards: **p**, **j**. These letters are plane line letters that go all the way down to the worm line.

WEEK 3 DAY ❷

Introduce Letter-Keyword-Sound with Large and Standard Sound Cards: **v**, **w**. These letters are plane line slide letters.

WEEK 3 DAY ❸

Introduce Letter-Keyword-Sound with Large and Standard Sound Cards: **z**, **qu**. The letter **z** is a plane line slide letter. The letter **q** is a plane line round letter. We call it the "chicken letter" because it will never ever go anywhere without his best buddy, **u**. Tell the students that **u** does not count as a vowel when it is with the letter **q**. It just sits there to keep **q** company.

Unit 1 **Lesson Activity Plan**

Introduce Letter-Keyword-Sound with Large and Standard Sound Cards: **y**, **x**. These letters are plane line slide letters.

 Student Notebook

Direct the students to find the letters that you are working on in the sound section of their Student Notebooks. Direct them to point to one letter at a time.

When students find the letter:

Ask

> What is the name of this letter?

> What is the picture to help us remember the sound?

> What is the sound that this letter makes?

Say the letter-keyword-sound and have them echo. Lastly, have the students color the corresponding keyword pictures.

 Drill Sounds

Do All The Introduced Sounds Each Day

First practice sounds with the Large Sound Cards (see Unit Resources).

Say the letter-keyword-sound and have the students echo. Next, point to the Standard Sound Cards (which are on display) with the Baby Echo pointer. You say the letter-keyword-sound and hold up Baby Echo to have the students repeat.

Note

As a new sound is taught, the Standard Sound Card should be added to your display to be drilled at each lesson.

 Sky Write/Letter Formation

Have the students stand. Always start this activity by shaking out arms and body and stretching.

Follow the Letter Formation Guide instructions and demonstrate how to make the letter you are going to practice. Be sure to face the Writing Grid and use the verbalization.

After you demonstrate, have students put their arms out "straight as a pencil" and point with two fingers. Do the letter again and have the students do it with you, following the verbalization. Do it together several times.

At least once, make the letter while saying the letter-keyword-sound (**t-top-/t/**). This helps to make an association between the formation and the sound.

You can have students shake out their arms before teaching or practicing a new letter.

 Echo/Letter Formation

Reinforce the correct pencil grip. Say a sound and hold up Echo the Owl.

Say

> /t/

Students repeat.

Ask

> What says /t/?

Select a student to give you the answer, naming the letter **t**.

Next have that student come up to the classroom board to make it on the Writing Grid. Then have all students write the answer on their Dry Erase Writing Tablets as you direct them with the letter formation verbalization.

Do the new sounds as well as two or three sounds from previous days.

(See Echo Sounds in Unit Resources.)

 ### Vowel Extension

Use the Keyword Pictures (see Appendix) to make a Vowel Extension activity on chart paper on your classroom board.

Vowels are open-mouth sounds and therefore they can be held. This activity helps the students extend the vowel sound. Model 'reading' the Keyword Picture: /ă/...**pple**. Extend the /ă/ sound while you trace the line and finish the word when you get to the picture.

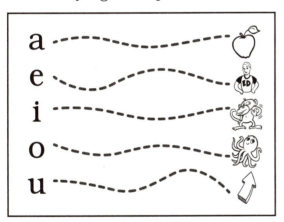

You can also have a student come trace the line while everyone extends the /ă/ sound.

Do only the vowels introduced thus far.

 ### Make It Fun

WEEK 1

Have a student come up to the front of the room. Whisper a letter name to him/her. Next have the student form the letter with their finger (not write it) on the Writing Grid. Do this on the overhead screen, if possible (or on your classroom board). Be sure the student follows the correct letter formation procedure.

The other students need to watch and decide which letter was formed. Call on a student to figure out which letter is being formed, by saying the letter-keyword-sound (**h-hat-/h/**). Whoever guesses correctly gets to do the next letter.

WEEK 2

Say a sound /t/ and have students repeat. Call on a student to come get the Standard Sound Card from your card display.

Ask

Who can come find /t/?

When they find it, have them say the letter-keyword-sound. Hold up Echo the Owl so all the students can repeat. Have the student sit down with the card. When all cards are taken, tell the children with the cards to hand their card to someone who doesn't have a card. Next, have the students bring back each card.

Ask

I'm looking for /b/. Who has /b/?

WEEK 3

Preparation

- Standard Sound Cards
- Baby Echo (on a pointer or ruler)

Call a student to the front of the room. Have the student close his (her) eyes and point to a letter with the Baby Echo pointer. Then have the student open eyes and see the selected letter.

Ask

  What is the name of the letter?

  What is the sound of the letter?

  Name three words that start with /__/.

Other students can help. Then allow the student to select the next student to come up and do the same.

Alphabetical Order

To do the Alphabetical Order activity, simply have the students start with their Magnetic Letter Tiles off their Letter Boards and have them put them in alphabetical order on their boards, matching them to the Alphabet Overlay. They should match and place letters in order (**a** first, then **b**) rather than randomly.

Students place tiles for each letter introduced thus far. If a letter has not yet been introduced, the Alphabet Overlay can simply hold the place for that Letter Tile.

When students have their tiles placed, say the entire alphabet altogether. Use the Baby Echo pointer to point to your card display and the students should point to their Letter Tiles. Emphasize each row, pausing for a deep breath at the end of each row: **a-b-c-d-e-f** (breathe).

You can also say a row, and have students echo. You can also have a student come up and use the Baby Echo pointer to say a row and then have students echo.

Echo/Find Letters

Students start with Letter Tiles on their Letter Board (with the Alphabet Overlay). Say a sound and hold up Echo. This is the students' cue to echo the sound.

Say

  /t/

Students repeat.

Say

  Find /t/.

The students then point to the Letter Tile that has the letter representing the sound.

Call on individual students to come to the sound card display at the front of the room to find and point to the letter corresponding to the sound.

Lastly,

Ask

  What says /t/?

A student should answer with the letter name.

The students can also make the letter with their index fingers on their desk to add a tactile-kinesthetic reinforcement.

Dictate new sounds and review some previously taught sounds.

See Echo Sounds - Unit Resources.

Drill Sounds

a - apple - /ă/	b - bat - /b/
c - cat - /k/	d - dog - /d/
e - Ed - /ĕ/	f - fun - /f/
g - game - /g/	h - hat - /h/
i - itch - /ĭ/	j - jug - /j/
k - kite - /k/	l - lamp - /l/
m - man - /m/	n - nut - /n/
o - octopus - /ŏ/	p - pan - /p/
qu - queen - /kw/	r - rat - /r/
s - snake - /s/	t - top - /t/
u - up - /ŭ/	v - van - /v/
w - wind - /w/	x - fox - /ks/
y - yellow - /y/	z - zebra - /z/

Echo Sounds

Sounds appear between / /. You say the sound. Students echo the sound and say the letter. Depending on the activity, students then either find or make the letter corresponding to that sound.

CONSONANTS

/b/ - b	/d/ - d	/f/ - f
/g/ - g	/h/ - h	/j/ - j
/k/ - c, k	/l/ - l	/m/ - m
/n/ - n	/p/ - p	/kw/ - qu
/r/ - r	/s/ - s	/t/ - t
/v/ - v	/w/ - w	/ks/ - x
/y/ - y	/z/ - z	

VOWELS

/ă/ - a	/ĕ/ - e	/ĭ/ - i
/ŏ/ - o	/ŭ/ - u	

For Unit 1, copy the Unit Test Page for each student (see Appendix). Subsequent Unit Test pages are located at the end of their Composition Books.

Have Students Write The Lower-Case Letters Of The Alphabet

Direct the students to write the alphabet in sequence. They should write the letters in four quadrants or lines:

a	b	c	d	e	f
g	h	i	j	k	l
m	n	o	p	qu	r	s
t	u	v	w	x	y	z

Dictate The Following Sounds

Dictate the sounds. Have students repeat and then write the letter independently.

/f/   /m/   /h/   /l/   /p/

/t/   /ĭ/   /v/   /ă/   /z/

Unit 2 Level 1

Introduction

In Unit 2 you will teach children how to blend and read three-sound short vowel words as well as how to segment and spell them. If the students did Fundations® in Kindergarten, this will be a review. These words are often called CVC words.

See the Unit Resources at the end of this Unit to gain an understanding of the words presented. You will see that the words for Week 1 begin with the consonants **f, l, m, n, r** and **s**. These consonants have sounds that can be 'held' into the vowel sound and thus are easier to blend.

You will also introduce the procedures for the various lesson activities in Fundations. The new activities will be added gradually to your lesson to help both you and your students learn the procedures. The first lessons will be shorter and they will grow in length as you introduce the additional lesson activities.

Note that the Fundations Fluency Kit provides the opportunity for students to further practice and apply their new skills. This can be used individually with students for charting or with a large group for practice. See the Fluency Kit instructions for further guidance.

In a Nutshell

NEW CONCEPTS

- Phonemic awareness skills: sound manipulation (initial, final, medial)

- Blending and reading three-sound short vowel words

- Segmenting and spelling three-sound short vowel words

- Sentence dictation procedures: capitalization, punctuation (period) and proofreading procedures

SAMPLE WORDS

map   sad   rat

TRICK WORDS

the   of   and

PLANNED TIME IN UNIT

2 WEEKS

If students had Fundations in Kindergarten

3-4 WEEKS

If students did not have Fundations in Kindergarten

Note

Extend the time in this Unit if student mastery is not demonstrated on the Unit test.

PREPARING YOUR MATERIALS

Have on hand **5" x 8" blank index cards** to use in the Word of the Day Activity (Weeks 2-4).

Arrange the Standard Sound Card display in the following manner

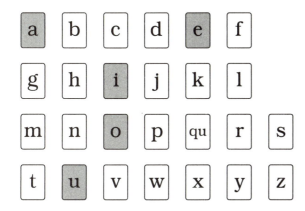

PREPARING YOUR STUDENTS

Students should have the **Magnetic Letter Tiles** (a-z) on their **Letter Boards**. Students place the **Alphabet Overlay** on their boards and then match the tiles to the corresponding square on the overlay.

PREPARING FOR HOME SUPPORT

Copy and send home the **Unit 2 Letter and Activity Packet**.

Getting Ready

VIEW THE CD-ROM

LEVEL 1
• Unit 2
   Lesson Activities (see below)

STUDY LESSON ACTIVITIES

Review the following activities in your manual's Lesson Activity Overview and on CD-ROM:

WEEK 1
• Echo/Find Sounds & Words

• Dictation

WEEK 2
• Trick Words

• Word of the Day

• Word Talk

Unit 2 **Lesson Activity Plan**

Week 1

DAY ❶	DAY ❷	DAY ❸	DAY ❹	DAY ❺
Drill Sounds	Drill Sounds	Drill Sounds	Drill Sounds	Drill Sounds
Introduce New Concepts	Introduce New Concepts	Introduce New Concepts	Introduce New Concepts	Introduce New Concepts
		Echo/Find Sounds & Words	Echo/Find Sounds & Words	Echo/Find Sounds & Words
			Dictation (Dry Erase)	Dictation (Dry Erase)

Week 2

DAY ❶	DAY ❷	DAY ❸	DAY ❹	DAY ❺
Drill Sounds	Drill Sounds	Drill Sounds	Drill Sounds	Drill Sounds
Introduce New Concepts	Echo/Find Sounds & Words	Word of the Day	Word of the Day	Word Talk
Trick Words	Introduce New Concepts	Echo/Find Sounds & Words	Echo/Find Sounds & Words	Trick Words
Dictation (Dry Erase)	Dictation (Composition Book)	Dictation (Composition Book)	Dictation (Composition Book)	Dictation (Day 5 Check-up)*

Weeks 3 • 4

DAY ❶	DAY ❷	DAY ❸	DAY ❹	DAY ❺
Drill Sounds	Drill Sounds	Drill Sounds	Drill Sounds	Drill Sounds
Trick Words	Word of the Day	Word of the Day	Word Talk	Word Talk
Echo/Find Sounds & Words	Echo/Find Sounds & Words	Echo/Find Sounds & Words	Echo/Find Sounds & Words	Dictation (Unit Test/Final Week)†
Dictation (Dry Erase)	Dictation (Composition Book)	Dictation (Dry Erase)	Dictation (Composition Book)	

* If Week 2 is the Unit's final week, then do Dictation (Unit Test)

† If Unit 2 continues for 4 weeks, then do Dictation (Day 5 Check-up) for Weeks 2 and 3, and Dictation (Unit Test) for Week 4.

Introduce New Concepts

TEACH TAPPING TO READ WORDS

Teach students how to blend words with three sounds.

If students have trouble with any sound, point to the corresponding Large Sound Card (or poster) and ask them to say the letter-key-word-sound. Then tap out the word, using the sounds.

Use your Standard Sound Card display to make the words.

Example

Say

> Say each sound separately, then blend the sounds together.
>
> Tap a finger to your thumb over each sound card while saying the sound.
>
> Tap your index finger to thumb while saying /m/,
>
> middle finger to thumb while saying /a/
>
> and ring finger to thumb while saying /t/.
>
> Then blend the sounds and say the word as you drag your thumb across your fingers beginning with the index finger.

Have the students do this. Explain that they can say sounds while tapping and blending them together to make words.

Continue with 8-10 other word examples. (See Unit Resources.) Each time, make the words with the Standard Sound Cards. Tap and blend sounds with your students.

RETEACH TAPPING TO READ WORDS

Use your Standard Sound Card display to make 8-10 Unit words. (See Unit Resources.)

Make each word then say and tap each sound. Have students tap with you. Then blend the sounds as you drag your thumb across your fingers.

Next, point under each card as you say each sound, then drag your finger under all three cards as you blend the sounds to read the word.

RETEACH TAPPING TO READ WORDS

See above. Continue to model until students can do this without your guidance.

Use your Standard Sound Card display to make 4-5 Unit words. (See Unit Resources.)

TEACH TAPPING TO SPELL

Use your Standard Sound Card display to teach sound tapping for segmentation and spelling skills.

Say

> Now we are going to do something a little bit different.
>
> I'm going to say a word and we are going to tap it without seeing the letters.
>
> Are you ready to try?

Say the word **map**, and tap out the three separate sounds without the cards. Tell the students to try to picture the three cards in their minds.

Now re-tap with fingers, but this time select the Standard Sound Cards with each tap to form the word **map**.

Unit 2 Lesson Activity Plan

Repeat this procedure dictating the word **lip**, then **mat**. Tap out sounds and have students repeat. Then find the corresponding cards and place them together to form the word.

Next, dictate the words **nap**, **mud** and **sat**. Have a student come to the front and try tapping out the sounds and finding the corresponding cards.

WEEK 1 DAY ❹

RETEACH TAPPING TO READ WORDS

Use your Standard Sound Card display to make 4-5 Unit words. (See Unit Resources.)

Have students try to tap and blend sounds independently.

RETEACH TAPPING TO SPELL

Dictate the word, **nut**. Have students echo. (Do not display the word yet.)

Say

> Tap out the sounds in nut.

Tap the word with students. Select a student to come find the corresponding cards from the card display as you tap each sound again. Explain to the students that tapping words will help them spell.

Say

> Spell the word nut.

Have the student spell the word by naming the letters while pointing to the cards. Tap the three taps again, this time naming letters, rather than sounds. Do several words. (See Unit Resources.)

WEEK 1 DAY ❺

RETEACH TAPPING TO READ WORDS

Follow Day 4 procedures.

TEACH SENTENCE READING

Write the following sentence on the board:

Meg is sad.

Help students tap out the words **Meg** and **sad**. Tell them the word **is** (do not tap it out).

Use Baby Echo to point to the words and read the sentence. Have students echo. Discuss the capital letter at the beginning of the sentence and the period at the end.

Do the same with the following sentences. (Explain the words **in** and **the** if they are unknown to the students.)

Rob sat in the sun.

The rat sat in the mud.

Next demonstrate how to read these sentences with fluency. Draw the scoops under the sentences. Read it in phrases as you scoop with Baby Echo.

Rob sat in the sun.

The rat sat in the mud.

WEEK 2 DAY ❶

TEACH TAPPING TO READ WORDS

In Week 2 move on to form words beginning with other consonants.

You can now change the final or initial consonant as well as the vowel to form new words. Make 8-10 words. Each time, tap and blend the word with your students.

Example

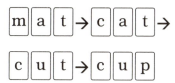

WEEK 2 DAY ❷

TEACH SENTENCE DICTATION

Teach sentence dictation using the Blue Word Frames on your magnetic board.

Say the sentence and have students echo. Then write the sentence on the Blue Word Frames.

Example

Explain that at the beginning of a sentence, the word must begin with a capital letter. That is why the frame at the beginning is tall.

Discuss period used to end the sentence.

Next dictate another sentence.

Say

Tom had a dog.

Have the students echo. Select a student to come forward and write each word on the Blue Word Frames. Tap each word before the student writes it. Be sure to discuss capital letter and punctuation.

Proofread the sentence with students, tapping each word to check the spelling. Do not tap the word **a.**

Drill Sounds

Always do the vowel sounds. You can select some consonants, but there is no need to do all of them. (See Unit Resources.)

There are no new sounds taught in this Unit.

Large Sound Cards

First practice sounds with the Large Sound Cards. Say the letter-keyword-sound and have students echo.

Standard Sound Cards

Next, point to the Standard Sound Cards (on display) with the Baby Echo pointer. You say the letter-keyword-sound and hold up Baby Echo to have students repeat.

Word of the Day

Select a Word of the Day from the words below. Make the word using your Standard Sound Card display. Also, write the word on a blank index card and add it to your Word of the Day packet.

Word Resource

WEEK 2

f i x   qu i t

WEEK 3

l o g   p e t

WEEK 4

l i p   y e t

Review Concepts

Reteach the current Unit concept using the Word of the Day.

Note

Although **qu** says /**kw**/ and **x** says /**ks**/ tap them out with one finger, not two fingers. Technically they have two sounds but it is more effective to teach students to give it one tap, corresponding to the one card.

Use The Word In A Sentence

Have a student (or students) use the word in a sentence and discuss the word's meaning.

Make Other Words

Then use sound cards to make several other words from this Unit. (See Unit Resources.) Have students tap and read each word.

Student Notebook Entry

Have students add the Word of the Day to the Vocabulary section of their Student Notebooks.

Students can circle the "chicken letter" **q** with the **u** to remind them that **q** never goes in a word without its buddy **u**.

Write a sentence on the board for students to copy. (This can be done at another time of the day.)

Word Talk

Review the Words of the Day from your Words of the Day index card packet.

Make and Discuss Words

Make words with your Standard Sound Card display.

Have students tap and read the words.

Ask a student to use the word in a sentence and another student to explain what the word means.

Read Words

Use your packet of words as flashcards. Have students quickly read them without tapping.

Display Words

Display current and review words. Have students find and read the words as directed.

Ask

How do you tap this word?

How many letters?

How many sounds?

What is the vowel sound?

Is there a "chicken letter" in this word? (for quit)

Trick Words

Trick Words require lots of practice. Sky write and finger write trick words, but **do not** tap them out or make them with the Magnetic Letter Tiles.

Word Resource

the   of   and

Students add these words to the Trick Word section of their Student Notebooks. Hold them accountable for the spelling of these words throughout the day. Direct students to look them up in the Trick Word section of their Student Notebooks.

After the introduction of new Trick Words, practice them with sky writing and tracing.

Echo/Find Sounds & Words

Echo/Find Sounds

Say a sound. Have students echo and find the letter on their Letter Board.

(See Echo Sounds in Unit Resources for expected student responses.)

Echo/Find Words

Dictate several words, such as **lap**. These words will get three taps: /l/ - /ă/ - /p/.

(See Current Unit Words in Unit Resources.)

Have students find their Magnetic Letter Tiles needed to make words on their Letter Boards. After finding a word, have a student spell it orally.

Dictation

Refer to this Unit's Resource List of Echo Sounds, Words and Sentences.

Proper Dictation Activity procedures are very important. Be sure to follow their demonstration on the CD-ROM.

DRY ERASE

Dictate 3 sounds, 3 current words and 3 trick words (trick words can be current or review).

This is a teaching time, not a testing time. Be sure students repeat each dictation. They should tap and orally spell the Unit words before writing. Students should write and orally spell trick words with their finger prior to writing them on their Dry Erase Writing Tablet.

Have students "mark up" the review and current words.

COMPOSITION BOOKS

Dictate 3 sounds, 2 review, 2 current words and 2 trick words (trick words can be current or review) and 1 sentence.

This is also a teaching time, not a testing time. Be sure students repeat each thing that you dictate. They should tap and orally spell the review and current Unit words before writing. Students should write and orally spell trick words with their finger prior to writing them in their Composition Books. Students independently write the sentence and then you lead them through the proofreading procedure.

Have students "mark up" the review and current words.

DAY 5 CHECK-UP

Students do Day 5 Dictation in their Composition Books. Have them check the Check-up box at the top of the page.

Dictate the sound, word, or sentence. Have students repeat and then write independently. Do not have students spell orally. Encourage them to tap as appropriate.

UNIT TEST

Have students find Unit Test pages at the end of their Composition Books.

Dictate the sound, word, or sentence. (See Unit Resources.) Have students repeat and then write independently. Do not have students spell aloud. Encourage them to tap as appropriate.

Drill Sounds

a - apple - /ă/   b - bat - /b/

c - cat - /k/   d - dog - /d/

e - Ed - /ĕ/   f - fun - /f/

g - game - /g/   h - hat - /h/

i - itch - /ĭ/   j - jug - /j/

k - kite - /k/   l - lamp - /l/

m - man - /m/   n - nut - /n/

o - octopus - /ŏ/   p - pan - /p/

qu - queen - /kw/   r - rat - /r/

s - snake - /s/   t - top - /t/

u - up - /ŭ/   v - van - /v/

w - wind - /w/   x - fox - /ks/

y - yellow - /y/   z - zebra - /z/

Echo Sounds

Sounds appear between / /. You say the sound. Students echo the sound and say the letter. Depending on the activity, students then either find or make the letter corresponding to that sound.

CONSONANTS

/b/ - b	/d/ - d	/f/ - f
/g/ - g	/h/ - h	/j/ - j
/k/ - c, k	/l/ - l	/m/ - m
/n/ - n	/p/ - p	/kw/ - qu
/r/ - r	/s/ - s	/t/ - t
/v/ - v	/w/ - w	/ks/ - x
/y/ - y	/z/ - z	

VOWELS

/ă/ - a	/ĕ/ - e	/ĭ/ - i
/ŏ/ - o	/ŭ/ - u	

Current Unit Trick Words

the   of   and

Current Unit Words

The following words begin with consonant sounds that can be "held" into the vowel sound. For this reason, these words facilitate blending. Begin with these words throughout Week 1:

WEEK 1

sad	sat	sap	mad	map	mat
rag	rap	rat	nag	Nat	nap
lad	lag	lap	sip	sit	rip
rig	lip	lit	fit	fig	nip
mop	not	nod	rug	rut	mud
mug	nut	lug	set	met	Meg
net	leg	let			

WEEKS 2 • 4

mop	map	tap	tab	tub	rub
led	lad	bad	bud	bug	rug
dig	dip	zip	zap	tax	wet
bet	bit	fit	fig	fog	rib
sob	job	cop	dot	lid	mud
Ted	fix	lap	web	not	ten
bed	at	hip	peg	had	pen
bat	hit	pet	bus	bun	bib
red	jab	kid	nod	but	cup
mix	pot	Ben	pat	Jim	tin
cob	rat	big	tip	cot	mad
den	gum	mug	sub	wig	yes
fun	cub	pup	lot	hut	sit
let	gap	sip	dug	cab	Sid
vet	wax	mat	lit	pig	nap
kit	did	pal	fox	nut	gas
him					

Sentences

*Write any **bold word** on the board for students to copy. A **bold word** has untaught components.*

Nat **is** sad.

The rag **is** on the mat.

The rat **had a** nap.

Mom **had a** map.

Rob **is** on **the** mat.

The rat sat in **the** mud.

Rob sat in **the** sun.

Meg **is** not sad.

Mom sat on **the** log.

The bug **is** in the pot.

The gum **is** in the bag.

Rob bit the fig.

Mom had **a** sip of pop.

Mom had **to** jog **to** the bus.

Deb met Tom.

Deb had **a** bad cut.

Meg had **a** red hat.

The cat hid in the box.

The wax **is** hot.

The pup had fun.

Max had **a** dog.

The wig **is** on Viv.

The fox **is** in the pen.

Pat **is** quick.

Tom had **a** quiz.

Have students find the Unit Test pages located at the end of their Composition Books. Dictate the sounds, words and sentences. Have students repeat and then write independently. Encourage them to tap, but they should not use their Student Notebooks.

Dictate The Following Sounds

/ĕ/   /ă/   /k/   /z/   /ks/

Dictate The Following Words

lug   nap   zap   yes   beg

fix   quit   rob   hit   mud

Dictate The Following Trick Words

the   of

Dictate The Following Sentences

Pat had a big quiz.

Bob had a red bug.

Have The Students Do The Following

Circle the "chicken letter" and his best buddy.

Answer Key

SOUNDS

1. e
2. a
3. k, c
4. z
5. x

WORDS

1. lug
2. nap
3. zap
4. yes
5. beg
6. fix
7. (qu)it
8. rob
9. hit
10. mud

TRICK WORDS

1. the
2. of

SENTENCES

1. Pat had a big (qu)iz.
2. Bob had a red bug.

Unit 3 Level 1

Introduction

In Unit 3, you will teach that the digraphs **wh**, **ch**, **sh**, **th**, and **ck** 'stick together' to form one sound, even though there are two letters. That is why they are on one card.

You will also explain that **wh** is only used at the beginning of a word and **ck** is only used at the end of a word right after a short vowel.

You will also explain to your students that some books that they read are "make-believe" whereas other books present them with true facts. At this point you do not need to name these fiction and non-fiction.

PREPARING YOUR MATERIALS

Add the digraphs (**wh**, **ch**, **sh**, **th**, and **ck**) along with **blank ivory** and the **blank orange** cards to your Standard Sound Card display.

You will also need the digraphs from your Large Sound Cards pack.

Arrange the Standard Sound Card display in the following manner

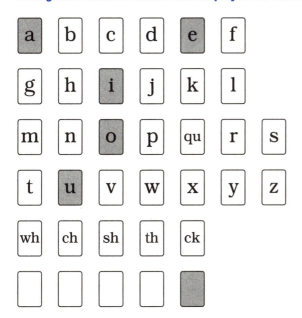

PREPARING YOUR STUDENTS

Students should have the **Magnetic Letter Tiles** (a-z) on their **Letter Boards**.

They should also add the blank ivory and the blank orange tiles, and the digraphs (**wh**, **ch**, **sh**, **th**, and **ck**).

PREPARING FOR HOME SUPPORT

Copy and send home the **Unit 3 Letter and Activity Packet**.

Unit 3 **Lesson Activity Plan**

Week 1

DAY ❶	DAY ❷	DAY ❸	DAY ❹	DAY ❺
Introduce New Concepts	Drill Sounds	Drill Sounds	Drill Sounds	Drill Sounds
Trick Words	Introduce New Concepts	Word of the Day	Word Talk	Word Talk
	Trick Words	Echo/Find Sounds & Words	Trick Words	Storytime
	Dictation (Dry Erase)	Make it Fun	Echo/Find Sounds & Words	
			Dictation (Dry Erase)	

Week 2

DAY ❶	DAY ❷	DAY ❸	DAY ❹	DAY ❺
Drill Sounds	Drill Sounds	Drill Sounds	Drill Sounds	Drill Sounds
Trick Words	Word of the Day	Word of the Day	Word Talk	Word Talk
Word of the Day	Echo/Find Sounds & Words	Make it Fun	Trick Words	Storytime
Introduce New Concepts	Dictation (Composition Book)	Dictation (Composition Book)	Dictation (Dry Erase)	Dictation (Day 5 Check-up)

Week 3

DAY ❶	DAY ❷	DAY ❸	DAY ❹	DAY ❺
Drill Sounds	Drill Sounds	Drill Sounds	Drill Sounds	Drill Sounds
Trick Words	Word of the Day	Word of the Day	Word Talk	Storytime
Word of the Day	Echo/Find Sounds & Words	Make it Fun	Trick Words	Dictation (Unit Test)
Echo/Find Sounds & Words	Dictation (Composition Book)	Dictation (Composition Book)	Dictation (Dry Erase)	
Dictation (Dry Erase)				

Introduce New Concepts

TEACH DIGRAPHS

wh, ch, sh, th, ck

Explain that these consonants 'stick together' to form one sound, even though there are two letters. That is why they are on one card. They are not separated.

Sh, for example, will not say /s/, /h/. These letters stay together to say /sh/.

Teach the digraphs **wh**, **ch**, **sh**, **th**, **ck** with the Large Sound Cards.

Form three-sound words (short vowels with digraphs) with the Standard Sound Cards. Use only the letters and sounds taught thus far. (See Current Unit Words in Unit Resources.)

Example

Make the word **mash**.

Digraphs Get One Tap, With One Finger

Say the sounds separately, and then blend them together.

Tap a finger to your thumb over each sound card while saying the sound.

Tap your index finger to your thumb while saying /m/, middle finger to thumb while saying /ă/, and ring finger to thumb while saying /sh/.

Then blend the sounds and say the word while dragging your thumb across your fingers, starting with the index finger.

Have students practice this with 8-10 words.

TEACH HOW TO MARK WORDS

Whenever a digraph is in a word, you can identify it by underlining it.

In the word **ship**, the letters **sh** are a digraph. To show that these letters stay together, you can underline them in the word: <u>sh</u>ip.

Examples

<u>ch</u>op   du<u>ck</u>   <u>th</u>at

Student Notebook Entry

Have the students color keyword pictures on the digraph page in their Student Notebooks.

Have students add the word **quick**, with a sentence to the Vocabulary section of their Student Notebooks.

TEACH SPELLING

Have students use their Magnetic Tiles and Letter Boards. (See Resources for Echo Sounds and Words.)

Echo/Find Sounds

Ask the students, **"What says /k/?"** Now they should answer **k**, **c**, and **ck**. Ask **"What says /w/?"** The answer should now be **w** and **wh**. Also, do Echo/Find Sounds for the other digraphs.

Echo/Find Words

Dictate a word with a digraph, such as **shop**, without first getting the corresponding sound cards. Tap out sounds and have students repeat. Then find the corresponding sound cards and place them together to form the word.

Next, dictate a word and have the students try tapping out the sounds. Call a student up to find the corresponding sound cards. Have the students tap out sounds and then name the corresponding letters.

Dictate several words, including words with digraphs such as **path**. These words will get three taps: /p/ - /ă/ - /th/.

Have students find the Magnetic Letter Tiles needed to make the word on their Letter Boards. Then have one student do the word for the class, by tapping the sounds, building the word at the Standard Sound Card display and naming the letters.

Explain to the students that **ck** is used only at the **end of words** right **after the short vowel**.

Example

Make the word **duck**.

Cover the **ck** with the letter **c**. Tell them that **c** says /k/ but does not end words. Cover the **ck** with the letter **k**. Tell them that **k** says /k/ but does not end words, right after a short vowel.

Tell students that even though **c** and **k** both say /k/, right after a short vowel, they should always use **ck**.

Tell students to arrange their digraph Letter Tiles with **ck** last to remind them that **ck** is only found at the end of words.

Student Notebook Entry

Have students add ways to spell /k/ in the Spelling Rules section of their Student Notebooks.

WEEK 2 DAY ❶

TEACH SENTENCE DICTATION

Do sentence dictation as a group using the Blue Word Frames on your magnetic board.

Say the sentence and have students echo. Then write the sentence on the Blue Word Frames.

Example

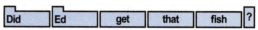

Explain that at the beginning of a sentence, the word must begin with a capital letter. That is why the frame at the beginning is tall. Next explain why the frame with Ed is also tall. Tell students that people's names always begin with a capital letter. Show students the tall punctuation frame and explain the question mark. Tell them that they will need to think about sentences to use a period or a question mark.

Next, dictate the following sentences.

Sentence Resources

Tim had a rash.

Did Jack hit his chin?

Have the students echo. Select a student to come forward and write each word on the Blue Word Frames. Be sure to discuss capital letter and punctuation.

Proofread the sentence with students, tapping each word to check the spelling. Do not tap the word **a**.

 Drill Sounds

Always do the vowel sounds. You can select some consonants, but there is no need to do all of them. (See Unit Resources.)

Include the digraphs with each drill.

Large Sound Cards

First practice sounds with the Large Sound Cards. Say the letter-keyword-sound and have students echo.

Standard Sound Cards

Next, point to the Standard Sound Cards (on display) with the Baby Echo pointer. You say the letter-keyword-sound and hold up Baby Echo to have students repeat.

Instruct Students

Name the digraphs.

Which three letters say /k/?

(k, c, ck)

Which letters say /w/?

(w, wh)

 Word of the Day

Select a Word of the Day from the words below. Make the word using your Standard Sound Card display. Also, write the word on a blank index card and add it to your Word of the Day packet.

Word Resource

WEEK 1

| qu | i | ck | | m | u | ch |

WEEK 2

| p | a | th | | l | u | ck | | r | u | sh |

WEEK 3

| th | u | d | | d | o | ck | | w | i | sh |

Review Concepts

Have students find and read words with digraphs. Also discuss **ck** at the end of words with **lu<u>ck</u>** and **do<u>ck</u>**.

Use The Word In A Sentence

Have a student (or students) use the word in sentence and discuss the word's meaning.

Make Other Words

Then use sound cards to make several other words from this Unit. (See Unit Resources.) Have students tap and read each word.

Student Notebook Entry

Have students add the Word of the Day to the Vocabulary section of their Student Notebooks.

Have students mark up words by underlining the digraph.

Write a sentence on the board for students to copy. (This can be done at another time of the day.)

Word Talk

Review the Words of the Day from your Words of the Day index card packet.

Make and Discuss Words

Make 4-5 words with your Standard Sound Card display.

Have students tap and read the words.

Ask a student to use a word in a sentence and another student to explain what the word means.

Read Words

Use your packet of words as flashcards. Have students quickly read them without tapping.

Display Words

Display current and review words. Have students find and read the words as directed.

Instruct Students

Find the words with a "chicken" letter.

Find a word that starts with a digraph.

Find a word that ends with a digraph.

 Trick Words

Trick words require lots of practice. Sky write and finger write trick words, but **do not** tap them out or make them with the Magnetic Letter Tiles.

Word Resource

WEEK 1

| to | a | was |

WEEK 2

| is | he | for |

WEEK 3

| as | his | has |

Students add these words to the Trick Word section of their Student Notebooks. Hold them accountable for the spelling of these words throughout the day. Direct students to look them up in the Trick Word section of their Student Notebooks.

After the introduction of new trick words, practice them with sky writing and tracing.

 Echo/Find Sounds & Words

Echo/Find Sounds

Say a sound. Have students echo and find the letter on their Letter Board.

(See Echo Sounds in Unit Resources for expected student responses.)

Echo/Find Words

Dictate several words, including words with digraphs such as **path**. These words will get three taps: /p/ - /ă/ - /th/.

(See Current Unit Words in Unit Resources.)

Have students find Magnetic Letter Tiles needed to make words on their Letter Boards. After finding a word, have a student spell it orally.

 Dictation

Refer to this Unit's Resource List of Echo Sounds, Words and Sentences.

Proper Dictation Activity procedures are very important. Be sure to follow their demonstration on the CD-ROM.

DRY ERASE

Dictate 3 sounds, 3 current words and 3 trick words (trick words can be current or review).

This is a teaching time, not a testing time. Be sure students repeat each dictation. They should tap and orally spell the Unit words before writing. Students should write and orally spell trick words with their finger prior to writing them on their Dry Erase Writing Tablets.

Have students "mark up" the review and current words.

COMPOSITION BOOKS

Dictate 3 sounds, 2 review, 2 current words and 2 trick words (trick words can be current or review) and 1 sentence.

This is also a teaching time, not a testing time. Be sure students repeat each thing that you dictate. They should tap and orally spell the review and current Unit words before writing. Students should write and orally spell trick words with their finger prior to writing them in their Composition Books. Students independently write the sentence and then you lead them through the proofreading procedure.

Have students "mark up" the review and current words.

DAY 5 CHECK-UP

Students do Day 5 Dictation in their Composition Books. Have them check the Check-up box at the top of the page.

Dictate the sound, word, or sentence. Have students repeat and then write independently. Do not have students spell orally. Encourage them to tap as appropriate.

UNIT TEST

Have students find Unit Test pages at the end of their Composition Books.

Dictate the sound, word, or sentence. (See Unit Resources.) Have students repeat and then write independently. Do not have students spell orally. Encourage them to tap as appropriate.

 **Make It Fun**

Preparation

- Resource List of Current and Review Words

DIGRAPH DETECTIVES

This activity will help students learn to find digraphs.

Instruct Students

Write 10-15 words on the classroom board, some with digraphs and some without. Tell the students they are **digraph detectives** and they need to find all the digraphs and underline them. Read the list of words together with the class.

Variation

Break the class into groups of 3 students and assign each group a digraph to look for. Have the students copy the words with their digraph onto their Dry Erase Writing Tablets. Then call on a student from each group to come and underline the digraph in the words with their designated digraph.

Storytime

WEEK 1

Preparation

- Baby Echo (on a pointer or ruler)
- Large Chart Paper

COD FISH

Write the following story, with the phrases scooped, on chart paper.

Instruct Students

Ask the students to read the title silently. (Tell students to tap words when reading silently, if necessary.) Discuss the title and predict what the story might be about.

Read Sentences

Continue reading one sentence at a time.

- Have students read silently. (Tell students to tap words when reading silently, if necessary.)
- Select a student to come read the sentence with the Baby Echo pointer. Be sure the student uses proper expression and phrasing. If not, model.
- Have the whole class repeat the sentence.

After the story has been read once in this manner, read it altogether with choral reading as you scoop the phrases with Baby Echo.

Make a Movie

Have students "make a movie" in their heads. Tell them to close their eyes and picture the story.

Ask someone to describe what they see in their movie, discussing each sentence.

Continue with the whole story. Then model retelling the story in your own words and ask a student to retell it in their own words.

Mark Words

Lastly, select students to come mark words as directed.

- Make a capital letter frame around words that have a capital letter and discuss why (at the beginning of a sentence or a person's name).
- Highlight the exclamation marks (briefly discuss them again).
- Underline digraphs.

WEEK 2

Preparation

- Baby Echo (on a pointer or ruler)
- Large Chart Paper with the story from Week 1
- Copy COD FISH story for each student from the Fluency Kit (in the Stories tab).

Instruct Students

Ask the students to read the title silently. Have them try to remember the "movie" in their mind. Have someone describe the story by re-telling it. Read chorally as you point with Baby Echo and determine if the retelling was accurate.

Next disseminate the story to the students. Have them draw pictures for each page and cut on the dotted lines. Staple these into booklets for the students to bring home.

WEEK 3

Preparation

- Find a non-fiction book about fish, such as **Hello Fish! Visiting the Coral Reef**, by Earle, Silvia A., Washington, DC: National Geographic Society, 1999
- If you do not have one about fish, substitute a non-fiction book about animals.

Instruct Students

Tell students that some books have stories that are pretend or make-believe. The story can be about people or animals, but it is make-believe.

Explain that other books tell us facts about things. They teach us things that are true. Show them your non-fiction book and tell the students that it is a book that teaches them true things about (name the subject).

Read the book (or part of the book) to your students. After each page, ask them to name one true fact that they have learned.

Note

When reading other books with your students, be sure to discuss whether they are pretend stories or if they teach true facts.

Drill Sounds

a - apple - /ă/   b - bat - /b/

c - cat - /k/   d - dog - /d/

e - Ed - /ĕ/   f - fun - /f/

g - game - /g/   h - hat - /h/

i - itch - /ĭ/   j - jug - /j/

k - kite - /k/   l - lamp - /l/

m - man - /m/   n - nut - /n/

o - octopus - /ŏ/   p - pan - /p/

qu - queen - /kw/   r - rat - /r/

s - snake - /s/   t - top - /t/

u - up - /ŭ/   v - van - /v/

w - wind - /w/   x - fox - /ks/

y - yellow - /y/   z - zebra - /z/

sh - ship - /sh/   ck - sock - /k/

wh - whistle - /w/   th - thumb - /th/

ch - chin - /ch/

Echo Sounds

Sounds appear between / /. You say the sound. Students echo the sound and say the letter. Depending on the activity, students then either find or make the letter corresponding to that sound.

CONSONANTS

/b/ - b	/d/ - d	/f/ - f
/g/ - g	/h/ - h	/j/ - j
/k/ - c, k, ck	/l/ - l	/m/ - m
/n/ - n	/p/ - p	/kw/ - qu
/r/ - r	/s/ - s	/t/ - t
/v/ - v	/w/ - w, wh	/ks/ - x
/y/ - y	/z/ - z	/ch/ - ch
/sh/ - sh	/th/ - th	

VOWELS

/ă/ - a	/ĕ/ - e	/ĭ/ - i
/ŏ/ - o	/ŭ/ - u	

Review Trick Words

the   of   and

Current Unit Trick Words

to   a   was   is   he   for

as   his   has

Review Words

mop	rib	sob	job	map	cop
dot	lid	mud	Ted	fix	lap
web	not	ten	tub	bed	at
hip	peg	shot	had	bug	pen
bat	hit	pet	bus	bun	bib
red	jab	kid	nod	but	cup
mix	pot	Ben	pat	tab	Jim
tin	cob	rat	big	tip	cot
mad	den	gum	dip	mug	sub
wig	yes	fun	cub	fit	rush
quit	pup	fog	lot	hut	sit
let	gap	sip	dug	dig	cab
Sid	vet	wax	led	mat	lit
pig	nap	kit	did	zap	rub
pal	fox	nut	gas	him	mob
nab	fib	lab	rob	lob	lug
rut	sun	run			

Current Unit Words

rash	such	chip	much	shot	moth
rich	lash	path	dash	whip	math
dish	shut	rush	shop	wish	fish
shed	chin	chop	chat	Beth	with
bath	Seth	thin	thud	ship	mash
whiz	lick	rock	lock	pick	kick
shock	Rick	neck	back	pack	chick
Jack	sock	quick	dock	deck	sick
thick	luck	puck	rack	duck	

Sentences

*Write any **bold word** on the board for students to copy. A **bold word** has untaught components.*

Write untaught trick words from this Unit on the board for students to copy. After you have taught a trick word, students should look it up in their Trick Word dictionary if they need help with the spelling.

Tim had a rash.

The fish is hot.

Dick is not back yet.

Tim sat on that big rock.

Bob has a cut on his neck.

Beth had a wig and a hat.

Dad met Bev at the shop.

A big moth is in the pot.

Did Rick hop on that bus?

He had a nap on the rug.

Did Tom nab the fish?

Did Jack rush to the bus?

Beth had to get the pup.

Did the dog lick him?

Rick had a dot on his **chair**.

The pen is in the den.

Mom sat on the deck.

Did Chet wish for a pup?

Bob had his hot bath.

That kid is sad.

Tim hit his chin.

The fish is for the cat.

Have students find the Unit Test pages located at the end of their Composition Books. Dictate the sounds, words and sentences. Have students repeat and then write independently. Encourage them to tap, but they should not use their Student Notebooks.

Dictate The Following Sounds

/sh/   /k/   /ĭ/   /ŭ/   /ch/

Dictate The Following Words

chat   shot   dash   math   thin

chop   neck   dock   whip   ship

Dictate The Following Trick Words

to   for

Dictate The Following Sentences

Rick had a hot bath.

Did Jack rush to get the bus?

Have The Students Do The Following

Underline all the digraphs in words and sentences.

Answer Key

SOUNDS

1. sh
2. k, c, ck
3. i
4. u
5. ch

WORDS

1. chat
2. shot
3. dash
4. math
5. thin
6. chop
7. neck
8. dock
9. whip
10. ship

TRICK WORDS

1. to
2. for

SENTENCES

1. Rick had a hot bath.
2. Did Jack rush to get the bus?

Unit 4   Level 1

Introduction

In Unit 4 you will teach the **ff**, **ll**, **ss** bonus letter rule.

At the end of a one syllable word, if the word has one vowel immediately followed by an **f**, **l** or **s** at the end, double that consonant.

The extra **f**, **l** or **s** is considered a **bonus letter** because it is extra. It does not make a sound. The word **miss**, for example, has the 3 sounds since the bonus letter **s** does not make a sound.

Examples

hill   **miss**   **puff**

The letter **a** followed by double **l** does not have the expected short vowel sound.

Examples

ball   **call**   **tall**

Sometimes the letter **z** does not get doubled (**quiz**, **whiz**, **Liz**) and sometimes it does (**fuzz**, **buzz**, **fizz**, **razz**, **jazz**). We do not consider **z** a bonus letter. It wants to be though!

In a Nutshell

NEW CONCEPTS

- Bonus Letter Spelling Rule: **ff**, **ll**, **ss** and sometimes **z**
- Glued Sound: **all**
- Punctuation: Exclamation Point

SAMPLE WORDS

hill	puff	bill
miss	call	

TRICK WORDS

you	we	I
they	one	said

PLANNED TIME IN UNIT

2 WEEKS

Note
Extend the time in this Unit if student mastery is not demonstrated on the Unit test.

PREPARING YOUR MATERIALS

Add the green **all** Standard Sound Card and the extra **f**, **l**, and **s** Sound Cards to your classroom card display. You will also need the **all** Large Sound Card.

Arrange the Standard Sound Card display in the following manner

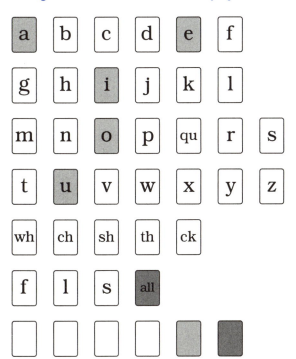

NOTE HOW THE CARD ROWS END IN THE BONUS LETTERS

The sound cards are arranged so that the rows end with the Bonus Letters, **f**, **l** and **s** and sometimes **z**. Be sure to show this to your students.

PREPARING YOUR STUDENTS

Have the students add the green **all**, and the extra **f**, **l** and **s** Magnetic Letter Tiles to their Letter Boards. Tell them that they will soon discover why they need an extra **f**, **l** and **s**. They should also add the blank green tile.

PREPARING FOR HOME SUPPORT

Copy and send home the **Unit 4 Letter and Activity Packet**.

Getting Ready

VIEW THE CD-ROM

LEVEL 1
- Unit 4
  Lesson Activities (see below)

STUDY LESSON ACTIVITIES

For each Unit you will review one or more lesson activities. This will help you master and internalize important activity procedures.

Review the following activities in your manual's Lesson Activity Overview and on CD-ROM:

- Drill Sounds
  (See especially Student Drill Leader.)

Week 1

DAY ❶	DAY ❷	DAY ❸	DAY ❹	DAY ❺
Drill Sounds	Drill Sounds	Drill Sounds	Drill Sounds	Drill Sounds
Introduce New Concepts	Introduce New Concepts	Word of the Day	Word of the Day	Word Talk
Trick Words	Dictation (Dry Erase)	Make it Fun	Trick Words	Storytime
		Echo/Find Sounds & Words	Dictation (Composition Book)	Dictation (Day 5 Check-up)

Week 2

DAY ❶	DAY ❷	DAY ❸	DAY ❹	DAY ❺
Drill Sounds	Drill Sounds	Drill Sounds	Drill Sounds	Drill Sounds
Trick Words	Word of the Day	Word of the Day	Word Talk	Storytime
Word of the Day	Echo/Find Sounds & Words	Make it Fun	Trick Words	Dictation (Unit Test)
Echo/Find Sounds & Words	Dictation (Composition Book)	Dictation (Composition Book)	Dictation (Dry Erase)	
Dictation (Dry Erase)				

Introduce New Concepts

WEEK 1 DAY ❶

TEACH BONUS LETTERS

ff, ll, ss

Put the letters **m i s** up on the Standard Sound Card display. Tap the sounds and blend it to read.

Tell the students that this word has three-sounds but it needs another **s**. Add the other **s** card to make the word **miss**.

| m | i | s | s |

Even though there are two **s**'s, there is only one /**s**/ sound. Tap out **miss** (three taps) and read the word aloud.

This happens when an **s** follows a short vowel to end the word. Demonstrate with other words such as **kiss**, **fuss**, etc.

Write the words **yes** and **bus** on the board and tell students that these are two very common words that **do not** get a bonus letter **s**, but other words do get it.

Repeat the bonus letter explanation with double **ll** and double **ff** words making the words with sound cards.

Show students that sometimes words ending in **z** get a bonus letter and sometimes they do not.

Word Resource

| bill | tell | buff | huff | quiz | fuzz |

Teach Students To Mark Words

In the word **miss**, the last letter, **s**, is a bonus letter. It is extra. It doesn't make a sound. To show that it is a bonus letter, you can put a star above it.

miss

Student Notebook Entry

Have students add the word **miss** to the Vocabulary section of their Student Notebooks.

Dictate the Sentence

Yes, do not miss the bus.

Write the word, **miss**, on an index card and add it to your Word of the Day Packet.

Have the students add word examples to the Bonus Letter Rule in the Spelling Rule section of their Student Notebooks.

WEEK 1 DAY ❷

TEACH THE GLUED SOUNDS

all

Put the letters **a**, **l**, and **l** up on the Standard Sound Card display.

Tell students that the bonus **ll** changes the short **a** sound to /ȯl/. Replace the **a**, **l**, and **l** cards with the green **all** card.

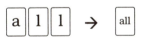

Show students the **all** Large Sound Card. Teach them to say the letter-keyword-sound: **all - ball - /ȯl/**

Green sound cards in Wilson programs are called **glued** (or **welded**) sounds because there are more than one sound, but they are glued very closely together.

The **all**, for example, is not one sound, it is two

sounds: /ò/ and /l/. The second **l** is silent.

First tap out /ò/, and then /l/, using middle finger, and then ring finger. Any sounds on green sound cards, however, get "glued" or "welded" together. Thus, to tap out /òl/, weld these two fingers together and tap them to the thumb at the same time: /òl/.

Example

Make **all** glued sound words with the cards on the board.

To tap out /b/ - /òl/, tap index finger to the thumb for /b/ and tap **two fingers**, (middle and ring, "glued" together) to the thumb for /òl/.

If a student is unable to do this, he or she can simply tap /b/ with one finger and /òl/ with one finger.

Practice with several current unit words, including **all** words and have students tap and read them with you. (See Unit Resources).

Teach Students To Mark Words

In a word with **all**, you can also show that there is a glued sound. **a-l-l** is glued. Box glued sounds like this:

Student Notebook Entry

Write the word, **call**, on an index card and add it to your Word of the Day Packet.

Have students add this word, with a sentence, to the Vocabulary section of their Student Notebooks.

Also, have the students color the keyword picture, **ball**, for the /òl/ sound in the Glued Sound section of their Student Notebooks.

TEACH SPELLING

Echo/Find Sounds

Say the sound /òl/, hold up Echo and have the students repeat.

Ask

What says /òl/?

Have a student come to the front and locate the **all** card.

Echo/Find Words

Next, dictate a current word such as **fill**. Have the students repeat the word and tap it out:

/f/ - /i/ - /l/.

It gets only three taps since it has three sounds.

Have a student find the letters **f, i, l** and add the other **l** for the bonus letter.

Lastly, the student must orally spell the word. Practice several current words.

Dictate several **all** words (see Resources). The students tap the word and find the cards. Remember to "glue" the /òl/ sound together when tapping. The green **all** card should be used for the /òl/ sound.

 Drill Sounds

Always do the vowel sounds. You can select some consonants, but there is no need to do all of them. (See Unit Resources.)

Include the green **all** Standard Sound Card in the quick drill.

Large Sound Cards

First practice sounds with the Large Sound Cards. Say the letter-keyword-sound and have students echo.

Standard Sound Cards

Next, point to the Standard Sound Cards (on display) with the Baby Echo pointer. You say the letter-keyword-sound and hold up Baby Echo to have students repeat. (Either you or a student can be the drill leader.)

Ask Students

What letters are the bonus letters?

(**f**, **l**, **s** and sometimes **z**)

What helps you remember this?

(These letters are at the end of each row.)

 ## Word of the Day

Select a Word of the Day from the words below. Make the word using your Standard Sound Card display. Also, write the word on a blank index card and add it to your Word of the Day packet.

Word Resource

WEEK 1

| m | i | s | s | | c | a | l | l | | o | f | f |

WEEK 2

| c | h | i | l | l | | y | e | l | l | | m | e | s | s |

Review Concepts

Reteach the bonus letter rule using the Word of the Day. Ask students to name all the bonus letters (**f**, **l**, **s** and sometimes **z**).

Use The Word In A Sentence

Have a student (or students) use the word in a sentence and discuss the word's meaning.

Make Other Words

Then use sound cards to make several other words from this Unit. (See Unit Resources.) Have students tap and read each word.

Student Notebook Entry

Have students add the Word of the Day to the Vocabulary section of their Student Notebooks.

Have students mark up the word with a star above the bonus letter.

Write a sentence on the board for students to copy. (This can be done at another time of the day.)

 ## Word Talk

Review the Words of the Day from your Words of the Day index card packet.

Make and Discuss Words

Make 4-5 words with your Standard Sound Card display.

Have students tap and read the words.

Ask a student to use a word in a sentence and another student to explain what the word means.

Read Words

Use your packet of words as flashcards. Have students quickly read them without tapping.

Display Words

Display current and review words. Have students find and read the words as directed.

Instruct Students

Find a word with a bonus letter.

Find a word with a glued sound.

Find a word with a digraph.

 Trick Words

Trick words require lots of practice. Sky write and finger write trick words, but **do not** tap them out or make them with the Magnetic Letter Tiles.

Word Resource

WEEK 1

you   we   I

WEEK 2

they   one   said

Students add these words to the Trick Word section of their Student Notebooks. Hold them accountable for the spelling of these words throughout the day. Direct students to look them up in the Trick Word section of their Student Notebooks.

After the introduction of new Trick Words, practice them with sky writing and tracing.

 Echo/Find Sounds & Words

Echo/Find Sounds

Say a sound. Have students echo and find the letter on their magnetic Letter Board.

Ask

What says /òl/?" (all)

(See Echo Sounds in Unit Resources for expected student responses.)

Echo/Find Words

Dictate the bonus letter words and include glued sound **all** words. The students tap the word and find the cards. Remember to "weld" or "glue" the /òl/ sound together when tapping. The green **all** Standard Sound Card should be used for the /òl/ sound.

(See Review and Current Unit Words in Unit Resources.)

Have students find Magnetic Letter Tiles needed to make words on their Letter Boards. After finding a word, have a student spell it orally.

 Dictation

Refer to this Unit's Resource List of Echo Sounds, Words and Sentences.

Proper Dictation Activity procedures are very important. Be sure to follow their demonstration on the CD-ROM.

DRY ERASE

Dictate 3 sounds, 3 current words and 3 trick words (trick words can be current or review).

This is a teaching time, not a testing time. Be sure students repeat each dictation. They should tap and orally spell the Unit words before writing. Students should write and orally spell trick words with their finger prior to writing them on their Dry Erase Writing tablets.

Have students "mark up" the review and current words.

COMPOSITION BOOKS

Dictate 3 sounds, 2 review, 2 current words and 2 trick words (trick words can be current or review) and 1 sentence.

This is also a teaching time, not a testing time. Be sure students repeat each thing that you dictate. They should tap and orally spell the review and current Unit words before writing. Students should write and orally spell trick words with their finger prior to writing them in their Composition Books. Students independently write the sentence and then you lead them through the proofreading procedure.

Have students "mark up" the review and current words.

DAY 5 CHECK-UP

Students do Day 5 Dictation in their Composition Books. Have them check the Check-up box at the top of the page.

Dictate the sound, word, or sentence. Have students repeat and then write independently. Do not have students spell orally. Encourage them to tap as appropriate.

UNIT TEST

Have students find Unit Test pages at the end of their Composition Books.

Dictate the sound, word, or sentence. (See Unit Resources.) Have students repeat and then write independently. Do not have students spell orally. Encourage them to tap as appropriate.

 **Make It Fun**

Preparation

- Building and Letter Boards
- Paper and Pencils

BUILDING WORDS

This activity will reinforce bonus letter spelling.

Instruct Students

Students see how many words they can build with bonus letters, **ff**, **ll**, **ss**. After they build the word with their Magnetic Letter Tiles, they can write each word on paper. They clear the Building Board to make another word.

Variation

Have students think of a word (each student can think of a different word) and make it with their Magnetic Letter Tiles. Then call on a student to come up to the front and make their word with the Standard Sound Cards. Have everyone "clear the Boards" and find letters to create another bonus letter word.

 **Storytime**

Preparation

- Baby Echo (on a pointer or ruler)
- Large Chart Paper

THE BIG MESS

Write the following story, with the phrases scooped, on chart paper.

The Big Mess

The hall was a big mess!

"What a mess!" said Mom.

"Pick this up."

Jill and Bill did the big job.

Did they fuss?

They did not fuss at all.

Instruct Students

Ask the students to read the title silently. (Tell students to tap words when reading silently, if necessary.) Discuss the title and predict what the story might be about.

Next, have the students read the first sentence silently. Have a student come to the front and read this aloud, scooping the words with Baby Echo.

Show students the exclamation point at the end of the first sentence. Tell the students about an exclamation point and explain how it changes voice expression.

Read the sentence with expression as you point with Baby Echo. Have students repeat.

Read Sentences

Continue reading one sentence at a time.

- Have students read silently. (Tell students to tap words when reading silently, if necessary.)
- Select a student to come read the sentence with the Baby Echo pointer. Be sure the student uses proper expression and phrasing. If not, model.
- Have the whole class repeat the sentence.

After the story has been read once in this manner, read it altogether with choral reading as you scoop the phrases with Baby Echo.

Make a Movie

Have students "make a movie" in their heads. Tell them to close their eyes and picture a really messy hall.

Ask someone to describe what they see in their movie, discussing each sentence.

Continue with the whole story. Then model retelling the story in your own words and ask a student to retell it in their own words.

Mark Words

Lastly, select students to come mark words as directed.

- Make a capital letter frame around words that have a capital letter and discuss why (at the beginning of a sentence or a person's name).

 The hall was a big mess!

- Highlight all punctuation marks (briefly discuss them again).
- Star bonus letters.
- Box welded or glued sounds.

WEEK 2

Preparation

- Baby Echo (on a pointer or ruler)
- Large Chart Paper with the story from Week 1
- Copy THE BIG MESS story for each student from the Fluency Kit (in the Stories tab)

Instruct Students

Ask the students to read the title silently. Have them try to remember the "movie" in their mind. Have someone describe the story by retelling it. Read chorally as you point with Baby Echo and determine if the retelling was accurate.

Next disseminate the story to the students. Have them draw pictures for each page and cut on the dotted lines. Staple these into booklets for the students to bring home.

Drill Sounds

a - apple - /ă/	b - bat - /b/
c - cat - /k/	d - dog - /d/
e - Ed - /ĕ/	f - fun - /f/
g - game - /g/	h - hat - /h/
i - itch - /ĭ/	j - jug - /j/
k - kite - /k/	l - lamp - /l/
m - man - /m/	n - nut - /n/
o - octopus - /ŏ/	p - pan - /p/
qu - queen - /kw/	r - rat - /r/
s - snake - /s/	t - top - /t/
u - up - /ŭ/	v - van - /v/
w - wind - /w/	x - fox - /ks/
y - yellow - /y/	z - zebra - /z/
sh - ship - /sh/	ck - sock - /k/
wh - whistle - /w/	th - thumb - /th/
ch - chin - /ch/	all - ball - /ȯl/

Echo Sounds

Sounds appear between / /. You say the sound. Students echo the sound and say the letter. Depending on the activity, students then either find or make the letter corresponding to that sound.

CONSONANTS

/b/ - b	/d/ - d	/f/ - f
/g/ - g	/h/ - h	/j/ - j
/k/ - c, k, ck	/l/ - l	/m/ - m
/n/ - n	/p/ - p	/kw/ - qu
/r/ - r	/s/ - s	/t/ - t
/v/ - v	/w/ - w, wh	/ks/ - x
/y/ - y	/z/ - z	/ch/ - ch
/sh/ - sh	/th/ - th	

VOWELS

/ă/ - a	/ĕ/ - e	/ĭ/ - i
/ŏ/ - o	/ŭ/ - u	

GLUED/WELDED SOUNDS
/ȯl/ - all

Review Trick Words

the	of	and	to	a	was
is	he	for	as	his	has

Current Unit Trick Words

you	we	I	they	one	said

Review Words

mop	rib	sob	job	rash	map
rock	cop	such	dot	lid	mud
Ted	fix	lap	web	not	lick
much	ten	chip	tub	bed	moth
at	hip	lock	peg	shot	had
rich	bug	pen	bat	hit	pet
lash	bus	bun	pick	path	bib
red	jab	kid	nod	but	cup
mix	pot	Ben	kick	pat	thick
tab	Jim	tin	cob	rat	big
tip	cot	Rick	dash	whip	mad
den	gum	math	neck	dip	mug
sub	dish	wig	yes	fun	this
cub	fit	shut	rush	wish	quit
back	pup	fog	shop	lot	hut
pack	sit	let	gap	fish	sip
dug	dig	cab	Sid	Dick	vet
wax	chin	sock	shed	led	mat

Current Unit Words

shell	cuff	fuss	miss	kiss	off
fill	puff	toss	doll	hill	fell
chill	Russ	Bess	well	mess	Nell
mass	bell	pill	will	huff	wall
fall	hall	call	ball	tall	mall

Sentences

*Write any **bold word** on the board for students to copy. A **bold word** has untaught components.*

I will huff and puff up the big hill.

Bill has **been** sick.

Did Chet get the red shell?

Bess had a big kiss for her dad.

Beth sat in the den with Bill.

Tim will fill the dish with fish.

We had to mop up the mess.

The bug fell in the web.

Did Dad yell at Tom?

I got a chill in the tub.

Jack had to sell his pig.

Ed will kill the big bug.

This hall is a mess!*

Mom did not miss the mud at all.

I fell on the path.

Toss the ball to Kim.

Will Jill and Russ **go** to the mall?

Can you call the pup?

Bess will **go** to the mall.

Dad had one ball for Jen.

You will fall!*

Did you get that at the mall?

The vet had a pill for the dog.

The vet got the quill off the dog.

They had bad luck on the quiz.

The duck will quack at Bill.

* Use the tall blue punctuation mark in the Sentence & Syllable Frames to demonstrate and explain the exclamation point.

Have students find the Unit Test pages located at the end of their Composition Books. Dictate the sounds, words and sentences. Have students repeat and then write independently. Encourage them to tap, but they should not use their Student Notebooks.

Dictate The Following Sounds

/ch/   /ĭ/   /ŏl/   /ă/   /z/

Dictate The Following Words

quiz   lash   puff   fall   zip

bell   miss   chop   tall   lock

Dictate The Following Trick Words

you   said

Dictate The Following Sentences

Bill will toss the ball.

This deck is a mess!

Have The Students Do The Following

• Put a star above the bonus letters.

• Put a box around the glued or welded sounds.

• Underline the digraphs.

Remind students that they do not need to mark up the trick words.

Answer Key

SOUNDS

1. ch
2. i
3. all
4. a
5. z

WORDS

1. quiz
2. la<u>sh</u>
3. puff*
4. f[all]*
5. zip
6. bell*
7. miss*
8. <u>ch</u>op
9. t[all]*
10. lo<u>ck</u>

TRICK WORDS

1. you
2. said

SENTENCES

1. Bill* will* toss* the b[all]*.
2. <u>Th</u>is de<u>ck</u> is a mess!*

Unit 5 Level 1

Introduction

In this Unit, you will present the students with two new sounds that we consider welded or **glued sounds**.

The first one is **am**, as in **ham** - /**am**/. The second is **an**, as in **fan** - /**an**/.

The vowels are somewhat changed from a pure short vowel to a more nasalized vowel. Depending upon the person's dialect, this is sometimes more pronounced.

For all students, however, we have found it is helpful to teach these as glued sounds. The words **ham** and **fan** contain the glued sounds you will teach in this Unit.

PREPARING YOUR MATERIALS

Add the green **am** and **an** Standard Sound Cards to your classroom card display.

Arrange the Standard Sound Card display in the following manner

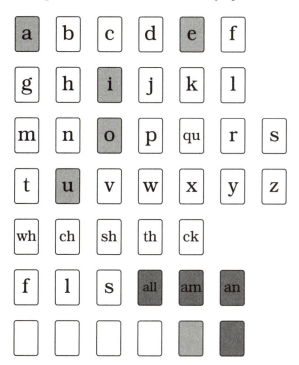

PREPARING YOUR STUDENTS

Have the students add the green **am** and **an** Magnetic Letter Tiles to their Letter Boards.

PREPARING FOR HOME SUPPORT

Copy and send home the **Unit 5 Letter and Activity Packet**.

Getting Ready

VIEW THE CD-ROM

LEVEL 1
- Unit 5
  Lesson Activities (see below)

STUDY LESSON ACTIVITIES

For each Unit you will review one or more lesson activities. This will help you master and internalize the important activity procedures.

Review the following activities in your manual's Lesson Activity Overview and on CD-ROM:

- Dictation (Dry Erase)

Week 1

DAY ❶	DAY ❷	DAY ❸	DAY ❹	DAY ❺
Introduce New Concepts	Drill Sounds	Drill Sounds	Drill Sounds	Drill Sounds
Trick Words	Word of the Day	Word of the Day	Word Talk	Storytime
	Echo/Find Sounds & Words	Make it Fun	Trick Words	Dictation (Unit Test)
	Dictation (Dry Erase)	Dictation (Composition Book)	Dictation (Dry Erase)	

 **Introduce New Concepts**

TEACH THE GLUED SOUNDS

am, an

Have students make the sound /m/. While making the sound, have them pinch their noses. The sound cannot be made with the nose blocked. Do the same with /n/.

Both **m** and **n** are called **nasal sounds** because the sound comes out of the nose. Due to this quality, **m** and **n** sometimes distort a vowel sound, especially **a**.

Produce the green **am** and **an** Large Sound Cards with the keyword pictures. Explain that these are **glued sounds**. The **n** and **m** change the short **a** sound from a pure short **a** to a nasal sound. The **a** is still considered short.

Most students have no difficulty with this. It is much easier to read and spell these words when **an** and **am** are glued together rather than segmented.

Use **b** and **a** magnetized Standard Sound Cards. Add **a** consonant at the end to make words, including **bat**, **back**, and **bad**. Tap and read each word. Now put **m** at the end.

Re-explain that **m** changes the sound of **a**. Replace the **a** and **m** with the green **am** Standard Sound Card.

Demonstrate tapping /b/ (tap index finger to thumb), /am/ (tap together middle and ring fingers to thumb).

Do words with **p** and **a** such as **pat**, **pad** and **pal**. Now make **p a n**. Change the **a** and **n** cards to the green **an** card.

Make **am** and **an** words using the Standard Sound Cards. Have the student tap and read these words.

Teach Students To Mark Words

The am and an sounds are glued sounds. You can box glued sounds like this:

Student Notebook Entry

Have the students color the keyword pictures for **am** and **an** in the Sounds section of their Student Notebooks.

Have students add the word **fan** (with a sentence) to the Vocabulary section of their Student Notebooks.

Write the word **fan** on an index card and add it to your Word of the Day packet.

TEACH SPELLING

Have students use their Magnetic Letter Tiles and Letter Boards. (See Resources for Echo Sounds and Words.)

Echo/Find Sounds

Be sure to include /**am**/ and /**an**/ as well as previous sounds. Say /**am**/ and have the students echo the sound.

Ask

What says /am/?

Have the students point to the tile. Select one student to give the answer, naming the letter(s). You can call the student up to your magnetic board in front of the class point to the Standard Sound Card. Do the same with /**an**/.

Echo/Find Words

Select current **am** and **an** words to dictate. For example, dictate the word, **pan**. Have students repeat the word. Then have them tap out the sounds: /**p**/ (one tap), /**an**/ (two fingers glued together in one tap).

The students then find the corresponding tiles to spell the words: **p** (ivory card), **an** (green card). Be sure the student(s) orally spell the word after tapping and finding cards. This can be done while tapping again: **p** - **an**.

Practice current words and also do some review words.

 Drill Sounds

Always do the vowel sounds. You can select some consonants, but there is no need to do all of them. (See Unit Resources.)

Include the green **am** and **an** Standard Sound Cards in the quick drill.

Large Sound Cards

First practice sounds with the Large Sound Cards. Say the letter-keyword-sound and have students echo.

Standard Sound Cards

Next, point to the Standard Sound Cards (on display) with the Baby Echo pointer. You say the letter-keyword-sound and hold up Baby Echo to have students repeat. (Either you or a student can be the drill leader.)

Examples

an - fan - /an/

am - ham - /am/

Instruct Students

Name some of the glued sounds.

(all, am, an)

 Word of the Day

Select a Word of the Day from the words below. Make the word using your Standard Sound Card display. Also, write the word on a blank index card and add it to your Word of the Day packet.

Word Resource

Review Concepts

Reteach the glued sounds **am** or **an**.

Use The Word In A Sentence

Have a student (or students) use the word in a sentence and discuss the word's meaning.

Make Other Words

Then use the Standard Sound Cards to make several other words from this Unit. (See Unit Resources.) Have students tap and read each word.

Student Notebook Entry

Have students add the Word of the Day to the Vocabulary section of their Student Notebooks.

Have students mark up the word by boxing the glued sounds.

Write a sentence on the board for students to copy. (This can be done at another time of the day.)

 **Word Talk**

Review the Words of the Day from your Words of the Day index card packet.

Make and Discuss Words

Make 4-5 words with your Standard Sound Card display.

Have students tap and read the words.

Ask a student to use a word in a sentence and another student to explain what the word means.

Read Words

Use your packet of words as flashcards. Have students quickly read them without tapping.

Display Words

Display current and review words. Have students find and read the words as directed.

Instruct Students

Find words with a bonus letter.

Find words with a glued sound.

 **Trick Words**

Trick words require lots of practice. Sky write and finger write trick words, but **do not** tap them out or make them with the Magnetic Letter Tiles.

Word Resource

from   or   have

Students add these words to the Trick Word section of their Student Notebooks. Hold them accountable for the spelling of these words throughout the day. Direct students to look them up in the Trick Word section of their Student Notebooks.

After the introduction of new Trick Words, practice them with sky writing and tracing.

 Echo/Find Sounds & Words

Echo/Find Sounds

Say a sound. Have students echo and find the letter on their Letter Board.

(See Echo Sounds in Unit Resources for expected student responses.)

Be sure to include /am/ and /an/ as well as previous sounds.

Echo/Find Words

Select current **am** and **an** words to dictate. Then have students tap out the sounds: /p/ (one tap), /an/ (two fingers "glued" together in one tap).

Practice current words and also do some review words.

(See Review and Current Unit Words in Unit Resources.)

Have students find Magnetic Letter Tiles needed to make words on their Letter Boards. After finding a word, have a student spell it orally.

Unit 5 Lesson Activity Plan

 Dictation

Refer to this Unit's Resource List of Echo Sounds, Words and Sentences.

Proper Dictation Activity procedures are very important. Be sure to follow their demonstration on the CD-ROM.

DRY ERASE

Dictate 3 sounds, 3 current words and 3 trick words (trick words can be current or review).

This is a teaching time, not a testing time. Be sure students repeat each dictation. They should tap and orally spell the Unit words before writing. Students should write and orally spell trick words with their finger prior to writing them on their Dry Erase Writing Tablets.

Have students "mark up" the review and current words.

COMPOSITION BOOKS

Dictate 3 sounds, 2 review, 2 current words and 2 trick words (trick words can be current or review) and 1 sentence.

This is also a teaching time, not a testing time. Be sure students repeat each thing that you dictate. They should tap and orally spell the review and current Unit words before writing. Students should write and orally spell trick words with their finger prior to writing them in their Composition Books. Students independently write the sentence and then you lead them through the proofreading procedure.

Have students "mark up" the review and current words.

DAY 5 CHECK-UP

Students do Day 5 Dictation in their Composition Books. Have them check the Check-up box at the top of the page.

Dictate the sound, word, or sentence. Have students repeat and then write independently. Do not have students spell orally. Encourage them to tap as appropriate.

UNIT TEST

Have students find Unit Test pages at the end of their Composition Books.

Dictate the sound, word, or sentence. (See Unit Resources.) Have students repeat and then write independently. Do not have students spell orally. Encourage them to tap as appropriate.

 Make It Fun

Preparation

• Review and Current Resource Word Lists in Unit Resources

STAND UP

This activity will help students learn to listen for glued sounds.

Instruct Students

Dictate a list of words, one at a time, some with glued sounds, some without. After you dictate a word, the students repeat the word and stand up if they hear a glued sound.

Storytime

Preparation

- Baby Echo (on a pointer or ruler)
- Large Chart Paper

PAM AND DAN

Write the following story, with the phrases scooped, on chart paper.

Pam and Dan

Pam and Dan sat in the sun.

Then Sam sat with them.

Pam had a red ball.

"Toss it to me," said Dan.

Sam, Pam and Dan

had fun with the red ball.

Instruct Students

Ask the students to read the title silently. (Tell students to tap words when reading silently, if necessary.) Discuss the title and predict what the story might be about.

Show the student the quotation marks and tell them what these indicate.

Read Sentences

Continue reading one sentence at a time.

- Have students read silently. (Tell students to tap words when reading silently, if necessary.)
- Select a student to come read the sentence

with the Baby Echo pointer. Be sure the student uses proper expression and phrasing. If not, model.

- Have the whole class repeat the sentence.

After the story has been read once in this manner, read it altogether with choral reading as you scoop the phrases with Baby Echo.

Make a Movie

Have students "make a movie" in their heads. Tell them to close their eyes and picture Pam and Dan.

Ask someone to describe what they see in their movie, discussing each sentence.

Continue with the whole story. Then model retelling the story in your own words and ask a student to retell it in his or her own words.

Mark Words

Lastly, select students to come mark words as directed.

- Highlight all quotation marks (briefly discuss them again).
- Box glued sound.

Note

You can copy and send home this story found in the Fluency Kit.

Drill Sounds

a - apple - /ă/	b - bat - /b/
c - cat - /k/	d - dog - /d/
e - Ed - /ĕ/	f - fun - /f/
g - game - /g/	h - hat - /h/
i - itch - /ĭ/	j - jug - /j/
k - kite - /k/	l - lamp - /l/
m - man - /m/	n - nut - /n/
o - octopus - /ŏ/	p - pan - /p/
qu - queen - /kw/	r - rat - /r/
s - snake - /s/	t - top - /t/
u - up - /ŭ/	v - van - /v/
w - wind - /w/	x - fox - /ks/
y - yellow - /y/	z - zebra - /z/
sh - ship - /sh/	ck - sock - /k/
wh - whistle - /w/	th - thumb - /th/
ch - chin - /ch/	all - ball - /öl/
an - fan - /an/	am - ham - /am/

Echo Sounds

Sounds appear between / /. You say the sound. Students echo the sound and say the letter. Depending on the activity, students then either find or make the letter corresponding to that sound.

CONSONANTS/CONSONANT DIGRAPHS

/b/ - b	/d/ - d	/f/ - f
/g/ - g	/h/ - h	/j/ - j
/k/ - c, k, ck	/l/ - l	/m/ - m
/n/ - n	/p/ - p	/kw/ - qu
/r/ - r	/s/ - s	/t/ - t
/v/ - v	/w/ - w, wh	/ks/ - x
/y/ - y	/z/ - z	/ch/ - ch
/sh/ - sh	/th/ - th	

VOWELS

/ă/ - a	/ĕ/ - e	/ĭ/ - i
/ŏ/ - o	/ŭ/ - u	

GLUED/WELDED SOUNDS

/öl/ - all	/am/ - am	/an/ - an

Review Trick Words

the	of	and	to	a	was
is	he	for	as	his	has
you	we	I	they	one	said

Current Unit Trick Words

from	or	have

Review Words

mop	rib	sob	job	rash	map
rock	cop	such	dot	lid	mud
Ted	fix	lap	web	not	lick
much	ten	chip	tub	bed	moth
at	hip	lock	peg	shot	had
rich	bug	pen	bat	hit	pet
lash	bus	bun	pick	path	bib
red	jab	kid	nod	but	cup
mix	pot	Ben	kick	pat	thick
tab	Jim	tin	fun	rat	big
tip	vet	Rick	dash	whip	mad
den	gum	math	neck	dip	mug
cub	fit	shut	rush	wish	quit
back	pup	fog	shop	dish	hut
pack	sit	let	wig	fish	sip
wax	chin	sock	shed	led	mat
fuss	miss	kiss	cuff	shell	puff
toss	huff	hill	fell	chill	Russ
Bess	well	mess	pill	mass	bell
call	ball	tall	wall	fall	hall

Current Unit Words

ham	Sam	can	than	pan	man
fan	Jan	am	jam	Dan	tan
Pam	ran	bam	ram	Nan	van

Sentences

*Write any **bold word** on the board for students to copy. A **bold word** has untaught components.*

Jill can nap on the bed.

Did Dan fall in the pig pen?

The dog ran on the path.

Chet had jam on his chin.

Did Beth get **a** fan for the den?

Jan will get **her** bath **at six**.

The ram on the hill is big.

Ben had a red and tan hat.

Pam and Bob have fun at the shop.

Sam has a bad rash on his leg.

Did Jack or Dan get the sock?

This is from Dan!

Have students find the Unit Test pages located at the end of their Composition Books. Dictate the sounds, words and sentences. Have students repeat and then write independently. Encourage them to tap, but they should not use their Student Notebooks.

Dictate The Following Sounds

/k/   /ks/   /am/   /ĕ/   /an/

Dictate The Following Words

quick   man   shed   Sam   mall

fan   wax   mud   rock   ham

Dictate The Following Trick Words

from   have

Dictate The Following Sentences

Pam ran up the big hill.

Beth can get the red ball.

Have The Students Do The Following

• Circle the "chicken letter" and his best buddy.
• Put a star above the bonus letters.
• Put a box around the glued sounds.
• Underline the digraphs.

Remind students that they do not mark up trick words.

Answer Key

SOUNDS

1. k, c, ck
2. x
3. am
4. e
5. an

WORDS

1. qu̲ick
2. m̲an̲
3. s̲hed
4. S̲am̲
5. m̲all̲
6. f̲an̲
7. wax
8. mud
9. ro̲ck̲
10. h̲am̲

TRICK WORDS

1. from
2. have

SENTENCES

1. P̲am̲ r̲an̲ up the big hill.
2. Be̲th c̲an̲ get the red b̲all̲.

Unit 6 Level 1

Introduction

In Unit 6, you will introduce the concept of a **baseword and suffix** in a very simple way, with just the suffix **-s**, using the **-s** Standard Sound Card and the Yellow Suffix Frame.

You will simply add the suffix **-s** to the words studied in previous Units. You will teach that when the suffix **-s** is added to a word, it sometimes says **/s/** as in the word **shops** or it sometimes says **/z/** as in the word **bugs**.

The students should be able to fluently read the words from previous Units before starting this Unit. If a word is unknown, the student should tap out and read the baseword first but should only tap when necessary. The suffix is not tapped.

To emphasize the concept of baseword and suffix, the word **shops** is read, **shop - shops**. **Bugs** is read, **bug - bugs**.

You will also introduce the students to the concept of **plurals**. For your information, some of the words in this Unit are plural nouns and other words are singular verbs. For now, focus on baseword and suffix and briefly discuss plurals.

In a Nutshell

NEW CONCEPTS

- Baseword and suffix with the suffix **-s**
- Plural words
- Narrative story structure
- Beginning composition skills

SAMPLE WORDS

hills	bugs	chills

TRICK WORDS

were	her	put
there	what	she
been	by	who

PLANNED TIME IN UNIT

3 WEEKS

Note
Extend the time in this Unit if student mastery is not demonstrated on the Unit test.

PREPARING YOUR MATERIALS

In addition to the listed materials, have on hand the **Yellow Suffix Frames** for use with your Standard Sound Cards.

Arrange the Standard Sound Card display in the following manner

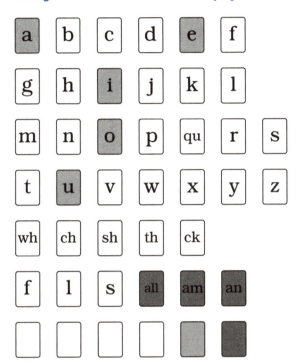

PREPARING YOUR STUDENTS

Have the students add the blank yellow Magnetic Tile to their Letter Boards.

PREPARING FOR HOME SUPPORT

Copy and send home the **Unit 6 Letter and Activity Packet**.

Getting Ready

VIEW THE CD-ROM

LEVEL 1
- Unit 6
  Lesson Activities (see below)

STUDY LESSON ACTIVITIES

For each Unit you will review one or more lesson activities. This will help you master and internalize important activity procedures.

Review the following activities in your manual's Lesson Activity Overview and on CD-ROM:

- Word of the Day

Unit 6 Lesson Activity Plan

Week 1

DAY ❶	DAY ❷	DAY ❸	DAY ❹	DAY ❺
Drill Sounds	Drill Sounds	Drill Sounds	Drill Sounds	Drill Sounds
Introduce New Concepts	Introduce New Concepts	Word of the Day	Word Talk	Word Talk
Trick Words	Dictation (Dry Erase)	Make it Fun	Trick Words	Storytime
		Dictation (Composition Book)	Echo/Find Sounds & Words	
			Dictation (Dry Erase)	

Week 2

DAY ❶	DAY ❷	DAY ❸	DAY ❹	DAY ❺
Drill Sounds	Drill Sounds	Drill Sounds	Drill Sounds	Drill Sounds
Trick Words	Word of the Day	Word of the Day	Word Talk	Storytime
Word of the Day	Echo/Find Sounds & Words	Make it Fun	Trick Words	Dictation (Day 5 Check-up)
Echo/Find Sounds & Words	Dictation (Composition Book)	Dictation (Composition Book)	Dictation (Dry Erase)	
Dictation (Dry Erase)				

Week 3

DAY ❶	DAY ❷	DAY ❸	DAY ❹	DAY ❺
Drill Sounds	Drill Sounds	Drill Sounds	Drill Sounds	Drill Sounds
Trick Words	Word of the Day	Word of the Day	Word Talk	Storytime
Word of the Day	Echo/Find Sounds & Words	Make it Fun	Trick Words	Dictation (Unit Test)
Echo/Find Sounds & Words	Dictation (Composition Book)	Dictation (Composition Book)	Dictation (Dry Erase)	
Dictation (Dry Erase)				

Introduce New Concepts

TEACH BASEWORD & THE -S SUFFIX

Begin by making the word **shop** with the Standard Sound Cards. Have the student read it. Add the **s** card to form the word **shops**. Tell students that **shop** is the **baseword** and the **suffix -s** can be added to it. Write **s** on the Yellow Suffix Frame and put it on the word shops.

Do the same thing with **bug**. Read the word **bug**, using the Standard Sound Cards. Write **s** on the Yellow Suffix Frame and add it to form **bugs**. Explain that sometimes the **s** sounds like a /**z**/ when added to words as a suffix. The suffix **-s** says /**z**/ in **bugs**. It says /**s**/ in **shops**.

Make the following words and have students read the baseword, then the baseword with the suffix. Have them tell you if the sound of the suffix is /**s**/ or /**z**/.

Word Resource

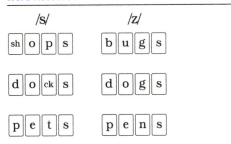

When reading the words, the students must always say the baseword, then the whole word (**shop - shops**, **bug - bugs**). This habit helps focus students' attention on the structure of the word. Only the baseword is tapped out. The suffix is not tapped. Students tap the baseword only if they have difficulty decoding.

Make the word **pen**. Tell students that you have one pen and hold up one pen. Add the suffix **-s** and hold up two or three pens. Tell them

that this means more than one. Explain that the fancy word of more than one is **plural**.

Teach Students To Mark Words

It is important to emphasize the baseword and suffix. You can do this by underlining the baseword and circling the suffix like this:

<u>bug</u>(s)

Have the students do this whenever they spell words with a suffix.

You can also have the students identify the sound of the suffix **-s**. Do it above the suffix like this:

　　/s/　　　　　　/z/
<u>hit</u>(s)　　　<u>bug</u>(s)

Student Notebook Entry

Have the students color the bugs for the sound of /**z**/ beside the consonant **s** in the Sounds section of their Student Notebooks.

Also, have students note the definition of a baseword and suffix in the Spelling section. Have them add two examples for words that form plurals by adding **-s**.

　　/s/　　　　　　/z/
<u>rock</u>(s)　　<u>pen</u>(s)

TEACH SPELLING

Have students use their Magnetic Tiles and Letter Board. (See Resources for Echo Sounds and Words.)

Echo/Find Sounds

Do this activity and include **"What says /z/?"** Now, both **z** and **s** should be the response.

Echo/Find Words

It is important to teach students to work from the baseword when spelling a word. Tell them this and teach them how to do it in the following manner. Make the word **bugs**. Use the Yellow Suffix Frame. Ask the students to read the word, including the suffix (**bugs**). Remove the suffix **-s**, and ask, **"What is the baseword?"** (bug).

Make another word with the suffix **-s**. Have the students read it, remove the **s** and name the baseword.

Next, do this orally, without the cards. You say a word such as **pens**. The students should repeat (**pens**) then name the baseword (**pen**). You can cue students by asking, **"What's the baseword?"** after students repeat the word.

When the students are able to do this, dictate a current Unit word such as **rugs**. The students should echo the word (**rugs**).

Then ask, **"What is the baseword?"** After they name the baseword, say, **"Let's tap it,"** and tap it out.

Then have students find the Magnetic Letter Tiles **r**, **u** and **g**. Next have students add the blank suffix card for the suffix **-s**.

Have one student do this on the magnetic board at the front. Lastly, have a student spell the word for students to check. Then **"clear the deck."**

Demonstrate that the baseword might have a bonus letter such as in the word **bells**. Students should name and spell the baseword first so they remember the bonus letters. Dictate several current words and have the students name the baseword, spell with the Magnetic Letter Tiles and then add the Yellow Suffix Frame.

Note

*The students tell you that the yellow card is **s**, but they do not write it on their cards.*

Drill Sounds

Always do the vowel sounds. You can select some consonants, but there is no need to do all of them. (See Unit Resources.)

Remember to do both sounds of **s** when you do the drill with the Standard Sound Cards. (See the back of the **s** sound card as a reminder.)

Large Sound Cards

First practice sounds with the Large Sound Cards. Say the letter-keyword-sound and have students echo.

Standard Sound Cards

Next, point to the Standard Sound Cards (on display) with the Baby Echo pointer. You say the letter-keyword-sound and hold up Baby Echo to have students repeat. (Either you or a student can be the drill leader.)

Ask Students

When does the s say /z/?

(Sometimes when it is a suffix.)

Word of the Day

Select a Word of the Day from the words on the following page. Make the word using your Standard Sound Card display. Also, write the word on a blank index card and add it to your Word of the Day packet.

Word Resource

WEEK 1

| l | o | g | s |

WEEK 2

| w | a | l | l | s | | s | o | ck | s | | sh | i | p | s |

WEEK 3

| j | u | g | s | | b | e | l | l | s | | h | u | g | s |

Review Concepts

Reteach baseword and suffix and discuss plurals (or more than one) using the Word of the Day.

Use The Word In A Sentence

Have a student (or students) use the word in a sentence and discuss the word's meaning.

Make Other Words

Then use sound cards to make several other words from this Unit. (See Unit Resources.) Have students tap and read each word.

Student Notebook Entry

Have students add the Word of the Day to the Vocabulary section of their Student Notebooks.

Have students mark up the word by underlining the baseword and circling the suffix.

Write a sentence on the board for students to copy. (This can be done at another time of the day.)

 **Word Talk**

Review the Words of the Day from your Words of the Day index card packet.

Make and Discuss Words

Make 4-5 words with your Standard Sound Card display.

Have students tap and read the words.

Ask a student to use a word in a sentence and another student to explain what the word means.

Read Words

Use your packet of words as flashcards. Have students quickly read them without tapping.

Display Words

Display current and review words. Have students find and read the words as directed.

Instruct Students

Find the words with a baseword and suffix.

Find a word that ends with a digraph.

Find a word that has a glued sound.

 **Trick Words**

Trick words require lots of practice. Sky write and finger write trick words, but **do not** tap them out or make them with the Magnetic Letter Tiles.

Word Resource

WEEK 1

were   her   put

WEEK 2

there   what   she

WEEK 3

been   by   who

Students add these words to the Trick Word section of their Student Notebooks. Hold them accountable for the spelling of these words throughout the day. Direct students to look them up in the Trick Word section of their Student Notebooks.

After the introduction of new Trick Words, practice them with sky writing and tracing. (See Resources.)

 Echo/Find Sounds & Words

Echo/Find Sounds

Say a sound. Have students echo and find the letter on their Letter Boards.

Include **"What says /z/?"** Now, both **z** and **s** should be the response.

(See Echo Sounds in Unit Resources for expected student responses.)

Echo/Find Words

It is important to teach students to work from the baseword when spelling a word.

Dictate several current words and have the students name the baseword, spell with the Magnetic Letter Tiles and then add the yellow suffix card.

(See Review and Current Unit Words in Unit Resources.)

After finding a word, have a student spell it orally.

 Dictation

Refer to this Unit's Resource List of Echo Sounds, Words and Sentences.

Proper Dictation Activity procedures are very important. Be sure to follow their demonstration on the CD-ROM.

DRY ERASE

Dictate 3 sounds, 3 current words and 3 trick words (trick words can be current or review).

This is a teaching time, not a testing time. Be sure students repeat each dictation. They should tap and orally spell the Unit words before writing. Students should write and orally spell trick words with their finger prior to writing them on their Dry Erase Writing tablets.

Have students "mark up" the review and current words.

COMPOSITION BOOKS

Dictate 3 sounds, 2 review, 2 current words and 2 trick words (trick words can be current or review) and 1 sentence.

This is also a teaching time, not a testing time. Be sure students repeat each thing that you dictate. They should tap and orally spell the review and current Unit words before writing. Students should write and orally spell trick words with their finger prior to writing them in their Composition Books. Students independently write the sentence and then you lead them through the proofreading procedure.

Have students "mark up" the review and current words.

DAY 5 CHECK-UP

Students do Day 5 Dictation in their Composition Books. Have them check the Check-up box at the top of the page.

Dictate the sound, word, or sentence. Have students repeat and then write independently. Do not have students spell orally. Encourage them to tap as appropriate.

UNIT TEST

Have students find Unit Test pages at the end of their Composition Books.

Dictate the sound, word, or sentence. (See Unit Resources.) Have students repeat and then write independently. Do not have students spell orally. Encourage them to tap as appropriate.

 Make It Fun

WEEK 1

Preparation

- Echo the Owl
- Blue Word Frame and Yellow Suffix Frame
- Resource List

IDENTIFYING WORDS WITH SUFFIXES

This activity will help students determine when words have a suffix.

Instruct Students

Write the word bag on the Blue Word Frame. Add the Yellow Suffix Frame and write **-s**. Have the students read the word. Tell them that you will use the Blue Word Frame for the baseword.

Read a word from the list above. Hold up Echo and have the students echo the whole word.

Ask a student to come to the magnetic board and put the Word and Suffix Frames needed to make the word on the board. Have the student tell you the baseword if there is one.

For example, if the word is **blocks**, the stu-

dent gets both the Blue Word and Yellow Suffix Frames and says, **block**, pointing to the Blue Frame.

If the word is **box**, the student gets only the Blue Frame and says, **box**. Each time, write the word to confirm the choice. Then erase and dictate another word.

Variation

You can also make teams and tally points if you want to make the activity into a game. Sometimes you will need to use the word in a sentence in order for the students to determine whether or not the word is made up of a baseword and suffix.

WEEKS 2 • 3

Preparation

- Echo the Owl
- Blue Word Frame and Yellow Suffix Frame
- List of Words: **blocks, dogs, box, rocks, miss, beds, chills, fox, docks, picks, fix, kiss, fuss, socks**

IDENTIFYING WORDS WITH SUFFIXES

This activity will help students determine when words have a suffix.

Instruct Students

Tell students that some words sound like they end with a suffix, but they do not. As an example, make the word **fox** with your Standard Sound Cards and read it. Next write it on the Blue Word Frame and explain that it does not need a suffix.

Next dictate the word **dogs**. Have a student erase the Blue Word Frame and write **dog** and then add the suffix **-s** to the Yellow Suffix Frame:

Erase the frames.

 **Storytime**

WEEK 1

Preparation

• Baby Echo (on a pointer or ruler)
• Large Chart Paper

JACK'S BAGS

Write the following story, with the phrases scooped, on chart paper.

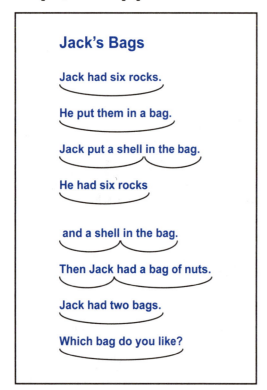

Jack's Bags

Jack had six rocks.

He put them in a bag.

Jack put a shell in the bag.

He had six rocks

and a shell in the bag.

Then Jack had a bag of nuts.

Jack had two bags.

Which bag do you like?

Instruct Students

Ask the students to read the title silently. (Tell students to tap words when reading silently, if necessary.) Discuss the title and predict what the story might be about.

Show students the question mark at the end of the last sentence. Explain how it changes voice expression.

Read the sentence with expression as you point with Baby Echo. Have students repeat.

Read Sentences

Continue reading one sentence at a time.

• Have students read silently. (Tell students to tap words when reading silently, if necessary.)

• Select a student to come read the sentence with the Baby Echo pointer. Be sure the student uses proper expression and phrasing. If not, model.

• Have the whole class repeat the sentence.

After the story has been read once in this manner, read it altogether with choral reading as you scoop the phrases with Baby Echo.

Make a Movie

Have students "make a movie" in their heads. Tell them to close their eyes and picture Jack's Bags.

Ask someone to describe what they see in their movie, discussing each sentence.

Continue with the whole story. Then model retelling the story in your own words and ask a student to retell it in their own words.

Mark Words

Lastly, select students to come mark words as directed.

• Highlight the question mark (briefly discuss it again).

• Underline basewords and circle suffixes.

WEEK 2

Preparation

- Baby Echo (on a pointer or ruler)
- Large Chart Paper with the story from Week 1
- Copy the JACK'S BAGS story for each student from the Fluency Kit (in the Stories tab)

Instruct Students

Ask the students to read the title silently. Have them try to remember the "movie" in their mind. Have someone describe the story by retelling it. Read chorally as you point with Baby Echo and determine if the retelling was accurate.

Next, disseminate the story to the students. Have them draw pictures for each page and cut on the dotted lines. Staple these into booklets for the students to bring home.

WEEK 3

Preparation

- Find a picture in a magazine that shows at least two characters doing something. Be sure it is a good picture to develop a story.
- Large Chart Paper - Divide it with lines into 4 boxes:

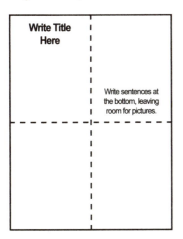

Instruct Students

Tell students that they are going to help you write a story. They are going to write a fiction story which is make-believe.

Show them the picture and talk about it. Explain that every story has characters. Explain that characters are the people in the story. Have them tell you who the characters are in the picture. (For example, a mother and a son). Help students make up names for the characters.

Explain that every story takes place somewhere. Tell them that the place where the story happens is called a setting. Ask the students where the characters in the picture are.

Next, paste the picture in the top left hand box.

Tell students they need to think of a Title. Help them come up with a title and put it above the picture.

Tell students that you will help them write a story. They will need to think of what happened first (point to the top right box), what happened next (point to the bottom left box), and what happened in the end. Ask students for ideas and guide them to come up with ideas for each box. Do only one or two sentences per box.

Write sentences at the bottom of the boxes, leaving room for pictures.

After you write a story, read each panel with Baby Echo. Have students echo after you.

Ask

Who are the characters in this story?

What is the setting? (Remind them this means where it took place).

What happened first?

What happened next?

What happened in the end?

Note

You can draw pictures for each panel at another time and re-read the story again.

Drill Sounds

a - apple - /ă/	b - bat - /b/
c - cat - /k/	d - dog - /d/
e - Ed - /ĕ/	f - fun - /f/
g - game - /g/	h - hat - /h/
i - itch - /ĭ/	j - jug - /j/
k - kite - /k/	l - lamp - /l/
m - man - /m/	n - nut - /n/
o - octopus - /ŏ/	p - pan - /p/
qu - queen - /kw/	r - rat - /r/
s - snake - /s/	s - bugs - /z/
t - top - /t/	u - up - /ŭ/
v - van - /v/	w - wind - /w/
x - fox - /ks/	y - yellow - /y/
z - zebra - /z/	sh - ship - /sh/
ck - sock - /k/	wh - whistle - /w/
th - thumb - /th/	ch - chin - /ch/
all - ball - /òl/	an - fan - /an/
am - ham - /am/	

Echo Sounds

Sounds appear between / /. You say the sound. Students echo the sound and say the letter. Depending on the activity, students then either find or make the letter corresponding to that sound.

CONSONANTS/CONSONANT DIGRAPHS

/b/ - b	/d/ - d	/f/ - f
/g/ - g	/h/ - h	/j/ - j
/k/ - c, k, ck	/l/ - l	/m/ - m
/n/ - n	/p/ - p	/kw/ - qu
/r/ - r	/s/ - s	/t/ - t
/v/ - v	/w/ - w, wh	/ks/ - x
/y/ - y	/z/ - z, s	/ch/ - ch
/sh/ - sh	/th/ - th	

VOWELS

/ă/ - a	/ĕ/ - e	/ĭ/ - i
/ŏ/ - o	/ŭ/ - u	

GLUED/WELDED SOUNDS

/òl/ - all	/am/ - am	/an/ - an

Review Trick Words

the	of	and	to	a	was
is	he	for	as	his	has
I	you	we	they	one	said
from	or	have			

Current Unit Trick Words

were	her	put	there	what	she
been	by	who			

Review Words

lash	bus	bun	pick	path	bib
red	jab	kid	nod	but	cup
mix	pot	Ben	kick	pat	thick
tab	Jim	tin	cob	rat	big
tip	cot	Rick	dash	whip	mad
dug	dig	cab	Sid	Dick	vet
wax	chin	sock	shed	led	mat
lit	pig	nap	kit	Jack	then
job	did	zap	rub	them	pal
fox	nut	gas	him	shell	cuff
fuss	miss	kiss	off	fill	puff
toss	doll	hill	fell	chill	Russ
Bess	well	mess	Nell	mass	bell
pill	will	huff	wall	fall	hall
call	ball	tall	mall	ham	Sam
can	than	pan	man	fan	Jan
am	jam	Dan	tan	Pam	ran
bam	ram	Nan	van		

Current Unit Words

dogs	pens	pups	shops	locks	webs
nets	pegs	hams	chins	backs	mats
mills	chills	maps	tops	sips	wets
bills	rubs	necks	bells	lugs	shuts
rugs	shells	fans	tins	kicks	huffs
sheds	wins	pins	runs	fills	nuts
packs	jugs	sits	bugs	pats	zags
naps	tubs	buds	sets	fibs	dads
socks	pills	chips	ships	dabs	kids
paths	pits	cans	quits	zaps	rocks
cops	lips	mops	tugs	beds	bets

Sentences

*Write any **bold word** on the board for students to copy. A **bold word** has untaught components.*

Dad sits in the den with his dog.

The kids will nap on the cot.

Tim put the mops in the shed.

The rugs had lots of mud on them.

Bob yells at the kids.

Seth runs to the dock with Tom.

The shells **are** red.

Did Rick get his socks?

Chet lugs the jug up the hill.

Pam hugs the pup when it is sad.

Mom shops and shops.

Did Jeff miss the kids?

Who has the pens?

Put it in the jugs.

There **are** six mops.

She sits on the deck.

The dogs have been fed.

Put her bells in the hall.

Fill the cups for the kids.

Ted will mop the decks.

The ship gets lots of sun.

Dan shops at the mall.

Sam has lots of fun.

The kids had chips and dip.

Mom fills the jugs in the shed.

Bob naps in the den on the rug.

Jim has bags of shells.

Chet gabs with Jill.

The kids had the ball in the bin.

Fill the jug with nuts.

The dog runs with Tim.

Did Rick get the bells for the shop?

The red pens **are** on the bed.

Chad calls his dogs.

Tim is sick and has the chills.

Have students find the Unit Test pages located at the end of their Composition Books. Dictate the sounds, words and sentences. Have students repeat and then write independently. Encourage them to tap, but they should not use their Student Notebooks.

Dictate The Following Sounds

/kw/   /z/   /th/   /ă/   /ŏ/

Dictate The Following Words

pans   huffs   ships   chins   bells

locks   bags   quits   nets   walls

Dictate The Following Trick Words

put   what

Dictate The Following Sentences

Did Ted fill the cups yet?

The dog runs with Jill.

Have The Students Do The Following

• Underline baseword and circle suffix
• Star bonus letters
• Box any glued sounds

Answer Key

SOUNDS

1. qu
2. s, z
3. th
4. a
5. o

WORDS

1. pan(s)
2. huff*(s)
3. ship(s)
4. chin(s)
5. bell*(s)
6. lock(s)
7. bag(s)
8. quit(s)
9. net(s)
10. wall*(s)

TRICK WORDS

1. put
2. what

SENTENCES

1. Did Ted fill* the cup(s) yet?
2. The dog run(s) with Jill*.

Unit 7 Level 1

Introduction

In Unit 7, you will introduce new glued sounds. There will be four new glued sounds ending with **ng** (**ang**, **ing**, **ong**, **ung**) and four ending with **nk** (**ank**, **ink**, **onk**, **unk**).

You will explain that these new sounds do have individual sounds but that they are closely glued together. To tap these out, you use three fingers glued together to represent the sounds working together.

PREPARING YOUR MATERIALS

Add the green **ang**, **ing**, **ong**, **ung**, **ank**, **ink**, **onk**, and **unk** cards to your Standard Sound Card display. Have on hand these new Large Sound Cards with keyword pictures as well.

Arrange the Standard Sound Card display in the following manner

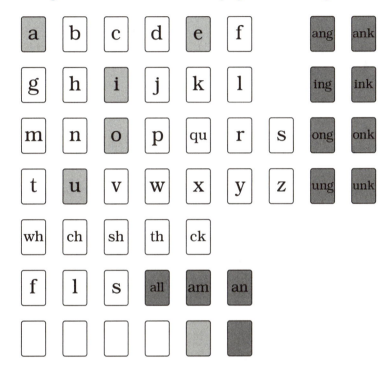

PREPARING YOUR STUDENTS

Have the students add the green **ang**, **ing**, **ong**, **ung**, **ank**, **ink**, **onk**, and **unk** Magnetic Letter Tiles to their Letter Boards.

PREPARING FOR HOME SUPPORT

Copy and send home the **Unit 7 Letter and Activity Packet**.

Getting Ready

VIEW THE CD-ROM

LEVEL 1
• Unit 7
  Lesson Activities (see below)

STUDY LESSON ACTIVITIES

For each Unit you will review one or more lesson activities. This will help you master and internalize important activity procedures.

Review the following activities in your manual's Lesson Activity Overview and on CD-ROM:

• Word Talk

Week 1

DAY ❶	DAY ❷	DAY ❸	DAY ❹	DAY ❺
Drill Sounds	Drill Sounds	Drill Sounds	Drill Sounds	Drill Sounds
Introduce New Concepts	Word of the Day	Word of the Day	Word Talk	Trick Words
Word of the Day	Introduce New Concepts	Dictation (Composition Book)	Trick Words	Word Talk
Trick Words	Dictation (Composition Book)	Make it Fun	Echo/Find Sounds & Words	Storytime
			Dictation (Dry Erase)	

Week 2

DAY ❶	DAY ❷	DAY ❸	DAY ❹	DAY ❺
Drill Sounds	Drill Sounds	Drill Sounds	Drill Sounds	Drill Sounds
Introduce New Concepts	Word of the Day	Word of the Day	Word Talk	Word Talk
Word of the Day	Introduce New Concepts	Make it Fun	Trick Words	Storytime
Trick Words	Dictation (Composition Book)	Dictation (Composition Book)	Echo/Find Sounds & Words	Dictation (Day 5 Check-up)
			Dictation (Dry Erase)	

Week 3

DAY ❶	DAY ❷	DAY ❸	DAY ❹	DAY ❺
Drill Sounds	Drill Sounds	Drill Sounds	Drill Sounds	Drill Sounds
Trick Words	Word of the Day	Word of the Day	Word Talk	Storytime
Word of the Day	Echo/Find Sounds & Words	Make it Fun	Trick Words	Dictation (Unit Test)
Echo/Find Sounds & Words	Dictation (Composition Book)	Dictation (Composition Book)	Echo/Find Sounds & Words	
Dictation (Dry Erase)			Dictation (Dry Erase)	

Introduce New Concepts

WEEK 1 DAY ❶

TEACH GLUED SOUNDS

ang, ing, ong, ung

Present the new sounds with the Large Sound Cards with keyword pictures. Teach the following letter combinations:

ang - fang - /ang/   ing - ring - /ing/

ong - song - /ong/   ung - lung - /ung/

Display the magnetic Standard Sound Cards:

Read them: /ang/, /ing/, /ong/, /ung/. Have the students practice after you.

Explain that the three letters do have individual sounds but that the sounds are very closely glued together and are therefore difficult to separate.

To tap this out, use **three fingers** tapping **together** at the same time.

Place the **s** card in front of **ang** to make the word **sang**. Students can tap on the table or the floor rather than to thumb if this is easier for them. Explain that the three fingers represent the three individual sounds. The sounds are said almost at the same time so it is easier to glue them together.

For example, **sang** is tapped /s/ (one tap with index finger), /ang/ (one tap with three fingers)

Now, place the **b** consonant card in front of

ang. Tap out the word: /b/ (one tap), /ang/ (one tap with three fingers).

Create words with all of the glued sounds. Have the students tap and blend each word.

Teach Students To Mark Words

When a vowel is combined with **ng** , we call it a glued sound. You can mark glued sounds with a box, like this:

s|ing|

Student Notebook Entry

Have the students color the pictures for the four new glued sounds in the Sounds section of their Student Notebooks: **ang**, **ing**, **ong**, **ung**.

WEEK 1 DAY ❷

TEACH SPELLING

Have students use their Magnetic Letter Tiles and Letter Boards. (See Resources for Echo Sounds and Words.)

Echo/Find Sounds

Ask "What Says____?" and include new sounds:

/ang/   / ing/   /ong/   /ung/

Echo/Find Words

Have students make review and current words with Magnetic Letter Tiles.

Dictate a current Unit word, such as **wing** and have the students echo.

Students tap out the word and then select the Magnetic Letter Tiles needed to form the word. Use the green Standard Sound Card for spelling glued sounds rather than the orange vowel card followed by two consonant cards. Be sure the students orally spell the word after finding the letters.

Dictate other words and have the students tap them out and find the corresponding tiles to make the words.

WEEK 2 DAY ❶

TEACH GLUED SOUNDS

ank, ink, onk, unk

Present the new sounds with the Large Sound Cards with keyword pictures. Teach the following letter combinations:

ank - bank - /ank/ **ink - pink - /ink/**

onk - honk - /onk/ **unk - junk - /unk/**

Display the magnetic Standard Sound Cards:

ang	ank
ing	ink
ong	onk
ung	unk

Read them: **/ang/, /ing/, /ong/, /ung/, /ank/, /ink/, /onk/, /unk/**. Have the students practice after you.

Explain that **-ng** words are tapped in the same way as **-nk** words.

To tap these words, use **three fingers** tapping **together** at the same time. Place the **s** card in front of **ank** to make the word **sank**.

For example, **sank** is tapped **/s/** (one tap with index finger), **/ank/** (one tap with three fingers)

Create words with all of the glued sounds. Have the students tap and blend each word.

Teach Students To Mark Words

When a vowel is combined with **ng** or **nk**, we call it a glued sound. You can mark glued sounds with a box, like this:

s**ing** s**ink**

If a word has **ank** in it, the **ank** rather than just the **an** is the glued sound.

Student Notebook Entry

Have the students color the pictures for the four new glued sounds in the Sounds section of their Student Notebooks: **ank**, **ink**, **onk**, **unk**.

WEEK 2 DAY ❷

TEACH SPELLING

Have students use their Magnetic Letter Tiles and Letter Boards. (See Resources.)

Echo/Find Sounds

Ask "What Says_____?" and include new sounds:

/ang/ /ing/ /ong/ /ung/

/ank/ /ink/ /onk/ /unk/

Echo/Find Words

Have students make review and current words with their Magnetic Letter Tiles.

Dictate a current Unit word, such as **wink** and have the students echo.

Students tap out the word and then select the Magnetic Letter Tiles needed to form the word. Use the green Standard Sound Card for spelling glued sounds rather than the orange vowel card followed by two consonant cards. Be sure the students orally spell the word after finding the letters.

Dictate other words and have the students tap them out and find the corresponding tiles to make the words.

WEEK 3 DAY **❶**

TEACH READING

Make 8-10 words with **ng** and **nk**. Add the suffix **-s** to each word. Have students read the words, naming the baseword first. The word **bangs** is read **bang** - **bangs**.

TEACH SPELLING

Teach students how to add the suffix **-s** to an **-ng** or **–nk** baseword. Follow the Unit 6 procedure for reading and spelling words with basewords and suffixes. (See Resources.)

 Drill Sounds

Always do the vowel sounds. You can select some consonants, but there is no need to do all of them. (See Unit Resources.)

Include the new glued sounds in each drill.

Large Sound Cards

First practice sounds with the Large Sound Cards. Say the letter-keyword-sound and have students echo.

Standard Sound Cards

Next, point to the Standard Sound Cards (on display) with the Baby Echo pointer. You say the letter-keyword-sound and hold up Baby Echo to have students repeat. (Either you or a student can be the drill leader.)

Ask (Week 1)

What glued sounds end with ng?

(/ang/, /ing/, /ong/, /ung/)

Ask (Week 2)

What glued sounds end with nk?

(/ank/, /ink/, /onk/, /unk/)

 Word of the Day

Select a Word of the Day from the words below. Make the word using your Standard Sound Card display. Also, write the word on a blank index card and add it to your Word of the Day packet.

Word Resource

WEEK 1

| r | ang | | h | ung | | l | ong |

WEEK 2

| j | unk | | p | ink | | th | ank |

WEEK 3

| k | ing | s | | w | ink | s | | f | ang | s |

Review Concepts

Reteach glued sounds using the Word of the Day.

Use The Word In A Sentence

Have a student (or students) use the word in a sentence and discuss the word's meaning.

Make Other Words

Then use sound cards to make several other words from this Unit. (See Unit Resources.) Have students tap and read each word.

Student Notebook Entry

Have students add the Word of the Day to the Vocabulary section of their Student Notebooks.

Have students mark up the word, boxing the glued sounds. Words with a suffix, have them underline the baseword and circle the suffix.

Write a sentence on the board for students to copy. (This can be done at another time of the day.)

Word Talk

Review the Words of the Day from your Words of the Day index card packet.

Make and Discuss Words

Make 4-5 words with your Standard Sound Card display.

Have students tap and read the words.

Ask a student to use a word in a sentence and another student to explain what the word means.

Read Words

Use your packet of words as flashcards. Have students quickly read them without tapping.

Display Words

Display current and review words. Have students find and read the words as directed.

Instruct Students

Find words with a baseword and suffix.

Find words with ng glued sounds.

Find words with nk glued sounds.

 Trick Words

Trick words require lots of practice. Sky write and finger write trick words, but **do not** tap them out or make them with the Magnetic Letter Tiles.

Resource Words

WEEK 1

out   so   are

WEEK 2

two   about   into

WEEK 3

only   other   new

Students add these words to the Trick Word section of their Student Notebooks. Hold them accountable for the spelling of these words throughout the day. Direct students to look them up in the Trick Word section of their Student Notebooks.

After the introduction of new trick words, practice them with sky writing and tracing.

 Echo/Find Sounds & Words

Echo/Find Sounds

Say a sound. Have students echo and find the letter on their Letter Board. Include some review and new sounds.

WEEK 1

/ang/   /ing/   /ong/   /ung/

WEEK 2

/ank/   /ink/   /onk/   /unk/

(See Echo Sounds in Unit Resources for expected student responses.)

Echo/Find Words

Dictate **-ng** and **-nk** words and have the students tap them out and find the corresponding tiles to make the words.

(See Review and Current Unit Words in Unit Resources.)

Have students find Magnetic Letter Tiles needed to make words on their Letter Boards. When proficient, have students make words with blank tiles, naming the letters that correspond to the selected tiles. After finding a word, have a student spell it orally.

Dictation

Refer to this Unit's Resource List of Echo Sounds, Words and Sentences.

Proper Dictation Activity procedures are very important. Be sure to follow their demonstration on the CD-ROM.

DRY ERASE

Dictate 3 sounds, 3 current words and 3 trick words (trick words can be current or review).

This is a teaching time, not a testing time. Be sure students repeat each dictation. They should tap and orally spell the Unit words before writing. Students should write and orally spell trick words with their finger prior to writing them on their Dry Erase Writing Tablets.

Have students "mark up" the review and current words.

COMPOSITION BOOKS

Dictate 3 sounds, 2 review, 2 current words and 2 trick words (trick words can be current or review) and 1 sentence.

This is also a teaching time, not a testing time. Be sure students repeat each thing that you dictate. They should tap and orally spell the review and current Unit words before writing. Students should write and orally spell trick words with their finger prior to writing them in their Composition Books. Students independently write the sentence and then you lead them through the proofreading procedure.

Have students "mark up" the review and current words.

DAY 5 CHECK-UP

Students do Day 5 Dictation in their Composition Books. Have them check the Check-up box at the top of the page.

Dictate the sound, word, or sentence. Have students repeat and then write independently. Do not have students spell orally. Encourage them to tap as appropriate.

UNIT TEST

Have students find Unit Test pages at the end of their Composition Books.

Dictate the sound, word, or sentence. (See Unit Resources.) Have students repeat and then write independently. Do not have students spell orally. Encourage them to tap as appropriate.

Make It Fun

WEEK 1

Preparation

• Students should have their Student Notebooks open to the **ng** page.

RHYMING

This activity will help students see the relationship between the key words for the glued sounds and other words that have that glued sound.

Instruct Students

Teacher dictates a word with an **ng** glued sound. Students repeat word and then give the rhyming key word and corresponding glued sound. Example: Teacher says, **"thing"** Students say, **"thing - ring - ing"**. Next, have students think of other words that rhyme. Write the list on the board. Finish the activity by chorally reading all the lists.

WEEK 2

Repeat the same activity above using **-nk** words.

WEEK 3

Disseminate the Word of the Day packet of cards, giving one card to each student. Have students stand and read their cards as you ask them to according to specific directions.

Instruct Students

Stand if you have a word that begins with a digraph.

Stand if you have a word with a suffix.

Stand if you have an ng glued sound.

Stand if you have an nk glued sound.

Students can stand more than once, if appropriate. In the end, ask if anyone did not stand yet. Have them stand and read the word and use it in a sentence.

 Storytime

WEEK 1

Preparation

• Baby Echo (on a pointer or ruler)
• Large Chart Paper

KING SAM

Write the following story, with the phrases scooped, on chart paper.

King Sam

King Sam sings to the kids.

The king can not sing.

His song is bad!

The kids say "Stop!"

The king winks

and the song stops.

The kids say,

"Thank you, King Sam."

Instruct Students

Ask the students to read the title silently. (Tell students to tap words when reading silently, if necessary.) Discuss the title and predict what the story might be about.

Show students quotation marks and discuss these again.

Read Sentences

Continue reading one sentence at a time.

• Have students read silently. (Tell students to tap words when reading silently, if necessary.)

• Select a student to come read the sentence with the Baby Echo pointer. Be sure the student uses proper expression and phrasing. If not, model.

• Have the whole class repeat the sentence.

After the story has been read once in this manner, read it altogether with choral reading as you scoop the phrases with Baby Echo.

Make a Movie

Have students "make a movie" in their heads. Tell them to close their eyes and picture King Sam.

Ask someone to describe what they see in their movie, discussing each sentence.

Continue with the whole story. Then model retelling the story in your own words and ask a student to retell it in their own words.

Mark Words

Lastly, select students to come mark words as directed.

- Circle quotation marks (briefly discuss).
- Highlight exclamation marks (briefly discuss them again).
- Box glued sounds.

WEEK 2

Preparation

- Baby Echo (on a pointer or ruler)
- Large Chart Paper with the story from Week 1
- Copy the KING SAM story for each student from the Fluency Kit (in the Stories tab)

Instruct Students

Ask the students to read the title silently. Have them try to remember the "movie" in their mind. Have someone describe the story by retelling it. Read chorally as you point with Baby Echo and determine if the retelling was accurate.

Next, disseminate the story to the students. Have them draw pictures for each page and cut on the dotted lines. Staple these into booklets for the students to bring home.

WEEK 3

Preparation

- Find a picture in a magazine that shows at least two characters doing something. Be sure it is a good picture to develop a story.

- Large Chart Paper - Divide it with lines into 4 boxes:

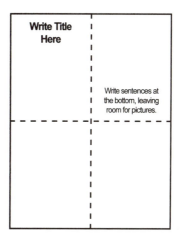

Instruct Students

Tell students that they are going to help you write a story. They are going to write a fiction story which is make-believe.

Show them the picture and talk about it. Explain that every story has characters. Explain that characters are the people in the story. Have them tell you who the characters are in the picture. (For example, a mother and a son). Help students make up names for the characters.

Explain that every story takes place somewhere. Tell them that the place where the story happens is called a setting. Ask the students where the characters in the picture are.

Next, paste the picture in the top left hand box.

Tell students they need to think of a Title. Help them come up with a title and put it above the picture.

Tell students that you will help them write a story. They will need to think of what happened first (point to the top right box), what happened next (point to the bottom left box), and what happened in the end. Ask students for ideas and guide them to come up with ideas for each box. Do only one or two sentences per box.

Write sentences at the bottom of the boxes, leaving room for pictures.

After you write a story, read each panel with Baby Echo. Have students echo after you.

Ask

Who are the characters in this story?

What is the setting? (Remind them this means where it took place).

What happened first?

What happened next?

What happened in the end?

Note

You can draw pictures for each panel at another time and re-read the story again.

Drill Sounds

a - apple - /ă/	b - bat - /b/
c - cat - /k/	d - dog - /d/
e - Ed - /ĕ/	f - fun - /f/
g - game - /g/	h - hat - /h/
i - itch - /ĭ/	j - jug - /j/
k - kite - /k/	l - lamp - /l/
m - man - /m/	n - nut - /n/
o - octopus - /ŏ/	p - pan - /p/
qu - queen - /kw/	r - rat - /r/
s - snake - /s/	s - bugs - /z/
t - top - /t/	u - up - /ŭ/
v - van - /v/	w - wind - /w/
x - fox - /ks/	y - yellow - /y/
z - zebra - /z/	sh - ship - /sh/
ck - sock - /k/	wh - whistle - /w/
th - thumb - /th/	ch - chin - /ch/
all - ball - /ȯl/	an - fan - /an/
am - ham - /am/	ang - fang - /ang/
ing - ring - /ing/	ong - song - /ong/
ung - lung - /ung/	ank - bank - /ank/
ink - pink - /ink/	onk - honk - /onk/
unk - junk - /unk/	

Echo Sounds

Sounds appear between / /. You say the sound. Students echo the sound and say the letter. Depending on the activity, students then either find or make the letter corresponding to that sound.

CONSONANTS/CONSONANT DIGRAPHS

/b/ - b	/d/ - d	/f/ - f
/g/ - g	/h/ - h	/j/ - j
/k/ - c, k, ck	/l/ - l	/m/ - m
/n/ - n	/p/ - p	/kw/ - qu
/r/ - r	/s/ - s	/t/ - t
/v/ - v	/w/ - w, wh	/ks/ - x
/y/ - y	/z/ - z, s	/ch/ - ch
/sh/ - sh	/th/ - th	

VOWELS

/ă/ - a	/ĕ/ - e	/ĭ/ - i
/ŏ/ - o	/ŭ/ - u	

GLUED/WELDED SOUNDS

/ȯl/ - all	/am/ - am	/an/ - an
/ang/ - ang	/ing/ - ing	/ong/ - ong
/ung/ - ung	/ank/ - ank	/ink/ - ink
/onk/ - onk	/unk/ - unk	

Review Trick Words

the	of	and	to	a	was
is	he	for	as	his	has
I	you	we	they	one	said
from	or	have	were	her	put
there	what	she	been	by	who

Current Unit Trick Words

out	so	are	two	about	into
only	other	new			

Review Words

mop	rib	sob	job	rash	map
much	ten	chip	tub	bed	moth
cub	fit	shut	rush	wish	quit
back	pup	fog	shop	lot	hut
pack	sit	let	gap	fish	sip
wax	chin	sock	shed	led	mat
lit	wig	nap	kit	Jack	then
fuss	miss	kiss	Bess	shell	cuff
toss	doll	hill	fell	chill	Russ
huff	well	mess	hall	mass	bell
can	than	pan	man	fan	Jan
bam	ram	Nan	van	dogs	pens
pups	shops	locks	webs	nets	pegs
hams	chins	vans	mats	mills	chills
maps	tops	sips	wets	bills	rubs
necks	bells	lugs	shuts	rugs	shells
fans	tins	kicks	huffs	sheds	wins
pins	runs	fills	nuts	packs	jugs
sits	bugs	pats	zags	naps	tubs
buds	sets	fibs	chips	paths	pills

Current Unit Words

bang	ring	sang	long	song	lung
king	wing	hang	sing	fang	hung
thing	rang	sung	pink	honk	gong

think	junk	rink	sink	thank	tank
chunk	bank	dunk	link	bunk	Hank
sunk	wink	yank	mink	bonk	sank

banks	rings	things	honks	songs	lungs
wings	hangs	kings	thinks	winks	sings
fangs	rinks	sinks	thanks	tanks	
chunks					

Sentences

*Write any **bold word** on the board for students to copy. A **bold word** has untaught components.*

WEEK 1

Tom sang the song to the kids.

What was that big bang?

It is a long run up the hill.

Kim will sing at the shop.

Did Bob hang this up?

The king has had bad luck.

My ring did not fit Meg.

What is the thing in this jug?

WEEK 2

Thank Dad for the gum.

Put the cash in the bank.

Ed sank the shot to win.

The cat has a big chunk of fish.

Ben had to get rid of the junk.

The ship sank in the bath tub.

Jim had the top bunk for his nap.

WEEK 3

The kids are at the rink.

Bob has bad lungs.

The wings on the bug **are** pink.

The kings had bad luck.

Mom has six rings.

Have students find the Unit Test pages located at the end of their Composition Books. Dictate the sounds, words and sentences. Have students repeat and then write independently. Encourage them to tap, but they should not use their Student Notebooks.

Dictate The Following Sounds

/ank/   /z/   /ung/   /e/   /ink/

Dictate The Following Words

thank wings bunk   fans   things

chill   rink   quits   songs fox

Dictate The Following Trick Words

out   into

Dictate The Following Sentences

Did Dan sing that song?

Ed will thank Tom and Jim.

Have The Students Do The Following

- Underline baseword and circle the suffix.
- Box all glued sounds.
- Put a star above the bonus letters.

Answer Key

SOUNDS

1. ank
2. z, s
3. ung
4. e
5. ink

WORDS

1. th⬚ank⬚
2. w⬚ing⬚(s)
3. b⬚unk⬚
4. f⬚an⬚(s)
5. th⬚ing⬚(s)
6. chill*
7. r⬚ink⬚
8. quit(s)
9. s⬚ong⬚(s)
10. fox

TRICK WORDS

1. out
2. into

SENTENCES

1. Did D⬚an⬚ s⬚ing⬚ that s⬚ong⬚?
2. Ed will* th⬚ank⬚ Tom ⬚an⬚d Jim.

Unit 8   Level 1

Introduction

In this Unit you will teach your students the difference between a **blend** and a **digraph**.

A digraph contains two consonants and only makes one sound, such as **sh, /sh/**.

A blend, however, contains two consonants but they each make their own sound, such as /**s**/ and /**l**/, /**sl**/.

The words in Unit 8 will contain blends. These words will have four sounds. You will also teach about **digraph blends**. A digraph blend is a digraph blended with another consonant such as **n** and **ch** in the word **lunch** or **sh** and **r** in the word **shred**. Words in this Unit with digraph blends will also have four sounds.

All of these words should be tapped to represent each separate sound.

In Week 3, be sure to practice these words with the suffix **-s** added (**flips** and **shreds**).

PREPARING YOUR MATERIALS

There are no new Standard Sound Cards to be displayed.

Arrange the Standard Sound Card display in the following manner

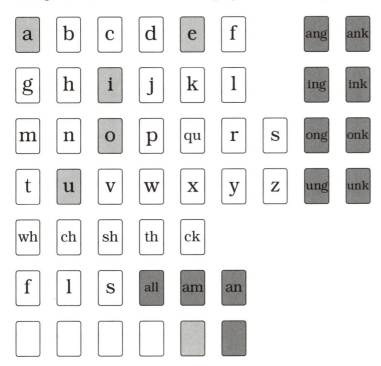

PREPARING YOUR STUDENTS

Students do not add any new Magnetic Letter Tiles to their Letter Boards.

PREPARING FOR HOME SUPPORT

Copy and send home the **Unit 8 Letter and Activity Packet**.

Week 1

DAY 1	DAY 2	DAY 3	DAY 4	DAY 5
Drill Sounds	Drill Sounds	Drill Sounds	Drill Sounds	Drill Sounds
Introduce New Concepts	Word of the Day	Word of the Day	Word Talk	Trick Words
Word of the Day	Introduce New Concepts	Dictation (Dry Erase)	Echo/Find Sounds & Words	Word Talk
Trick Words	Dictation (Composition Book)	Make it Fun	Dictation (Dry Erase)	Storytime
			Trick Words	Dictation (Day 5 Check-up)

Week 2

DAY 1	DAY 2	DAY 3	DAY 4	DAY 5
Drill Sounds	Drill Sounds	Drill Sounds	Drill Sounds	Drill Sounds
Introduce New Concepts	Word of the Day	Word of the Day	Word Talk	Trick Words
Word of the Day	Introduce New Concepts	Dictation (Dry Erase)	Echo/Find Sounds & Words	Word Talk
Trick Words	Dictation (Composition Book)	Make it Fun	Dictation (Dry Erase)	Storytime
			Trick Words	Dictation (Day 5 Check-up)

Week 3

DAY 1	DAY 2	DAY 3	DAY 4	DAY 5
Drill Sounds	Drill Sounds	Drill Sounds	Drill Sounds	Drill Sounds
Introduce New Concepts	Word of the Day	Word of the Day	Word Talk	Trick Words
Word of the Day	Echo/Find Sounds & Words	Dictation (Dry Erase)	Echo/Find Sounds & Words	Storytime
Trick Words	Dictation (Composition Book)	Make it Fun	Dictation (Dry Erase)	Dictation (Unit Test)
			Trick Words	

Introduce New Concepts

WEEK 1 DAY ❶

TEACH BLENDS

Using the Standard Sound Cards, form the word **ship**:

The students must read the word and identify the digraph.

Now, form the word **slip**:

Explain that this word is also formed by two consonants, a vowel and another consonant.

There is, however, a big difference between the words **ship** and **slip**.

Tap out **ship** (three taps). Tap out **slip** by tapping one finger over each card in the word.

Explain that slip has four sounds because the letters **s** and **l** each have their own sound. That is why **s** and **l** have their own cards, unlike the **sh** card.

Tell the students that when there are two or more consonants together, each making its own sound, that is called a **blend**. These sounds can be pulled apart. Pull the **s** and **l** cards apart to demonstrate. Show that even though the two consonants can be separated, the two consonants blend together nicely.

Separate the **s** and **l** cards, then push them together as students practice saying sounds individually and then blended.

Follow this example with several other Unit 8 words. Pull blends apart (separating sound cards) while students say each individual sound. Put blends together (joining sound cards) as students read letters to blend them together.

Show students that blends may appear before a vowel (**brag**) or after a vowel (**sent**).

Have the students tap out sounds and read the words.

Teach Students To Mark Words

A blend has separate sounds. You can show this by underlining each sound in the blend with a separate line, like this:

s <u>l</u> i p   m a <u>s</u> k

The **nk** in **pink** is a blend. Technically, the student could mark it like this:

p <u>i</u> <u>n</u> <u>k</u>

However, do not encourage the students to mark the **nk** blend (although it is correct if they do mark it). Instead, emphasize the glued sound. For your information, technically the **nk** is considered a **blend** and the **ng** is a **digraph**. This is confusing to students and therefore unnecessary to teach.

Remember, it isn't necessary to mark everything in all words. Usually you will want to emphasize specific concepts, especially anything new.

Student Notebook Entry

The students should see the definition of a blend in the Sounds section of their Student Notebooks. Have them add words with a blend: <u>f</u>l a g, t e <u>s</u> t

WEEK 1 DAY ❷

TEACH SPELLING

Have students use their Magnetic Letter Tiles and Letter Boards. (See Resources for Echo Sounds and Words.)

Unit 8 **Lesson Activity Plan**

Sounds

There are no new sounds. Review previous sounds.

Words

For spelling, students must now learn to pull apart four sounds. Do this with the Standard Sound Cards, tapping above each card:

Then take away cards and say the same word (**step**). Instruct students to tap sounds, visualizing cards in their minds. Repeat this with several current words.

Dictate a word. Have the students repeat the word and tap it out. Ask the students to try to picture the cards in their mind as they say each sound separately. They should then find the cards to correspond with each tap. Dictate 4-5 words.

WEEK 2 DAY ❶

TEACH DIGRAPH BLENDS

Demonstrate a digraph blend with the Standard Sound Cards:

These words also have four sounds. A digraph is blended with another consonant. Call this a **digraph blend**.

Teach Students To Mark Words

A digraph blend can be marked like this:

l u <u>n</u> <u>ch</u>

Student Notebook Entry

The students should see the definition of a digraph blend in the Sound section of their Student Notebooks. Have them add the word **lunch** as an example.

WEEK 2 DAY ❷

TEACH SPELLING WITH BLANK CARDS

The blank phoneme Standard Sound Cards can also be used rather than the actual letter cards.

Students spell the word with the correct color blank cards to represent sounds in the word dictated. The correct representation of a word with blank cards shows that the students have internalized the phoneme segmentation skills that are critical for success.

To use blank cards, dictate a word such as **shred**. Show the students how to use blank cards to spell this word. Then name the letters as you point to the corresponding cards:

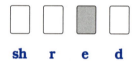

sh   r   e   d

Use the green cards to represent glued sounds. For example, demonstrate **clam** with:

c   l   am

WEEK 3 DAY ❶

REVIEW BASEWORD AND SUFFIX

Use the Standard Sound Cards to review the reading of a baseword and suffix. Make the word **drum** and add the suffix **-s**. This word should be read as **drum - drums**. Make 5-6 words. (See Resource List.)

 **Drill Sounds**

Always do the vowel sounds. You can select some consonants, but there is no need to do all of them. (See Unit Resources.)

There are no new sounds taught in this Unit.

Large Sound Cards

First practice sounds with the Large Sound Cards. Say the letter-keyword-sound and have students echo.

Standard Sound Cards

Next, point to the Standard Sound Cards (on display) with the Baby Echo pointer. You say the letter-keyword-sound and hold up Baby Echo to have students repeat. (Either you or a student can be the drill leader.)

 **Trick Words**

Trick words require lots of practice. Sky write and finger write trick words, but **do not** tap them out or make them with the Magnetic Letter Tiles.

Word Resource

WEEK 1

some   could   want

WEEK 2

say   do   first

WEEK 3

any   my   now

Students add these words to the Trick Word section of their Student Notebooks. Hold them accountable for the spelling of these words throughout the day. Direct students to look them up in the Trick Word section of their Student Notebooks.

After the introduction of new Trick Words, practice them with sky writing and tracing.

 Word of the Day

Select a Word of the Day from the words below. Make the word using your Standard Sound Card display. Also, write the word on a blank index card and add it to your Word of the Day packet.

Word Resource

WEEK 1

| a | s | k | | e | n | d |

| k | e | p | t |

WEEK 2

| b | u | n | ch | | r | an | ch |

| sh | r | u | g |

WEEK 3

| n | e | s | t | s | | f | l | a | g | s |

| qu | i | l | t | s |

Review Concepts

Reteach blend or digraph blend using the Word of the Day.

Use The Word In A Sentence

Have a student (or students) use the word in a sentence and discuss the word's meaning.

Make Other Words

Then use sound cards to make several other words from this Unit. (See Unit Resources.) Have students tap and read each word.

Student Notebook Entry

Have students add the Word of the Day to the Vocabulary section of their Student Notebooks.

Have students mark up the word with separate lines under the consonant blends.

Write a sentence on the board for students to copy. (This can be done at another time of the day.)

 ## Word Talk

Review the Words of the Day from your Words of the Day index card packet.

Make and Discuss Words

Make 4-5 words with your Standard Sound Card display.

Have students tap and read the words.

Ask a student to use a word in a sentence and another student to explain what the word means.

Read Words

Use your packet of words as flashcards. Have students quickly read them without tapping.

Display Words

Display current and review words. Have students find and read the words as directed.

Instruct Students

Find words that end with a blend.

Find digraph blends (Week 2).

 ## Echo/Find Sounds & Words

Echo/Find Sounds

Say a sound. Have students echo and find the letter on their Letter Board.

There are no new sounds. Review previous sounds.

(See Echo Sounds in Unit Resources for expected student responses.)

Echo/Find Words

Dictate a word.

(See Review and Current Unit Words in Unit Resources.)

Have students find Magnetic Letter Tiles needed to make words on their Letter Boards. After finding a word, have a student spell it orally.

 ## Dictation

Refer to this Unit's Resource List of Echo Sounds, Words and Sentences.

Proper Dictation Activity procedures are very important. Be sure to follow their demonstration on the CD-ROM.

DRY ERASE

Dictate 3 sounds, 3 current words and 3 trick words (trick words can be current or review).

This is a teaching time, not a testing time. Be sure students repeat each dictation. They should tap and orally spell the Unit words before writing. Students should write and orally spell trick words with their finger prior to writing them on their Dry Erase Writing Tablets.

Have students "mark up" the review and current words.

COMPOSITION BOOKS

Dictate 3 sounds, 2 review, 2 current words and 2 trick words (trick words can be current or review) and 1 sentence.

This is also a teaching time, not a testing time. Be sure students repeat each thing that you dictate. They should tap and orally spell the review and current Unit words before writing. Students should write and orally spell trick words with their finger prior to writing them in their Composition Books. Students independently write the sentence and then you lead them through the proofreading procedure.

Have students "mark up" the review and current words.

DAY 5 CHECK-UP

Students do Day 5 Dictation in their Composition Books. Have them check the Check-up box at the top of the page.

Dictate the sound, word, or sentence. Have students repeat and then write independently. Do not have students spell orally. Encourage them to tap as appropriate.

UNIT TEST

Have students find Unit Test pages at the end of their Composition Books.

Dictate the sound, word, or sentence. (See Unit Resources.) Have students repeat and then write independently. Do not have students spell orally. Encourage them to tap as appropriate.

 **Make It Fun**

WEEK 1

Preparation

- Sentences From Current Unit
- Blue Word Frames
- Punctuation Frames

SCRAMBLED SENTENCES

This activity will help students gain a better understanding of sentence structure, capitalization, punctuation and grammar usage.

Instruct Students

Write the words from a selected sentence on the word frames. Put these in a column in a mixed order. A student must rearrange sentences in correct order and add the correct punctuation mark. Have a student find and mark any word with a blend.

Variation

Hand students the scrambled words on word frames. Students must rearrange themselves into a sentence.

 **Storytime**

WEEK 1

Preparation

- Baby Echo (on a pointer or ruler)
- Large Chart Paper

THE PINK DRESS

Write the following story, with the phrases scooped, on chart paper.

The Pink Dress

Jill and her mom

went to the shop.

At the shop, Jill saw a pink dress.

It was the best dress

at the shop.

"Can I get this dress?" asked Jill.

What do you think

Jill's mom said?

Instruct Students

Ask the students to read the title silently. (Tell students to tap words when reading silently, if necessary.) Discuss the title and predict what the story might be about.

Read Sentences

Continue reading one sentence at a time.

- Have students read silently. (Tell students to tap words when reading silently, if necessary.)

- Select a student to come read the sentence with the Baby Echo pointer. Be sure the student uses proper expression and phrasing. If not, model.

- Have the whole class repeat the sentence.

After the story has been read once in this manner, read it altogether with choral reading as you scoop the phrases with Baby Echo.

Make a Movie

Have students "make a movie" in their heads. Tell them to close their eyes and picture the pink dress.

Ask someone to describe what they see in their movie, discussing each sentence.

Continue with the whole story. Then model re-telling the story in your own words and ask a student to retell it in their own words.

Mark Words

Lastly, select students to come mark words as directed.

- Make a capital letter frame around words that have a capital letter and discuss why (at the beginning of a sentence or a person's name).

- Highlight all punctuation marks (briefly discuss them again).

- Star bonus letters.

- Box glued sound.

WEEK 2

Preparation

- Baby Echo (on a pointer or ruler)
- Large Chart Paper with the story from Week 1
- Copy THE PINK DRESS story for each student from the Fluency Kit (in the Stories tab)

Instruct Students

Ask the students to read the title silently. Have them try to remember the "movie" in their mind. Have someone describe the story by re-telling it. Read chorally as you point with Baby Echo and determine if the retelling was accurate.

Next disseminate the story to the students. Have them draw pictures for each page and cut on the dotted lines. Staple these into booklets for the students to bring home.

WEEK 3

Preparation

- Find a picture in a magazine that shows at least two characters doing something. Be sure it is a good picture to develop a story.

- Large Chart Paper - Divide it with lines into 4 boxes:

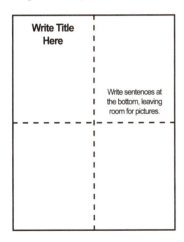

Instruct Students

Tell students that they are going to help you write a story. They are going to write a fiction story which is make-believe.

Show them the picture and talk about it. Explain that every story has characters. Explain that characters are the people in the story. Have them tell you who the characters are in the picture. (For example, a mother and a son). Help students make up names for the characters.

Explain that every story takes place some-where. Tell them that the place where the story happens is called a setting. Ask the students where the characters in the picture are.

Next, paste the picture in the top left hand box.

Tell students they need to think of a Title. Help them come up with a title and put it above the picture.

Tell students that you will help them write a story. They will need to think of what happened first (point to the top right box), what happened next (point to the bottom left box), and what happened in the end. Ask students for ideas and guide them to come up with ideas for each box. Do only one or two sentences per box.

Write sentences at the bottom of the boxes, leaving room for pictures.

After you write a story, read each panel with Baby Echo. Have students echo after you.

Ask

Who are the characters in this story?

What is the setting? (Remind them this means where it took place).

What happened first?

What happened next?

What happened in the end?

Notes

You can draw pictures for each panel at another time and re-read the story again.

The books in the Fluency Kit are now decodable. Students can independently read these books. Provide assistance as needed.

Drill Sounds

a - apple - /ă/	b - bat - /b/
c - cat - /k/	d - dog - /d/
e - Ed - /ĕ/	f - fun - /f/
g - game - /g/	h - hat - /h/
i - itch - /ĭ/	j - jug - /j/
k - kite - /k/	l - lamp - /l/
m - man - /m/	n - nut - /n/
o - octopus - /ŏ/	p - pan - /p/
qu - queen - /kw/	r - rat - /r/
s - snake - /s/	s - bugs - /z/
t - top - /t/	u - up - /ŭ/
v - van - /v/	w - wind - /w/
x - fox - /ks/	y - yellow - /y/
z - zebra - /z/	sh - ship - /sh/
ck - sock - /k/	wh - whistle - /w/
th - thumb - /th/	ch - chin - /ch/
all - ball - /ŏl/	an - fan - /an/
am - ham - /am/	ang - fang - /ang/
ing - ring - /ing/	ong - song - /ong/
ung - lung - /ung/	ank - bank - /ank/
ink - pink - /ink/	onk - honk - /onk/
unk - junk - /unk/	

Echo Sounds

Sounds appear between / /. You say the sound. Students echo the sound and say the letter. Depending on the activity, students then either find or make the letter corresponding to that sound.

CONSONANTS/CONSONANT DIGRAPHS

/b/ - b	/d/ - d	/f/ - f
/g/ - g	/h/ - h	/j/ - j
/k/ - c, k, ck	/l/ - l	/m/ - m
/n/ - n	/p/ - p	/kw/ - qu
/r/ - r	/s/ - s	/t/ - t
/v/ - v	/w/ - w, wh	/ks/ - x
/y/ - y	/z/- z, s	/ch/ - ch
/sh/ - sh	/th/ - th	

VOWELS

/ă/ - a	/ĕ/ - e	/ĭ/ - i
/ŏ/ - o	/ŭ/ - u	

GLUED/WELDED SOUNDS

/ŏl/ - all	/am/ - am	/an/ - an
/ang/ - ang	/ing/ - ing	/ong/ - ong
/ung/ - ung	/ank/ - ank	/ink/ - ink
/onk/ - onk	/unk/ - unk	

Review Trick Words

the	of	and	to	a	was
is	he	for	as	his	has
I	you	we	they	one	said
from	or	have	were	her	put
there	what	she	been	by	who
out	so	are	two	about	into
only	other	new			

Current Unit Trick Words

some	could	want	say	do	first
any	my	now			

Review Words

mop	rib	sob	job	rash	map
rock	cop	such	dot	lid	mud
Ted	fix	lap	web	not	lick
much	ten	chip	tub	bed	moth
tip	cot	Rick	dash	whip	mad
den	gum	math	neck	dip	mug
sub	dish	wig	yes	fun	this
cub	fit	shut	rush	wish	quit
back	pup	fog	shop	lot	hut
pack	sit	let	gap	fish	sip
wax	chin	sock	shed	led	mat
did	zap	rub	them	pal	fox
nut	gas	him	shell	cuff	fuss
miss	kiss	off	fill	puff	toss
doll	hill	fell	chill	Russ	pil
will	huff	wall	fall	hall	can
than	pan	man	fan	Jan	bam
ram	Nan	van	dogs	pens	pups
shops	locks	webs	nets	pegs	hams
chins	backs	mats	mills	chills	pins
runs	fills	nuts	packs	jugs	sits
bugs	pats	zags	naps	tubs	buds
sets	fibs	dads	socks	pills	

chips	ships	dabs	kids	paths	pits
mops	tugs	beds	bets	bang	ring
sang	long	song	lung	king	wing
hang	sing	fang	hung	thing	rang
rink	sink	thank	tank	chunk	bank
things	honks	songs	lungs	wings	hangs
kings	thinks	winks	sings	fangs	rinks

Current Unit Words

WEEK 1

sent	must	best	lend	drop	loft
pest	pond	flap	crib	bent	grab
jump	bend	chest	last	dent	trash
raft	stub	gust	grip	clock	brag
flop	stash	belt	stuck	cost	glad
grin	crab	plug	sand	drum	slush
trot	wept	dust	rest	hunt	vest
step	flag	swish	drag	drip	black
past	stick	vent	dump	ramp	brush

WEEK 2

punch	bunch	task	flip	test	ranch
camp	frog	crack	bench	soft	fast
squish	trap	crash	cloth	thump	stack
lost	nest	bled	mast	next	list
snip	spot	limp	block	lump	damp
spill	skin	flock	crop	plan	flat
west	snap	hint	cluck	blush	click
skip	pluck	kept	spin	clap	fled

chimp	small	mask	crush	pinch	band
fist	chomp	pump	clip	mint	slam
twig	shrug	trim	munch	rust	mend
slim	scab	melt	shelf	felt	help
silk	golf	milk	gulf	self	tilt
film	gulp	held	wilt	smog	flash
stop	snug	shrub	pant	went	just
gift	Fran	Brad	swim	glass	cross
press	spell	grass	fluff	class	dress
bless	still	stuff	cliff	drill	sniff

WEEK 3

clams	drops	ponds	pests	dents	stubs
grips	clocks	plugs	drums	vests	steps
flags	drags	drips	flips	tests	clicks
camps	frogs	cracks	stacks	shrubs	pumps

Sentences

*Write any **bold word** on the board for students to copy. A **bold word** has untaught components.*

WEEK 1

The belt is on the shelf in the den.

Did Beth step on that frog?

This clock is the best gift!

Bill fell in the wet sand.

Stan must dump the trash.

Ted will jump in the pond and swim.

Mom will mend the rip in the dress.

I wish that Kim did not brag.

Ben went on the ship.

The class must get a flag.

Tim will get the cloth on the shelf.

Jan got the drill for her dad.

WEEK 2

Jill will munch on the plum.

Bob went with Dad to the ranch.

The tot fell on the wet bench.

Bob had the last mint.

Trot up to the flag and then run **over** there!

Ben got a pinch on his leg from the trap.

Beth had a pink silk dress.

Did Tom brag about his six big fish?

Get the trash to the dump.

We will hunt for the lost raft.

Stan will lift that big pump.

Did Tom trip on that twig?

I held my pup as he got a shot.

Brad is sick so he can not help.

WEEK 3

Ed swims at the club with Tom.

Ben will sell the clams.

Pass the red blocks to Jed.

Did Jill get the frogs?

Fred trims the tall grass.

Can we bang on the drums?

Have students find the Unit Test pages located at the end of their Composition Books. Dictate the sounds, words and sentences. Have students repeat and then write independently. Encourage them to tap, but they should not use their Student Notebooks.

Dictate The Following Sounds

/unk/   /w/   /ĭ/   /öl/   /th/

Dictate The Following Words

spin   stuff   press   pinch   brag

chunks hang   blocks   vest   camps

Dictate The Following Trick Words

could   do

Dictate The Following Sentences

The pink shell was on the sand.

Did the dog sniff the clam?

Have The Students Do The Following

- Underline baseword and circle the suffix.
- Underline blends and digraph blends with two separate lines.

Answer Key

SOUNDS

1. unk
2. w, wh
3. i
4. all
5. th

WORDS

1. s<u>p</u>in
2. <u>s</u>tuff
3. <u>pr</u>ess
4. pin<u>ch</u>
5. <u>br</u>ag
6. chun k(s)
7. hang
8. <u>bl</u>ock(s)
9. ve<u>st</u>
10. cam <u>p</u>(s)

TRICK WORDS

1. could
2. do

SENTENCES

1. This pin <u>k</u> shell was on the san <u>d</u>.
2. Did the dog <u>s</u> niff the <u>cl</u> am?

Unit 9 Level 1

Introduction

This Unit reviews the reading and spelling of previous word patterns. No new word patterns are taught, just a new concept.

In Unit 9, you will teach students about a **closed syllable**:

1. Closed syllables can only have one vowel.

2. The vowel is followed by one or more consonants (closed in).

3. The vowel sound is short. To indicate the short sound, the vowel is marked with a **breve** (˘)

All the words presented thus far have been closed syllables. In English, there are six types of syllables (see Appendix). Closed syllables are the most common type. Whenever you have a short vowel sound, it will likely be a closed syllable.

It is important to teach students how to visually recognize a closed syllable so that they can then apply the short vowel sound to decode the word.

PREPARING YOUR MATERIALS

There are no new Standard Sound Cards to be displayed.

Arrange the Standard Sound Card display in the following manner

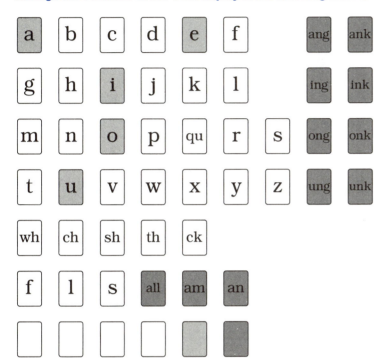

PREPARING YOUR STUDENTS

Students do not add any new Magnetic Letter Tiles to their Letter Boards.

PREPARING FOR HOME SUPPORT

Copy and send home the **Unit 9 Letter and Activity Packet**.

Getting Ready

VIEW THE CD-ROM

LEVEL 1
- Unit 9
  Lesson Activities (see below)

STUDY LESSON ACTIVITIES

For each Unit you will review one or more lesson activities. This will help you master and internalize important activity procedures.

Review the following activities in your manual's Lesson Activity Overview and on CD-ROM:

- Echo/Find Sounds & Words

Unit 9 **Lesson Activity Plan**

Week 1

DAY ❶	DAY ❷	DAY ❸	DAY ❹	DAY ❺
Drill Sounds	Drill Sounds	Drill Sounds	Drill Sounds	Drill Sounds
Introduce New Concepts	Word of the Day	Word of the Day	Word Talk	Storytime
Word of the Day	Introduce New Concepts	Dictation (Dry Erase)	Echo/Find Sounds & Words	Dictation (Day 5 Check-up)
Trick Words	Dictation (Composition Book)	Make it Fun	Dictation (Dry Erase)	
			Trick Words	

Week 2

DAY ❶	DAY ❷	DAY ❸	DAY ❹	DAY ❺
Drill Sounds	Drill Sounds	Drill Sounds	Drill Sounds	Drill Sounds
Introduce New Concepts	Word of the Day	Word of the Day	Word Talk	Trick Words
Word of the Day	Trick Words	Dictation (Dry Erase)	Echo/Find Sounds & Words	Word Talk
Echo/Find Sounds & Words	Echo/Find Sounds & Words	Make it Fun	Dictation (Dry Erase)	Storytime
Dictation (Dry Erase)	Dictation (Composition Book)		Trick Words	Dictation (Unit Test)

Introduce New Concepts

WEEK 1 DAY ❶

TEACH CLOSED SYLLABLE CONCEPT

In this unit, you will teach students the concept of a closed syllable. Explain that words have parts that go together called syllables. A syllable is part of a word that can be pushed out in one breath.

Cat is one syllable. **Catnip** has two syllables.

There are six kinds of syllables. All the words so far have been closed syllables.

Form the word **bat** with your Standard Sound Cards.

Tell the student that a closed syllable has one vowel only (point to **a**) and must be closed in (move the **t** closer to the **a** to show how it closes it in). A closed syllable gives the vowel the short sound; /ă/ is the short sound of **a**.

Now remove the **b** to leave the word **at**. Tell the student that there need not be a consonant in front of the vowel. The important point is that one vowel (point to **a** and stress **one**) is closed in (move **t**) by at least one consonant.

Make the word **bath**.

Tell the student that it can be closed in with more than one consonant (point to **th**).

Use the Standard Sound Cards to form the following words:

Ask the student to point to the closed syllables (**such**, **it**). Discuss each word, asking the student to explain why or why not it is a closed syllable.

such   has one vowel closed in with ch

she   has one vowel but it is not closed in

it   has one vowel closed in by t, no need for any letter before the vowel

boat   has two vowels

The Standard Sound Cards must be used to teach the closed syllable concept in a multisensory way. Use the procedure described to continually review this concept.

Avoid using **h**, **r**, **y**, and **w** at the end (**ah**, **bar**, **bay**, **saw**). These are not closed syllables. Do not explain them yet, just avoid them!

Teach Students To Mark Words

You mark closed syllables like this:

căt   or   căt
‾‾
c   c

Be sure to practice marking closed syllables often. Underline or scoop the syllable first.

cat

Then, identify the type of syllable with a **c** for closed.

cat
‾
c

Lastly, mark the vowel with a **breve** to show that it makes a short sound as in **apple**, like this:

$$\underline{c\breve{a}t}$$
c

Be sure to mark the vowel last, emphasizing **if** it is closed, **then** it is short.

Student Notebook Entry

Have the students look up the definition of a closed syllable in the Syllable section of their Student Notebook. As examples, have them add the following words:

$$\underline{c\breve{a}t} \qquad \underline{\breve{u}p} \qquad \underline{fl\breve{a}g}$$
c   c   c

WEEK 1 DAY ❷

TEACH SPELLING WITH BLANK TILES

Practice review words. There are no new words. Have students use blank Magnetic Letter Tiles to spell words. They should echo and tap the word, find blank tiles and then point to the tiles and name the corresponding letters. See words below for example:

Word	Blank tiles needed for word			
cash	white	orange	white	
thump	white	orange	white	white
song	white	green		
shops	white	orange	white	yellow

Drill Sounds

Always do the vowel sounds. You can select some consonants, but there is no need to do all of them. (See Unit Resources.)

There are no new sounds taught in this Unit.

Large Sound Cards

First practice sounds with the Large Sound Cards. Say the letter-keyword-sound and have students echo.

Standard Sound Cards

Next, point to the Standard Sound Cards (on display) with the Baby Echo pointer. You say the letter-keyword-sound and hold up Baby Echo to have students repeat. (Either you or a student can be the drill leader.)

Trick Words

Trick words require lots of practice. Sky write and finger write trick words, but **do not** tap them out or make them with the Magnetic Letter Tiles.

Resource Words

WEEK 1

our   over   come

WEEK 2

would   after   also

Students add these words to the Trick Word section of their Student Notebooks. Hold them accountable for the spelling of these words throughout the day. Direct students to look them up in the Trick Word section of their Student Notebooks.

After the introduction of new Trick Words, practice them with sky writing and tracing.

Word of the Day

Select a Word of the Day from the words below. Make the word using your Standard Sound Card display. Also, write the word on a blank index card and add it to your Word of the Day packet.

Word Resource

WEEK 1

| m | e | l | t |

| b | r | u | sh |

| a | c | t |

WEEK 2

| p | u | n | ch |

| i | l | l |

| s | t | i | f | f |

Review Concepts

Reteach closed syllable concept using the Word of the Day. Discuss why it is closed. Take away cards and ask if it is still closed. For example, take the **m** off **melt**. (It is still closed.) Take the **sh** off of **brush**. (It is not closed). Be sure to emphasize, if it is closed, **then** it is short.

Use The Word In A Sentence

Have a student (or students) use the word in a sentence and discuss the word's meaning.

Make Other Words

Then use sound cards to make several other words from this Unit. (See Unit Resources.) Have students tap and read each word.

Student Notebook Entry

Have students add the Word of the Day to the Vocabulary section of their Student Notebooks.

Have students mark up the word as a closed syllable.

Write a sentence on the board for students to copy. (This can be done at another time of the day.)

Word Talk

Review the Words of the Day from your Words of the Day index card packet.

Make and Discuss Words

Make 4-5 words with your Standard Sound Card display.

Have students tap and read the words.

Ask a student to use a word in a sentence and another student to explain what the word means.

Read Words

Use your packet of words as flashcards. Have students quickly read them without tapping.

Display Words

Display current and review words. Have students find and read the words as directed.

Have students select a word and explain why it is a closed syllable. Be sure they say something like, "It is closed because it has one vowel followed by a consonant." Remind them that it tells them that the vowel is short.

Echo/Find Sounds & Words

Echo/Find Sounds

Say a sound. Have students echo and find the letter on their Letter Board.

(See Echo Sounds in Unit Resources for expected student responses.)

Echo/Find Words

(See Current Unit Words in Unit Resources.)

Have students find Magnetic Letter Tiles needed to make words on their Letter Boards. After finding a word, have a student spell it orally.

 Echo/Find Sounds & Words

Echo/Find Sounds

Say a sound. Have students echo and find the letter on their Letter Board.

There are no new sounds. Review previous sounds.

(See Echo Sounds in Unit Resources for expected student responses.)

Echo/Find Words

Dictate a word.

(See Review and Current Unit Words in Unit Resources.)

Have students find Magnetic Letter Tiles needed to make words on their Letter Boards. After finding a word, have a student spell it orally.

 Dictation

Refer to this Unit's Resource List of Echo Sounds, Words and Sentences.

Proper Dictation Activity procedures are very important. Be sure to follow their demonstration on the CD-ROM.

DRY ERASE

Dictate 3 sounds, 3 current words and 3 trick words (trick words can be current or review).

This is a teaching time, not a testing time. Be sure students repeat each dictation. They should tap and orally spell the Unit words before writing. Students should write and orally spell trick words with their finger prior to writing them on their Dry Erase Writing Tablets.

Have students "mark up" the review and current words.

COMPOSITION BOOKS

Dictate 3 sounds, 2 review, 2 current words and 2 trick words (trick words can be current or review) and 1 sentence.

This is also a teaching time, not a testing time. Be sure students repeat each thing that you dictate. They should tap and orally spell the review and current Unit words before writing. Students should write and orally spell trick words with their finger prior to writing them in their Composition Books. Students independently write the sentence and then you lead them through the proofreading procedure.

Have students "mark up" the review and current words.

DAY 5 CHECK-UP

Students do Day 5 Dictation in their Composition Books. Have them check the Check-up box at the top of the page.

Dictate the sound, word, or sentence. Have students repeat and then write independently. Do not have students spell orally. Encourage them to tap as appropriate.

UNIT TEST

Have students find Unit Test pages at the end of their Composition Books.

Dictate the sound, word, or sentence. (See Unit Resources.) Have students repeat and then write independently. Do not have students spell orally. Encourage them to tap as appropriate.

 ## Make It Fun

Preparation

- Use Resource List for closed syllable words. Intersperse with other one-syllable words that are not closed syllables. These include double vowel words, vowel-consonant-e words and open syllables such as **she**.

CLOSED SYLLABLE HUNT

This activity will reinforce the concept of closed syllables and practice reading closed syllable words.

Instruct Students

Write a variety of words on the board. Select a student to come hunt for and cross out any word that is not a closed syllable. Have another student hunt for and mark a closed syllable word with syllable marking.

Continue until all words are either crossed off or marked as a closed syllable. Lastly, have students read the closed syllable words on the list.

Example

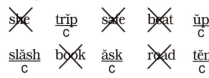

Storytime

WEEK 1

Preparation

- Baby Echo (on a pointer or ruler)
- Large Chart Paper

FRED THE FROG

Write the following story, with the phrases scooped, on chart paper.

Fred the Frog

This is Fred, the frog.

Fred likes to hop.

Did Fred hop up on the bench?

Yes he did.

Did Fred hop up on my bed?

Yes he did.

"Yuck. Get off Fred!"

Instruct Students

Ask the students to read the title silently. (Tell students to tap words when reading silently, if necessary.) Discuss the title and predict what the story might be about.

Discuss the question marks. Review how these will change voice expression.

Read Sentences

Continue reading one sentence at a time.

- Have students read silently. (Tell students to tap words when reading silently, if necessary.)

- Select a student to come read the sentence with the Baby Echo pointer. Be sure the student uses proper expression and phrasing. If not, model.

- Have the whole class repeat the sentence.

After the story has been read once in this manner, read it altogether with choral reading as you scoop the phrases with Baby Echo.

Make a Movie

Have students "make a movie" in their heads. Tell them to close their eyes and picture Fred the Frog.

Ask someone to describe what they see in their movie, discussing each sentence.

Continue with the whole story. Then model re-telling the story in your own words and ask a student to retell it in their own words.

Mark Words

Lastly, select students to come mark words as directed.

- Circle all quotation marks (briefly discuss them).

- Make a capital letter frame around words that have a capital letter and discuss why (at the beginning of a sentence or a person's name).

- Underline blends and digraph blends.

WEEK 2

Preparation

- Baby Echo (on a pointer or ruler)
- Large Chart Paper with the story from Week 1
- Copy FRED THE FROG story for each student from the Fluency Kit (in the Stories tab)

Instruct Students

Ask the students to read the title silently. Have them try to remember the "movie" in their mind. Have someone describe the story by re-telling it. Read chorally as you point with Baby Echo and determine if the retelling was accurate.

Next, disseminate the story to the students. Have them draw pictures for each page and cut on the dotted lines. Staple these into booklets for the students to bring home.

Drill Sounds

a - apple - /ă/	b - bat - /b/
c - cat - /k/	d - dog - /d/
e - Ed - /ĕ/	f - fun - /f/
g - game - /g/	h - hat - /h/
i - itch - /ĭ/	j - jug - /j/
k - kite - /k/	l - lamp - /l/
m - man - /m/	n - nut - /n/
o - octopus - /ŏ/	p - pan - /p/
qu - queen - /kw/	r - rat - /r/
s - snake - /s/	s - bugs - /z/
t - top - /t/	u - up - /ŭ/
v - van - /v/	w - wind - /w/
x - fox - /ks/	y - yellow - /y/
z - zebra - /z/	sh - ship - /sh/
ck - sock - /k/	wh - whistle - /w/
th - thumb - /th/	ch - chin - /ch/
all - ball - /òl/	an - fan - /an/
am - ham - /am/	ang - fang - /ang/
ing - ring - /ing/	ong - song - /ong/
ung - lung - /ung/	ank - bank - /ank/
ink - pink - /ink/	onk - honk - /onk/
unk - junk - /unk/	

Echo Sounds

Sounds appear between / /. You say the sound. Students echo the sound and say the letter. Depending on the activity, students then either find or make the letter corresponding to that sound.

CONSONANTS/CONSONANT DIGRAPHS

/b/ - b	/d/ - d	/f/ - f
/g/ - g	/h/ - h	/j/ - j
/k/ - c, k, ck	/l/ - l	/m/ - m
/n/ - n	/p/ - p	/kw/ - qu
/r/ - r	/s/ - s	/t/ - t
/v/ - v	/w/ - w, wh	/ks/ - x
/y/ - y	/z/- z, s	/ch/ - ch
/sh/ - sh	/th/ - th	

VOWELS

/ă/ - a	/ĕ/ - e	/ĭ/ - i
/ŏ/ - o	/ŭ/ - u	

GLUED/WELDED SOUNDS

/òl/ - all	/am/ - am	/an/ - an
/ang/ - ang	/ing/ - ing	/ong/ -ong
/ung/ - ung	/ank/ - ank	/ink/ - ink
/onk/ - onk	/unk/ - unk	

Review Trick Words

the	of	and	to	a	was
is	he	for	as	his	has
I	you	we	they	one	said
from	or	have	were	her	put
there	what	she	been	by	who
out	so	are	two	about	into

only	other	new	some	could	want
say	do	first	any	my	now

Current Unit Trick Words

our	over	come	would	after	also

Review/Current Words

lash	bus	bun	pick	path	bib
red	jab	kid	nod	but	cup
mix	pot	Ben	kick	pat	thick
tab	Jim	tin	cob	rat	big
tip	cot	Rick	dash	whip	mad
den	gum	math	neck	dip	mug
sub	dish	wig	yes	fun	this
cans	quits	zaps	rocks	cops	lips
mops	tugs	beds	bets	bang	ring
sang	long	song	lung	king	wing
hang	sing	fang	hung	thing	rang
sung	pink	honk	sank	think	junk
rink	sink	thank	tank	chunk	bank
dunk	link	bunk	Hank	sunk	wink
yank	mink	bonk	gong	banks	rings
things	honks	songs	lungs	wings	hangs
kings	thinks	winks	sings	fangs	rinks
sinks	thanks	tanks	chunks	sent	must
best	lend	drop	loft	pest	pond
flap	crib	bent	grab	jump	bend

chest	last	dent	trash	raft	stub
gust	grip	clock	brag	flop	stash
belt	stuck	cost	glad	grin	crab
plug	sand	drum	slush	trot	wept
dust	rest	hunt	vest	step	flag
swish	drag	drip	black	past	stick
vent	dump	ramp	brush	fist	bunch
task	flip	test	click	camp	frog
crack	spin	soft	fast	squish	trap
crash	cloth	thump	stack	lost	nest
bled	mast	next	list	snip	spot
limp	block	lump	damp	clam	skin
flock	crop	plan	flat	west	snap
hint	cluck	blush	ranch	skip	pluck
kept	bench	clap	fled	chimp	small
mask	crush	pinch	band	punch	chomp
pump	clip	mint	slam	twig	shrug
trim	munch	rust	mend	slim	scab
melt	shelf	felt	help	silk	golf
milk	gulf	self	tilt	film	gulp
held	wilt	smog	flash	stop	snug
shrub	pant	went	just	gift	Fran
Brad	swim	glass	cross	press	spell
grass	fluff	class	dress	bless	still
stuff	cliff	drill	sniff	spill	drops
ponds	pests	dents	stubs	grips	clocks
plugs	drums	vests	steps	flags	drags
drips	flips	tests	clicks	camps	frogs

Sentences

*Write any **bold word** on the board for students to copy. A **bold word** has untaught components.*

It was fun to go on that trip!

The kids dug in the soft sand.

Dad was cross about the mess.

Did Ed win at golf?

Did the ball swish in the net?

Gram will mend the vest.

Grab a lunch and go to the pond.

Jill will get the doll in the crib.

Do not dump that stuff on the bed!

Tom sets up drums for the band.

Jim must not miss that class.

Stan must sit on the bench.

The twin wept.

Fran will romp on the grass.

Pam did not step on the crab.

Did Fran bump her leg?

Gram can get this spot off the mask.

The belt is on the shelf in the den.

Did Beth step on that frog?

This clock is the best gift!

Bill fell in the wet sand.

Stan must dump the trash.

Ted will jump in the pond and swim.

Mom will mend the rip in the dress.

I wish that Kim did not brag.

Ben went on the ship.

The class must get a flag.

Tim will get the cloth on the shelf.

Pass the small block to Jed.

Jill had the plum.

Bob went with Dad to the ranch.

The tot fell in the wet slush.

Bob had the last mint.

Trot up to the flag and then run.

Ben got a cut on his leg from the trap.

Beth had a pink silk dress.

Did Tom brag about his six big fish?

Get the trash to the dump.

We will hunt for the lost raft.

Stan will lift that big pump.

Did Tom trip on that twig?

I held my pup as he got a shot.

Brad is sick so he can not help.

Bill is at the swim club with Tom.

Jan got the drill for her dad.

We will trim the tall grass.

Ben will sell the clams.

This pink shell was on the sand.

Did the dog sniff the fish?

Have students find the Unit Test pages located at the end of their Composition Books. Dictate the sounds, words and sentences. Have students repeat and then write independently. Encourage them to tap, but they should not use their Student Notebooks.

Dictate The Following Sounds

/z/   /ch/   /ung/   /ĕ/   /ă/

Dictate The Following Words

test   puffs   Hank   vent   plugs

drill   lunch   lungs   rocks   brings

Dictate The Following Trick Words

come   also

Dictate The Following Sentences

Jack will sell golf clubs to Stan.

Did he trip on the block?

Have The Students Do The Following

• Underline the baseword and circle the suffix in the first sentence.

• Mark all closed syllable words in both sentences.

Answer Key

SOUNDS

1. z, s
2. ch
3. ung
4. e
5. a

WORDS

1. test
2. puffs
3. Hank
4. vent
5. plugs
6. drill
7. lunch
8. lungs
9. rocks
10. brings

TRICK WORDS

1. come
2. also

SENTENCES

1. Jăck wĭll sĕll gŏlf clŭbs)
    c   c   c   c   c
    to Stăn.
    c

2. Dĭd he trĭp ŏn the
    c   c   c
    blŏck?
    c

Unit 10 Level 1

Introduction

Unit 10 does not introduce any new sounds.

In this Unit, you will teach your students to blend and segment up to five sounds in a closed syllable.

Some words containing five sounds have a blend with a glued sound, such as the word **skunk**:

Some five-sound words have a blend before the vowel and a blend at the end, such as in the word **blimp**:

PREPARING YOUR MATERIALS

There are no new Standard Sound Cards to be displayed.

Arrange the Standard Sound Card display in the following manner

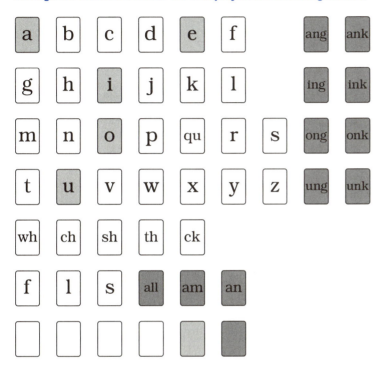

PREPARING YOUR STUDENTS

Students do not add any new Magnetic Letter Tiles to their Letter Boards.

PREPARING FOR HOME SUPPORT

Copy and send home the **Unit 10 Letter and Activity Packet**.

Week 1

DAY ❶	DAY ❷	DAY ❸	DAY ❹	DAY ❺
Drill Sounds	Drill Sounds	Drill Sounds	Drill Sounds	Drill Sounds
Introduce New Concepts	Word of the Day	Echo/Find Sounds & Words	Word Talk	Word Talk
Word of the Day	Introduce New Concepts	Dictation (Dry Erase)	Trick Words	Storytime
Trick Words	Dictation (Composition Book)	Make it Fun	Echo/Find Sounds & Words	
			Dictation (Dry Erase)	

Week 2

DAY ❶	DAY ❷	DAY ❸	DAY ❹	DAY ❺
Drill Sounds	Drill Sounds	Drill Sounds	Drill Sounds	Drill Sounds
Trick Words	Word of the Day	Word of the Day	Word Talk	Storytime
Word of the Day	Echo/Find Sounds & Words	Make it Fun	Trick Words	Dictation (Day 5 Check-up)
Echo/Find Sounds & Words	Dictation (Composition Book)	Dictation (Dry Erase)	Echo/Find Sounds & Words	
Dictation (Dry Erase)			Dictation (Dry Erase)	

Week 3

DAY ❶	DAY ❷	DAY ❸	DAY ❹	DAY ❺
Drill Sounds	Drill Sounds	Drill Sounds	Drill Sounds	Drill Sounds
Introduce New Concepts	Word of the Day	Word of the Day	Word Talk	Storytime
Trick Words	Introduce New Concepts	Make it Fun	Trick Words	Dictation (Unit Test)
	Dictation (Composition Book)	Dictation (Dry Erase)	Echo/Find Sounds & Words	
			Dictation (Dry Erase)	

Introduce New Concepts

WEEK 1 DAY ❶

TEACH BLENDING WORDS WITH 5 SOUNDS

Explain that some words have five sounds in a syllable. Form the word **lump** with Standard Sound Cards.

The students must tap out the sounds.

Ask

How many sounds are in this word? (4)

Add **c** to make **clump**. Point out that the word now has five sounds, with a blend before the vowel (**cl**) and a blend after the vowel (**mp**).

To tap words with five sounds, reuse the index finger or tap on the board and desktop using the thumb for first tap.

In some words, a digraph will combine with a consonant to form a digraph blend. Make the word **shrimp** to demonstrate:

Tap and count the sounds (5).

Make the word **skunk** with the Standard Sound Cards. This word has five sounds, even though the **unk** gets glued together. Practice tapping and reading words with five sounds including a glued sound.

Teach Students To Mark Words

Words in this section have nothing new to mark. However, they may have more than one blend. Be sure to identify both blends when marking words such as

b̲last̲

Also, words may have a blend and a glued sound such as

t̲r̲unk

If a student realizes **nk** is also a blend, it is fine to identify it and mark it like this:

t̲r̲un̲k̲

WEEK 1 DAY ❷

TEACH SPELLING WORDS WITH 5 SOUNDS

Some words in this Unit have glued sounds. The green glued Letter Tiles should be used to spell these words. Also, use the blank tiles: **ivory - ivory - green** for words such as **flunk**. Students must then name the letter(s) that correspond with each blank card.

With words that have two blends, students must learn to tap each sound separately.

Dictate a current word such as **stunt**. Students must repeat the word and then tap out the individual sounds. Tell students to be sure they tap out five sounds.

Spell the word out with your Standard Sound Cards and tap over each sound. After tapping the sounds, the students should find the Letter Tiles that correspond with each tap and then spell orally.

Blank cards can also be used: **ivory - ivory - orange - ivory - ivory**. Students then must name the letters to go on each blank card.

Dictate several current words for the students to practice. Then do 3-4 review words.

Unit 10 **Lesson Activity Plan**

TEACH READING WORDS WITH A SUFFIX

Make the word **clumps** with the Standard Sound Cards and the Yellow Suffix Frame. Have the students read the baseword, then read the whole word: **clump - clumps**.

Students should only tap the baseword if needed. Make 8-10 Unit words with a suffix. (See Unit Resources).

Remember, if a word has a suffix, always underline or scoop the baseword and circle the suffix such as

This syllable is also closed. It can be marked like this:

clŭmp(s)
ᴄ

TEACH SPELLING WORDS WITH A SUFFIX

Remember, whenever you dictate a word with a suffix, the students name and spell the baseword first. You can cue the students to do this. They do not tap out the suffix.

Dictate the word **plants** and have students echo. Have someone name the baseword and then come up to the front of the class to spell the word with your Standard Sound Card display. Next have the student get the Yellow Suffix Frame and write the suffix **-s**.

Dictate 4-5 words with a suffix and select other students to come form the word. Be sure students orally spell the word after finding the letters.

 Drill Sounds

Always do the vowel sounds. You can select some consonants, but there is no need to do all of them. (See Unit Resources.)

There are no new sounds. Review previous sounds.

Large Sound Cards

First practice sounds with the Large Sound Cards. Say the letter-keyword-sound and have students echo.

Standard Sound Cards

Next, point to the Standard Sound Cards (on display) with the Baby Echo pointer. You say the letter-keyword-sound and hold up Baby Echo to have students repeat. (Either you or a student can be the drill leader.)

 Word of the Day

Select a Word of the Day from the words below. Make the word using your Standard Sound Card display. Also, write the word on a blank index card and add it to your Word of the Day packet.

Word Resource

WEEK 1

| t | r | u | s | t | | b | l | ink |

WEEK 2

| s | t | u | m | p | | s | t | an | d |

| c | r | u | n | ch |

Note

*The letters **n** and **d** are a blend in the word **stand**. However, be sure to tap the glued sounds.*

WEEK 3

Review Concepts

Reteach the concepts of blends, digraph blends (**nch**), and baseword and suffix.

Use The Word In A Sentence

Have a student (or students) use the word in a sentence and discuss the word's meaning.

Make Other Words

Then use sound cards to make several other words from this Unit. (See Unit Resources.) Have students tap and read each word.

Student Notebook Entry

Have students add the Word of the Day to the Vocabulary section of their Student Notebooks.

Have students mark up the word by underlining blends and boxing glued sounds. For words with a baseword, have them also underline the baseword and circle the suffix.

Write a sentence on the board for students to copy. (This can be done at another time of the day.)

Word Talk

Review the Words of the Day from your Words of the Day index card packet.

Make and Discuss Words

Make 4-5 words with your Standard Sound Card display.

Have students tap and read the words.

Ask a student to use a word in a sentence and another student to explain what the word means.

Read Words

Use your packet of words as flashcards. Have students quickly read them without tapping.

Display Words

Display current and review words. Have students find and read the words as directed.

Instruct Students

Find a word that means "_____."

Find a word with a blend and a glued sound.

Find a word with two blends.

Trick Words

Trick words require lots of practice. Sky write and finger write trick words, but **do not** tap them out or make them with the Magnetic Letter Tiles.

Word Resource

WEEK 1

| many | before | called |

WEEK 2

| how | your | down |

WEEK 3

| should* | because | each |

Students add these words to the Trick Word section of their Student Notebooks. Hold them accountable for the spelling of these words throughout the day. Direct students to look them up in the Trick Word section of their Student Notebooks.

After the introduction of new trick words, practice them with sky writing and tracing.

*Tell students that since they already know how to spell **would** and **could**, they can spell **should**. They just need to change the first letters.

Echo/Find Sounds & Words

Echo/Find Sounds

Say a sound. Have students echo and find the letter on their Letter Board.

There are no new sounds. Review previous sounds.

(See Echo Sounds in Unit Resources for expected student responses.)

Echo/Find Words

Practice current review words. Have students use blank tiles to spell words. They should echo and tap word, find blank tiles and then point to the tiles and name the corresponding letters.

(See Review and Current Unit Words in Unit Resources.)

 Dictation

Refer to this Unit's Resource List of Echo Sounds, Words and Sentences.

Proper Dictation Activity procedures are very important. Be sure to follow their demonstration on the CD-ROM.

DRY ERASE

Dictate 3 sounds, 3 current words and 3 trick words (trick words can be current or review).

This is a teaching time, not a testing time. Be sure students repeat each dictation. They should tap and orally spell the Unit words before writing. Students should write and orally spell trick words with their finger prior to writing them on their Dry Erase Writing Tablets.

Have students "mark up" the review and current words.

COMPOSITION BOOKS

Dictate 3 sounds, 2 review, 2 current words and 2 trick words (trick words can be current or review) and 1 sentence.

This is also a teaching time, not a testing time. Be sure students repeat each thing that you dictate. They should tap and orally spell the review and current Unit words before writing. Students should write and orally spell trick words with their finger prior to writing them in their Composition Books. Students independently write the sentence and then you lead them through the proofreading procedure.

Have students "mark up" the review and current words.

DAY 5 CHECK-UP

Students do Day 5 Dictation in their Composition Books. Have them check the Check-up box at the top of the page.

Dictate the sound, word, or sentence. Have students repeat and then write independently. Do not have students spell orally. Encourage them to tap as appropriate.

UNIT TEST

Have students find Unit Test pages at the end of their Composition Books.

Dictate the sound, word, or sentence. (See Unit Resources.) Have students repeat and then write independently. Do not have students spell orally. Encourage them to tap as appropriate.

Make It Fun

Preparation

• Word of the Day packet

STAND UP

Instruct Students

Disseminate the Word of the Day cards, giving one card to each student. Divide the class into two teams.

Have students stand as you direct them.

Say

Stand if you have a word that begins with a blend.

Have students that stand read their word to confirm. They should remain standing. Say other directives until all students from one team are standing. The winning team is the first team to have all members standing.

Hint

When you are close to the time when a team might win, use the meaning of words as the directive so that both teams do not finish at the same time.

 Storytime

WEEK 1

Preparation

• Baby Echo (on a pointer or ruler)

• Large Chart Paper

THE SKUNK

Write the following story, with the phrases scooped, on chart paper.

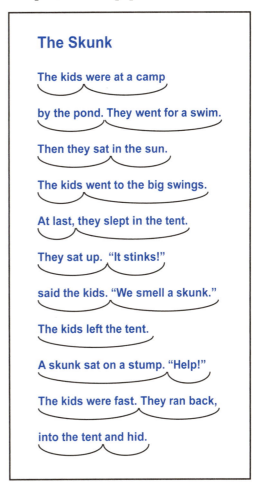

The Skunk

The kids were at a camp

by the pond. They went for a swim.

Then they sat in the sun.

The kids went to the big swings.

At last, they slept in the tent.

They sat up. "It stinks!"

said the kids. "We smell a skunk."

The kids left the tent.

A skunk sat on a stump. "Help!"

The kids were fast. They ran back,

into the tent and hid.

Instruct Students

Ask the students to read the title silently. (Tell students to tap words when reading silently, if necessary.) Discuss the title and predict what the story might be about.

Read Sentences

Continue reading one sentence at a time.

- Have students read silently. (Tell students to tap words when reading silently, if necessary.)
- Select a student to come read the sentence with the Baby Echo pointer. Be sure the student uses proper expression and phrasing. If not, model.
- Have the whole class repeat the sentence.

After the story has been read once in this manner, read it altogether with choral reading as you scoop the phrases with Baby Echo.

Make a Movie

Have students "make a movie" in their heads. Tell them to close their eyes and picture the skunk.

Ask someone to describe what they see in their movie, discussing each sentence.

Continue with the whole story. Then model re-telling the story in your own words and ask a student to retell it in their own words.

Mark Words

Lastly, select students to come mark words as directed.

- Circle quotation marks.
- Highlight exclamation point.
- Underline basewords, circle the suffixes.
- Star the bonus letter (small).

WEEK 2

Preparation

- Baby Echo (on a pointer or ruler)
- Large Chart Paper with the story from Week 1
- Copy THE SKUNK story for each student from the Fluency Kit (in the Stories tab)

Instruct Students

Ask the students to read the title silently. Have them try to remember the "movie" in their mind. Have someone describe the story by re-telling it. Read chorally as you point with Baby Echo and determine if the retelling was accurate.

Next disseminate the story to the students. Have them draw pictures for each page and cut on the dotted lines. Staple these into booklets for the students to bring home.

WEEK 3

Preparation

- Rather than box the story, you will write it in paragraph form.
- Find a picture in a magazine that shows at least two characters doing something. Be sure it is a good picture to develop a story.
- Large Chart Paper - Do not divide.

Instruct Students

Tell students that they are going to help you write a story. They are going to write a fiction story which is make-believe. Explain that today you will do it in a paragraph.

Have them tell you who the characters are in the picture. (For example, a mother and a son). Help students make up names for the characters.

Next explain that every story takes place somewhere. Tell them the place where the story happens is called a setting. Ask the students where the characters in the picture are. Tell them that is the setting.

Next paste the picture in the top left hand box.

Tell students you need to think of a Title. Help them come up with a title and put it above the picture.

Tell students that you will help them write a story.

Write sentences on the chart paper, indenting the first one.

After you write a story, read it with Baby Echo. Have students echo after you.

Ask

Who are the characters in this story?

What is the setting? (Remind them this means where it took place).

What happened first?

What happened next?

What happened in the end?

Next show the students how you indented the first sentence. Tell them that you wrote a paragraph and that paragraphs are always indented.

Put an arrow at the indentation to remind students:

→ **Once upon a time**

Lastly, have a student come highlight each punctuation mark.

Drill Sounds

a - apple - /ă/	b - bat - /b/
c - cat - /k/	d - dog - /d/
e - Ed - /ĕ/	f - fun - /f/
g - game - /g/	h - hat - /h/
i - itch - /ĭ/	j - jug - /j/
k - kite - /k/	l - lamp - /l/
m - man - /m/	n - nut - /n/
o - octopus - /ŏ/	p - pan - /p/
qu - queen - /kw/	r - rat - /r/
s - snake - /s/	s - bugs - /z/
t - top - /t/	u - up - /ŭ/
v - van - /v/	w - wind - /w/
x - fox - /ks/	y - yellow - /y/
z - zebra - /z/	sh - ship - /sh/
ck - sock - /k/	wh - whistle - /w/
th - thumb - /th/	ch - chin - /ch/
all - ball - /ȯl/	an - fan - /an/
am - ham - /am/	ang - fang - /ang/
ing - ring - /ing/	ong - song - /ong/
ung - lung - /ung/	ank - bank - /ank/
ink - pink - /ink/	onk - honk - /onk/
unk - junk - /unk/	

Echo Sounds

Sounds appear between / /. You say the sound. Students echo the sound and say the letter. Depending on the activity, students then either find or make the letter corresponding to that sound.

CONSONANTS/CONSONANT DIGRAPHS

/b/ - b	/d/ - d	/f/ - f
/g/ - g	/h/ - h	/j/ - j
/k/ - c, k, ck	/l/ - l	/m/ - m
/n/ - n	/p/ - p	/kw/ - qu
/r/ - r	/s/ - s	/t/ - t
/v/ - v	/w/ - w, wh	/ks/ - x
/y/ - y	/z/ - z, s	/ch/ - ch
/sh/ - sh	/th/ - th	

VOWELS

/ă/ - a	/ĕ/ - e	/ĭ/ - i
/ŏ/ - o	/ŭ/ - u	

GLUED/WELDED SOUNDS

/ȯl/ - all	/am/ - am	/an/ - an
/ang/ - ang	/ing/ - ing	/ong/ - ong
/ung/ - ung	/ank/ - ank	/ink/ - ink
/onk/ - onk	/unk/ - unk	

Review Trick Words

the	of	and	to	a	was
is	he	for	as	his	has
I	you	we	they	one	said
from	or	have	were	her	put
there	what	she	been	by	who

out	so	are	two	about	into
only	other	new	some	could	want
say	do	first	any	my	now
our	over	come	would	after	also

sung	pink	honk	sank	think	junk
rink	sink	thank	tank	chunk	bank
things	honks	songs	lungs	wings	hangs
fangs	rinks	sinks	thanks	tanks	chunks

Current Unit Trick Words

many	before	called	how	
your	down	should	each	because

Current Unit Words

WEEKS 1 • 2

blast	grunt	stump	crunch	drift	twist
crisp	draft	print	slant	trust	rump
blend	craft	slept	slump	stamp	stand
stunt	blimp	cramp	plump	plant	shrimp
squint	grand	crust	spend	crept	ranch
stung	blank	swing	stink	bring	skunk
sting	trunk	prank	blink	drink	shrink
Frank	drank	shrunk			

WEEK 3

brings	skunks	stings	trunks	pranks
blinks	drinks	grunts	stumps	drifts
blends	crafts	slumps	blimps	plants

Review Words

tab	Jim	tin	cob	rat	big
tip	cot	Rick	dash	whip	mad
den	gum	math	neck	dip	mug
sub	dish	wig	yes	fun	this
cub	fit	shut	rush	wish	quit
fox	nut	gas	him	shell	cuff
fuss	miss	kiss	off	fill	puff
pill	will	huff	wall	fall	hall
am	jam	Dan	tan	Pam	ran
pups	shops	locks	webs	nets	pegs
necks	bells	lugs	shuts	rugs	shells
fans	tins	kicks	huffs	sheds	wins
pins	runs	fills	nuts	packs	jugs
sits	bugs	pats	zags	naps	tubs
cans	quits	zaps	rocks	cops	lips
mops	tugs	beds	bets	bang	ring
hang	sing	fang	hung	thing	rang

Sentences

*Write any **bold word** on the board for students to copy. A **bold word** has untaught components.*

WEEKS 1 • 2

I got a chill from that bad draft.

Peg swept the rug with the brush.

The shrimp is on the top shelf.

Tim slept in the tent.

I will print on the pad.

Bob felt his leg twist.

Stan had ten shrimp **for** lunch.

Brad will blend that drink.

Russ slept on the cot.

We must stand to sing this song.

Ben will twist off that lid.

Stop to rest and get a drink.

The frost did not help the crops.

We must get a stamp to send this.

The stump is in **your** path.

The tot crept to her dad.

The blimp did not go fast at all.

The kids sat on the big clump of grass.

The big prank was a blast.

WEEK 3

Bill trusts his kids with his cash.

Did the plants in the den get sun?

The skunk stinks!

Have students find the unit test pages located at the end of their Composition Books. Dictate the sounds, words and sentences. Have students repeat and then write independently. Encourage them to tap, but they should not use their Student Notebooks.

Dictate The Following Sounds

/sh/   /ks/   /ĕ/   /onk/   /am/

Dictate The Following Words

trunk   shrink   slant   twist   grump

slumps   chills   drinks   blimps   blinks

Dictate The Following Trick Words

called   down

Dictate The Following Sentences

I had a cramp in my left leg.

Did Frank get stung?

Have The Students Do The Following

- Underline blends with two lines and digraphs with one line.
- Box the glued sounds.

Unit 11 Level 1

Introduction

In Unit 11, you will change your focus from **sounds** to **syllables**. You will tune your students in to looking at words in larger orthographic parts, i.e. syllables, rather than individual sounds.

In this Unit, you will teach your students how to read and spell two-syllable words with closed syllables. Look at the word **cat-nip**:

cat	nip

This word has two syllables. Both of these syllables are closed with short vowels.

<u>căt</u> <u>nĭp</u>
 c   c

You will teach students how to segment or divide two syllable words between consonants such as <u>c a t</u> <u>n i p</u>. Do not slash between syllables **cat/nip**. This is visually distracting. It is also better to work from left to right underlining or scooping the syllables rather than slashing the middle of the word.

This unit sets the groundwork for all multisyllabic reading and spelling.

For spelling, it will be very important to establish proper procedures. Students will now segment syllables and then name and spell one syllable at a time. This will be key for their success with these longer words.

In a Nutshell

NEW CONCEPTS

- Concept of syllable in multisyllabic words
- Compound words
- Syllable division rules for closed syllables: compound words and between two vowels
- Reading and spelling words with two closed syllables
- Paragraph structure

SAMPLE WORDS

sunset   catnip

TRICK WORDS

people	Mr.	Mrs.
years	says	little
good	very	own

PLANNED TIME IN UNIT

3 WEEKS

Note

Extend the time in this Unit if student mastery is not demonstrated on the Unit test.

PREPARING YOUR MATERIALS

Have the White Syllable Frames on hand to use in syllable building activities.

Arrange the Standard Sound Card display in the following manner

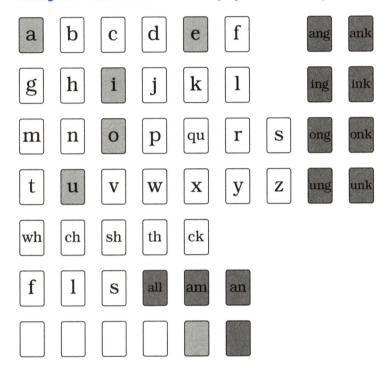

PREPARING YOUR STUDENTS

Tape the Syllable Overlays to students' Building Boards as a placeholder for two-syllable word construction.

PREPARING FOR HOME SUPPORT

Copy and send home the **Unit 11 Letter and Activity Packet**.

Week 1

DAY ❶	DAY ❷	DAY ❸	DAY ❹	DAY ❺
Drill Sounds	Drill Sounds	Drill Sounds	Drill Sounds	Drill Sounds
Introduce New Concepts	Word of the Day	Word of the Day	Word Talk	Word Talk
Trick Words	Introduce New Concepts	Make it Fun	Trick Words	Storytime
	Dictation (Composition Book)	Dictation (Dry Erase)	Echo/Find Sounds & Words	Dictation (Day 5 Check-up)
			Dictation (Composition Book)	

Week 2

DAY ❶	DAY ❷	DAY ❸	DAY ❹	DAY ❺
Drill Sounds	Drill Sounds	Drill Sounds	Drill Sounds	Drill Sounds
Word of the Day	Word of the Day	Word of the Day	Word Talk	Word Talk
Trick Words	Echo/Find Sounds & Words	Make it Fun	Trick Words	Storytime
Echo/Find Sounds & Words	Dictation (Composition Book)	Dictation (Dry Erase)	Echo/Find Sounds & Words	Dictation (Day 5 Check-up)
Dictation (Dry Erase)			Dictation (Composition Book)	

Weeks 3

DAY ❶	DAY ❷	DAY ❸	DAY ❹	DAY ❺
Drill Sounds	Drill Sounds	Drill Sounds	Drill Sounds	Drill Sounds
Trick Words	Word of the Day	Word of the Day	Word Talk	Word Talk
Introduce New Concepts	Echo/Find Sounds & Words	Make it Fun	Trick Words	Storytime
Echo/Find Sounds & Words	Dictation (Composition Book)	Dictation (Dry Erase)	Dictation (Composition Book)	Dictation (Unit Test)
Dictation (Dry Erase)				

Introduce New Concepts

WEEK 1 DAY ❶

TEACH SYLLABLE DIVISION

Tell students that **words are made up of parts**. Sounds go together to make each part. Sometimes there is only one part and other times, more than one.

The word **cat** has **one part** made up of **three sounds**. The word **catnip** has **two parts**. You can hear it.

Each part is **one push of breath**. Explain that this is called a syllable. When another push of breath is needed it is a new part or syllable.

Dictate words to the students. Students should listen and name the number of parts.

Say

> To read or spell longer words with more than one syllable, you just have to do one part at a time.
>
> You can already read the parts separately, so it will be easy to read and spell longer words one part at a time.

Write ⬚ bath ⬚ on the White Syllable Frame and put on the magnetic board. Let the students read it.

Next, put ⬚ tub ⬚ on another White Syllable Frame and have them read this part.

Now combine the parts to form:

| bath | | tub |

Read each part; then read it together. Scoop your finger under each part as it is read. Explain that each part is said in one push of breath.

Use both Standard Sound Cards and White Syllable Frames to demonstrate various Unit words, dividing the words for your students.

Next, make the word napkin with the Standard Sound Cards but do not split it into two syllables.

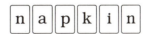

Point out that the two vowels in this word are separated by consonants. This is easy to see with the different colored cards used to represent vowels and consonants. The orange vowel cards are not together.

Say

> Whenever vowels are separated, the word must be split into two parts or syllables somewhere between the two separated vowels.
>
> If there are two consonants between the vowels,
>
> *(point to p and k)*
>
> then split or divide between the two consonants.

Move the word into the two syllables:

Demonstrate this rule with example words such as **sunfish**, **catnip** and **cactus**.

Make the word with the Standard Sound Cards.

Ask

> Should we divide this word?
>
> **Why?** (two vowels are separated)
>
> **Where would you divide?**

Then have a student separate the sound cards to make two syllables.

Student Notebook Entry

Students should add the word **nap kin** on the closed syllable page of their Student Notebooks

Unit 11 **Lesson Activity Plan**

for an example of a multisyllabic word.

TEACH SPELLING

Students will use their Magnetic Letter Tiles and Letter Boards.

The most important thing with multisyllabic spelling is the change in procedure. Now students **segment syllables** rather than sounds. Students no longer tap out individual sounds unless they have difficulty.

It is easiest to teach this with the White Syllable Frames to represent each syllable. Initially, have students simply learn to say a two-syllable word in two parts or two separate breaths.

Be careful not to 'feed' the students one syllable at a time. You must dictate the entire word and the students must learn to segment it into its parts.

Two blank White Syllable Frames can be used, and the students can simply repeat the dictated words while touching each Syllable Frame to represent each syllable. When the students understand this, use two White Syllable Frames to make the word | bath | tub |bath tub. Then erase the frames and do the following:

- Say the word **bathtub** and have students echo, **bathtub**.

- Students then divide the word into parts, saying each part or syllable as you point to the blank syllable frame representing the syllable part.

- Students say the first syllable (**bath**). Then have someone orally spell the first syllable. Write it on one White Syllable Frame. Then students say the second syllable (**tub**). Someone orally spells the second syllable and you write it on the second Frame.

- Students then immediately read the word back while you scoop syllables from left to right with your index finger. This is a proofreading technique that will be applied when the students write the words.

Next, have the students spell current unit words on their Letter Boards.

Initially, have students get the Magnetic Letter Tiles to spell the words, putting the tiles in the Syllable Overlay (on their Letter Boards).

Later, students can simply place blank tiles in the Syllable Overlay.

Be sure students say each syllable before finding the corresponding tiles. After the word is displayed, students should orally spell the word, syllable by syllable.

"catnip"

"cat c - a - t"

"nip n - i - p"

TEACH THE SPELLING OF IC

Make the word **public** with the Standard Sound Cards. Explain that any multisyllabic word ending with **-ic** is spelled with the letter **c**. Use the Syllable Frames. Write a unit word. Have a student scoop the syllables and read it. Do 8-10 unit words.

Student Notebook Entry

Have students add **public** as another **-ic** word example of how to spell /**k**/ at the end of multisyllabic words. This is done in the Spelling section of their Student Notebooks.

Drill Sounds

Always do the vowel sounds. You can select some consonants, but there is no need to do all of them. (See Unit Resources.)

There are no new sounds taught in this Unit.

Large Sound Cards

First practice sounds with the Large Sound Cards. Say the letter-keyword-sound and have students echo.

Standard Sound Cards

Next, point to the Standard Sound Cards (on display) with the Baby Echo pointer. You say the letter-keyword-sound and hold up Baby Echo to have students repeat. (Either you or a student can be the drill leader.)

Word of the Day

Select a Word of the Day from the words below. Make the word using your Standard Sound Card display. Also, write the word on a blank index card and add it to your Word of the Day packet.

Word Resource

WEEK 1

| s | u | n | s | e | t |

| u | p | s | e | t |

WEEK 2

| e | x | p | e | c | t |

| u | n | t | i | l |

| v | e | l | v | e | t |

WEEK 3

| p | u | b | l | i | c |

| f | r | an | t | i | c |

Review Concepts

Reteach syllable division with the Sound Cards using the Word of the Day. Also review closed syllable concept and show that each syllable is closed. In Week 3, reteach the **ic** at the end of words.

Use The Word In A Sentence

Have a student (or students) use the word in a sentence and discuss the word's meaning.

Make Other Words

Then use sound cards to make several other words from this Unit. (See Unit Resources.) Have students divide and read each word.

Student Notebook Entry

Have students add the Word of the Day to the Vocabulary section of their Student Notebooks.

Have students mark up the word by scooping the word into two syllables such as **sun set**. Mark the syllables closed:

sŭn sĕt
 c   c

Write a sentence on the board for students to copy. (This can be done at another time of the day.)

 **Word Talk**

Review the Words of the Day from your Words of the Day index card packet.

Make and Discuss Words

Make 4-5 words with your Standard Sound Card display.

Have students tap and read the words.

Ask a student to use a word in a sentence and another student to explain what the word means.

Read Words

Use your packet of words as flashcards. Have students quickly read them without tapping.

Display Words

Display current and review words. Have students find and read the words as directed.

Instruct Students

Find a word that means, "_____."

Find a word with one vowel. Do you divide this word? Why not?

Find a word with two syllables. How do you know it has two syllables? Where would you divide it? Why? Have the student scoop the word into syllables while reading it.

 Trick Words

Trick words require lots of practice. Sky write and finger write trick words, but **do not** tap them out or make them with the Magnetic Letter Tiles.

Word Resource

WEEK 1

| people | Mr. | Mrs. |

WEEK 2

| years | says | little |

WEEK 3

| good | very | own |

Students add these words to the Trick Word section of their Student Notebooks. Hold them accountable for the spelling of these words throughout the day. Direct students to look them up in the Trick Word section of their Student Notebooks.

After the introduction of new Trick Words, practice them with sky writing and tracing.

 Echo/Find Sounds & Words

Echo/Find Sounds

Say a sound. Have students echo and find the letter on their Letter Board.

(See Echo Sounds in Unit Resources for expected student responses.)

Echo/Find Words

(See Review and Current Unit Words in Unit Resources.)

Have one student use your Syllable Frame at the board. Have students find Magnetic Letter Tiles or blank Tiles needed to make words on their Letter Boards. They place the letters into the Syllable Overlay. After finding a word, have a student spell it orally. Be sure they name and spell one syllable at a time for multisyllabic words.

Dictation

Refer to this Unit's Resource List of Echo Sounds, Words and Sentences.

Proper Dictation Activity procedures are very important. Be sure to follow their demonstration on the CD-ROM.

Note

Be sure students name and spell one syllable at a time for the multisyllabic words. Have them immediately scoop the word into syllables and read it as a proofreading procedure.

DRY ERASE

Dictate 3 sounds, 3 current words and 3 trick words (trick words can be current or review).

Have one student do the multisyllabic words on your Syllable Frame. Students tap individual sounds only if they get stuck.

Have students "mark up" the review and current words.

COMPOSITION BOOKS

Dictate 3 sounds, 2 review, 2 current words and 2 trick words (trick words can be current or review) and 1 sentence.

Students repeat the word in syllables. They should only tap if needed. Students should immediately scoop multisyllabic words to proofread. Students should write and orally spell trick words with their finger prior to writing them in their Composition Books. Students independently write the sentence and then you lead them through the proofreading procedure.

Have students "mark up" the review and current words.

DAY 5 CHECK-UP

Students do Day 5 Dictation in their Composition Books. Have them check the Check-up box at the top of the page.

Dictate the sound, word, or sentence. Have students repeat and then write independently. Do not have students spell orally. Encourage them to tap as appropriate.

UNIT TEST

Have students find Unit Test pages at the end of their Composition Books.

Dictate the sound, word, or sentence. (See Unit Resources.) Have students repeat and then write independently. Do not have students spell orally. Encourage them to tap as appropriate.

 **Make It Fun**

WEEK 1

Preparation

- White Syllable Frames
- Resource List of Current and Review Words

SYLLABLE MATCH

This activity will help students match syllables to make a word. They will also practice segmenting syllables in words.

Instruct Students

Write the first syllable of a word in a left hand and the second syllable in a right hand column creating a match game. Put four syllables in each column.

Have a student find a match and draw a line from the first syllable to the second syllable.

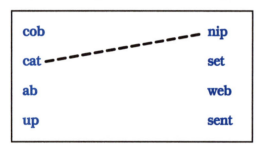

If the student is correct, have another student write it on the White Syllable Frames.

Have everyone read the word.

Ask

What would it be if I took away cat ?

Remove the cat frame. After students answer, put it back.

Ask

What would it be if I took away nip?

Remove the nip frame. After students answer, erase the frames.

Ask

What was the word?

Point to blank syllable frames as the word is said.

Say

Now, say catnip without cat.

Cover the first blank frame with your hand. (nip)

Say catnip without nip.

Cover the second frame with your hand. (cat)

Continue with matching of words. Be sure to do the whole activity with your students.

Storytime

WEEK 1

Preparation

- Baby Echo (on a pointer or ruler)
- Large Chart Paper

JACKSON

Write the following story, with the phrases scooped, on chart paper.

Jackson

Ed had a pet dog, Jackson.

Jackson had fun with the ball.

Jackson dug in the sandbox.

Jackson went for a swim

in the pond. He was all wet.

He was a mess! At sunset,

Jackson and Ed had a nap.

It was a fun day.

Instruct Students

Ask the students to read the title silently. (Tell students to tap words when reading silently, if necessary.) Discuss the title and predict what the story might be about.

Read Sentences

Continue reading one sentence at a time.

- Have students read silently. (Tell them to tap words when reading silently, if necessary.)
- Select a student to come read the sentence with the Baby Echo pointer. Be sure the student uses proper expression and phrasing. If not, model.
- Have the whole class repeat the sentence.

After the story has been read once in this manner, read it altogether with choral reading as you scoop the phrases with Baby Echo.

Make a Movie

Have students "make a movie" in their heads. Tell them to close their eyes and picture Jackson.

Ask someone to describe what they see in their movie, discussing each sentence.

Continue with the whole story. Then model re-telling the story in your own words and ask a student to retell it in their own words.

Mark Words

Lastly, select students to come mark words as directed.

- Make the word Jackson with the Standard Sound Cards. Show the students that this word has three consonants between the two vowels, but remind them that the **ck** is a digraph and it sticks together. Have them scoop it into syllables:

Jackson

- Scoop Jackson and all other multisyllabic words into syllables. Do this with a different color than you used to scoop phrases. Briefly discuss the syllable division.

Unit 11 **Lesson Activity Plan**

WEEK 2

Preparation

- Baby Echo (on a pointer or ruler)
- Large Chart Paper with the story from Week 1
- Copy JACKSON story for each student from the Fluency Kit (in the Stories tab).

Instruct Students

Ask the students to read the title silently. Have them try to remember the "movie" in their mind. Have someone describe the story by retelling it. Read chorally as you point with Baby Echo and determine if the retelling was accurate.

Next disseminate the story to the students. Have them draw pictures for each page and cut on the dotted lines. Staple these into booklets for the students to bring home.

WEEK 3

Preparation

- Find a non-fiction book about any animal
- Chart Paper

Instruct Students

Remind students that some books that have stories that are pretend or make-believe.

Explain that other books tell us facts about things. They teach us things that are true. Show them your non-fiction book and tell the students that it is a book that teaches them true things about (name the subject).

Read the book (or part of the book) to your students. After each page, ask them to name one true fact that they have learned.

Next, tell the students that they will help you write a non-fiction paragraph about (name the subject).

Have the students retell several facts. Write the sentences to create a paragraph. Be sure to indent.

Next have a student come and put an arrow to show the indented first sentence:

→ **Beavers build dams.**

Have another student highlight the punctuation marks.

Tell students that a paragraph has several sentences that all talk about the same topic.

Ask

What do you do at the beginning of the sentence?

(Indent)

What do you put at the end of every sentence?

(a period, a question mark or an exclamation point)

Unit 11 **Resources**

Drill Sounds

a - apple - /ă/	b - bat - /b/
c - cat - /k/	d - dog - /d/
e - Ed - /ĕ/	f - fun - /f/
g - game - /g/	h - hat - /h/
i - itch - /ĭ/	j - jug - /j/
k - kite - /k/	l - lamp - /l/
m - man - /m/	n - nut - /n/
o - octopus - /ŏ/	p - pan - /p/
qu - queen - /kw/	r - rat - /r/
s - snake - /s/	s - bugs - /z/
t - top - /t/	u - up - /ŭ/
v - van - /v/	w - wind - /w/
x - fox - /ks/	y - yellow - /y/
z - zebra - /z/	sh - ship - /sh/
ck - sock - /k/	wh - whistle - /w/
th - thumb - /th/	ch - chin - /ch/
all - ball - /òl/	an - fan - /an/
am - ham - /am/	ang - fang - /ang/
ing - ring - /ing/	ong - song - /ong/
ung - lung - /ung/	ank - bank - /ank/
ink - pink - /ink/	onk - honk - /onk/
unk - junk - /unk/	

Echo Sounds

Sounds appear between / /. You say the sound. Students echo the sound and say the letter. Depending on the activity, students then either find or make the letter corresponding to that sound.

CONSONANTS/CONSONANT DIGRAPHS

/b/ - b	/d/ - d	/f/ - f
/g/ - g	/h/ - h	/j/ - j
/k/ - c, k, ck	/l/ - l	/m/ - m
/n/ - n	/p/ - p	/kw/ - qu
/r/ - r	/s/ - s	/t/ - t
/v/ - v	/w/ - w, wh	/ks/ - x
/y/ - y	/z/ - z, s	/ch/ - ch
/sh/ - sh	/th/ - th	

VOWELS

/ă/ - a	/ĕ/ - e	/ĭ/ - i
/ŏ/ - o	/ŭ/ - u	

GLUED/WELDED SOUNDS

/òl/ - all	/am/ - am	/an/ - an
/ang/ - ang	/ing/ - ing	/ong/ - ong
/ung/ - ung	/ank/ - ank	/ink/ - ink
/onk/ - onk	/unk/ - unk	

Review Trick Words

the	of	and	to	a	was
is	he	for	as	his	has
I	you	we	they	one	said
from	or	have	were	her	put
there	what	she	been	by	who

out	so	are	two	about	into
only	other	new	some	could	want
say	do	first	any	my	now
our	over	come	would	after	also
many	before	called	how	your	down
should	each	because			

Current Unit Trick Words

people	Mr.	Mrs.	years	says	little
good	very	own			

Review Words

man	kiss	quits	junk	fell	lips
buds	sets	fibs	thinks	sings	bills
chunks	webs	balls	bank	puff	socks
stung	blank	swing	stink	bring	skunk
sting	trunk	prank	blink	drink	shrink
crunch	drift	twist	crisp	draft	print
slant	trust	grump	blend	craft	slept
plump	plant	shrimp	squint	grand	crust
trunks	pranks	blinks	drinks	grunts	stumps
drifts	blends	crafts	slumps	blimps	plants

Current Unit Words

WEEKS 1 • 2

upset	pigpen	hotrod	tomcat
sunfish	public	bathmat	uphill
hatbox	catfish	Batman	humbug
nutmeg	tenpin	suntan	tiptop
lapdog	sunlit	cobweb	undid
bathtub	sunset	sunbath	zigzag
catnip	bedbug	backstop	backpack
mascot	whiplash	unzip	laptop
napkin	publish	goblin	dentist
himself	insist	contest	chipmunk
expect	disrupt	insult	spandex
invent	absent	misfit	combat
admit	submit	until	Justin
sunsets	bedbugs	dishpans	napkins
unzips	tenpins	tomcats	cobwebs

WEEK 3

public	panic	tonic	plastic
frantic	picnic		

Unit 11 **Resources**

Sentences

*Write any **bold word** on the board for students to copy. A **bold word** has untaught components.*

WEEKS 1 • 2

Sid did not miss the sunset.

Ben had catnip for the tomcat.

Bob got a sunfish with his rod.

Dad will dust the cobweb in the den.

The dog in the bathtub is a mess.

The kids went to rent the Batman flick.

The bobcat hid in the shed.

Beth did not get upset when she lost.

Do not drop the album in the slush.

Did Kim admit that she felt a chill?

Stan put the napkin on his lap.

Ted did not get upset with Jill.

Jim went to get catnip for the tomcat.

Jan will **come** as a goblin.

Did Bob get a suntan on his trip?

Justin must dust the cobweb off the shelf.

Did Bob get in the bathtub?

Bill fell but did not get upset.

That chipmunk hid in the grass.

We sat on the cliff at sunset.

Do not step in the pigpen!

The big blast upset the pup.

The sunfish is in the bathtub.

Did you invent this thing?

Justin was absent from class.

I think I will win the next contest.

Did Stan **go** to the dentist?

Mom will insist that we help.

WEEK 3

Tom and Jan will **go** on a picnic.

The plastic jug is on the shelf.

Have students find the Unit Test pages located at the end of their Composition Books. Dictate the sounds, words and sentences. Have students repeat and then write independently. Encourage them to tap, but they should not use their Student Notebooks.

Dictate The Following Sounds

/z/   /g/   /k/   /j/   /ă/

Dictate The Following Words

upset	cobwebs	admit	cramps	public
stings	picnic	call	strap	bathtub

Dictate The Following Trick Words

Mr.   people

Dictate The Following Sentences

Is the napkin on his lap?

Justin was absent from class.

Have The Students Do The Following

- Multisyllabic words: scoop or underline into two syllables and circle any suffix **-s**.
- One syllable word: scoop word and circle the suffix **-s**.
- Find and underline the three-letter blend.

Answer Key

SOUNDS

1. z, s
2. g
3. k, c, ck
4. j
5. a

WORDS

1. up set
2. cob web(s)
3. ad mit
4. cramp(s)
5. pub lic
6. sting(s)
7. pic nic
8. call
9. s t r a p
10. bath tub

TRICK WORDS

1. Mr.
2. people

SENTENCES

1. Is the nap kin on his lap?
2. Jus tin was ab sent from class.

Unit 12 Level 1

Introduction

In this Unit, you teach your students about the new suffix ending -es. You will also review the concept of plural words with your students.

In order to present the appropriate words in this Unit, be sure to form those found in the Resource List provided in this Unit.

PREPARING YOUR MATERIALS

There are no new Standard Sound Cards to be displayed. Have on hand the Blue Word Frames and Yellow Suffix Frames.

Arrange the Standard Sound Card display in the following manner

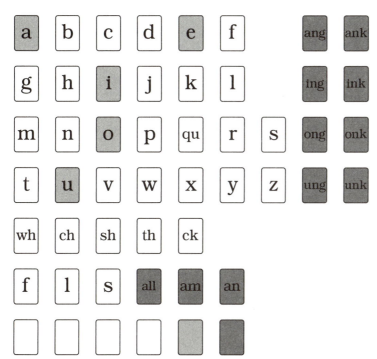

PREPARING YOUR STUDENTS

Students do not add any new Magnetic Letter Tiles to their Letter Boards.

PREPARING FOR HOME SUPPORT

Copy and send home the **Unit 12 Letter and Activity Packet**.

Getting Ready

VIEW THE CD-ROM

LEVEL 1
• Unit 12
  Lesson Activities (see below)

STUDY LESSON ACTIVITIES

Review the following on CD-ROM:

• Unit 6 video for the suffix procedures.

Week 1

DAY ❶	DAY ❷	DAY ❸	DAY ❹	DAY ❺
Drill Sounds	Drill Sounds	Drill Sounds	Drill Sounds	Drill Sounds
Introduce New Concepts	Word of the Day	Word Talk	Word Talk	Storytime
Word of the Day	Introduce New Concepts	Make it Fun	Trick Words	Dictation (Day 5 Check-up)
Trick Words	Dictation (Composition Book)	Dictation (Dry Erase)	Dictation (Composition Book)	

Week 2

DAY ❶	DAY ❷	DAY ❸	DAY ❹	DAY ❺
Drill Sounds	Drill Sounds	Drill Sounds	Drill Sounds	Drill Sounds
Word of the Day	Word of the Day	Word Talk	Word Talk	Storytime
Trick Words	Echo/Find Sounds & Words	Make it Fun	Trick Words	Dictation (Unit Test)
Echo/Find Sounds & Words	Dictation (Composition Book)	Dictation (Dry Erase)	Dictation (Composition Book)	
Dictation (Dry Erase)				

Introduce New Concepts

WEEK 1 DAY ❶

TEACH THE -ES SUFFIX

Students will learn about the suffix **-es**. Tell them that endings can be added to a baseword to make longer words.

Using the Standard Sound Cards, demonstrate with the word **bug**. Add **s** to form **bugs**.

Tell them that **bugs** means more than one thing. It is a plural word which means more than one. **Bug** is the baseword and **s** is added to it; **s** is a suffix.

A suffix is an ending that can be added to a baseword.

Say

> There are two kinds of suffixes: *vowel suffixes* begin with vowels and *consonant suffixes* begin with consonants.
>
> Today we will learn a new suffix.

Write **es** on the Yellow Suffix Frame and explain that the suffix **-es** is a **vowel suffix** because it begins with a vowel. Tell student it says /**əz**/ and have them echo.

Write basewords such as **box** or **lunch** on Blue Word Frames. Add the Yellow Suffix Frame with **es**. Have the students read the baseword and then read the entire word with the baseword and the suffix together: **box - boxes**.

Ask

> What is the baseword?
>
> What is the suffix?

Instruct students to read these words naming just the baseword first and then the baseword and suffix. This helps students solidify the concept and also prepares them for spelling.

Next explain that **-es** is another suffix that might make a word mean more than one thing.

Write the word **bench** on a Blue Word Frame. Have a student read the word.

Say

This means that there is one bench.

> If I add es (add suffix), what does the word say? (benches)
>
> This means that there is more than one bench.

Lastly, tell students that words that end in certain letters need to have **-es** rather than **-s**. Words that end in **ch**, **sh**, **s**, **x** and **z**, all add **-es**.

Student Notebook Entry

Write the words, **dresses**, **benches** and **rashes** on your classroom board. Students add these word examples to the **-es** suffix endings page in the Spelling section of their Student Notebooks.

Teach Students To Mark Words

In the word **boxes**, the letters **es** are a suffix. Underline the baseword and circle the suffix like this:

WEEK 1 DAY ❷

TEACH SPELLING

Dictate current Unit words. (See Unit Resources.)

Students must spell the baseword first. When the word **boxes** is dictated, the students must first repeat the word (**boxes**), name the baseword (**box**), spell this (**b-o-x**), and then add the suffix **-es**.

Use the Yellow Suffix Frame to represent either the **-s** or the **-es** suffix. Be sure they then orally spell the entire word.

It is vital that you establish the habit of naming and spelling the baseword before adding the suffix. You may cue the students to name the baseword by asking them, **"What's the baseword?"** after students repeat the whole word.

After students make several words on their Building Boards, have them write several words on their Dry Erase Writing Tablets.

 Drill Sounds

Always do the vowel sounds. You can select some consonants, but there is no need to do all of them. (See Unit Resources.)

There are no new sounds. Review previous sounds.

Large Sound Cards

First practice sounds with the Large Sound Cards. Say the letter-keyword-sound and have students echo.

Standard Sound Cards

Next, point to the Standard Sound Cards (on display) with the Baby Echo pointer. You say the letter-keyword-sound and hold up Baby Echo to have students repeat. (Either you or a student can be the drill leader.)

 Word of the Day

Select a Word of the Day from the words below. Make the word using your Standard Sound Card, and Yellow Suffix Frame. Also, write the word on a blank index card and add it to your Word of the Day packet.

Word Resource

WEEK 1

| i | n | ch | **es** | | d | i | sh | **es** |

WEEK 2

| f | o | x | **es** | | g | l | a | s | s | **es** |

Review Concepts

Reteach the **-es** suffix.

Use The Word In A Sentence

Have a student (or students) use the word in a sentence and discuss the word's meaning.

Make Other Words

Then use sound cards and the Yellow Suffix Frame to make several other words from this Unit. (See Unit Resources.) Have students read each word, naming the baseword first.

Student Notebook Entry

Have students add the Word of the Day to the Vocabulary section of their Student Notebooks.

Have students mark up the word by underling the baseword and circling the suffix.

Write a sentence on the board for students to copy. (This can be done at another time of the day.)

Word Talk

Review the Words of the Day from your Words of the Day index card packet.

Make and Discuss Words

Make 4-5 words with your Standard Sound Card display.

Have students read the words.

Ask a student to use a word in a sentence and another student to explain what the word means.

Read Words

Use your packet of words as flashcards. Have students quickly read them without tapping.

Display Words

Display current and review words. Have students find and read the words as directed.

Instruct Students

Find words with a suffix.

(Read the word inch-inches)

Find words with two syllables.

(Have the student scoop the syllables with his/her finger and read it to you).

 Trick Words

Trick words require lots of practice. Sky write and finger write trick words, but **do not** tap them out or make them with the Magnetic Letter Tiles.

Word Resource

WEEK 1

see   work   between

WEEK 2

both   being   under

Students add these words to the Trick Word section of their Student Notebooks. Hold them accountable for the spelling of these words throughout the day. Direct students to look them up in the Trick Word section of their Student Notebooks.

After the introduction of new trick words, practice them with sky writing and tracing.

 Echo/Find Sounds & Words

Echo/Find Sounds

Say a sound. Have students echo and find the letter on their Letter Boards.

There are no new sounds. Review previous sounds.

Echo/Find Words

(See Review and Current Unit Words in Unit Resources.)

Have students find Magnetic Letter Tiles needed to make words on their Letter Boards. They should add the yellow suffix card for words with a suffix. Be sure they use the Syllable Overlay for multisyllabic words. After finding the letters, have a student spell the word orally.

Dictation

Refer to this Unit's Resource List of Echo Sounds, Words and Sentences.

Proper Dictation Activity procedures are very important. Be sure to follow their demonstration on the CD-ROM.

Note

Be sure students name and spell one syllable at a time for the multisyllabic words. Have them immediately scoop the word into syllables and read it as a proofreading procedure.

DRY ERASE

Dictate 3 sounds, 3 current words and 3 trick words (trick words can be current or review).

Have one student do the multisyllabic words on your Syllable Frame. Students tap individual sounds only if they get stuck.

Have students "mark up" the review and current words.

COMPOSITION BOOKS

Dictate 3 sounds, 2 review, 2 current words and 2 trick words (trick words can be current or review) and 1 sentence.

Students repeat the word in syllables. They should only tap if needed. Students should immediately scoop multisyllabic words to proofread. Students should write and orally spell trick words with their finger prior to writing them in their Composition Books. Students independently write the sentence and then you lead them through the proofreading procedure.

Have students "mark up" the review and current words.

DAY 5 CHECK-UP

Students do Day 5 Dictation in their Composition Books. Have them check the Check-up box at the top of the page.

Dictate the sound, word, or sentence. Have students repeat and then write independently. Do not have students spell orally. Encourage them to tap as appropriate.

UNIT TEST

Have students find Unit Test pages at the end of their Composition Books.

Dictate the sound, word, or sentence. (See Unit Resources.) Have students repeat and then write independently. Do not have students spell orally. Encourage them to tap as appropriate.

Make It Fun

Preparation

- Blue Word Frames
- Yellow Suffix Frames
- Resource List of Current and Review Words

SUFFIX TEAMS

This activity will help students practice adding -**es** or -**s** suffix to a word.

Instruct Students

Write **es** on one suffix frame and **s** on another. Divide the class into two teams. Select a word with a suffix from the Resource List. Say it and have all students repeat.

Call on a student from Team One to select the correct suffix, -**es** or -**s**. If they point to the correct suffix, that team gets a point. After they select the suffix, ask if someone else from Team One can name the baseword for a bonus point.

Write the baseword on the Word Frame and read the baseword, then baseword and suffix. Have all students repeat. Erase the blue Word Frame and select another word for Team Two.

 Storytime

WEEK 1

Preparation

- Baby Echo (on a pointer or ruler)
- Large Chart Paper

BRAD'S LOST GLASSES

Write the following story, with the phrases scooped, on chart paper.

Brad's Lost Glasses

Brad, Stan and Jeff had their lunches

in a bag for a picnic. At the picnic

they played tag. Brad lost his glasses.

Stan, Brad and Jeff went on a hunt

for the glasses. Brad's glasses

were not on the steps.

Brad's glasses were not in the hotrod.

The kids must get the glasses.

Brad's mom would be upset.

Brad's glasses were in the branches

of a tree! At last, Brad was all set.

Instruct Students

Ask the students to read the title silently. (Tell students to tap words when reading silently, if necessary.) Discuss the title and predict what the story might be about.

Show the students the word played. Underline the baseword and circle the suffix and tell the students this word.

Read Sentences

Continue reading one sentence at a time.

- Have students read silently. (Tell students to tap words when reading silently, if necessary.)

- Select a student to come read the sentence with the Baby Echo pointer. Be sure the student uses proper expression and phrasing. If not, model.

- Have the whole class repeat the sentence.

After the story has been read once in this manner, read it altogether with choral reading as you scoop the phrases with Baby Echo.

Make a Movie

Have students "make a movie" in their heads. Tell them to close their eyes and picture Brad's Lost Glasses.

Ask someone to describe what they see in their movie, discussing each sentence.

Continue with the whole story. Then model retelling the story in your own words and ask a student to retell it in their own words.

Mark Words

Lastly, select students to come mark words as directed.

- Make a capital letter frame around words that have a capital letter and discuss why (at the beginning of a sentence or a person's name).

- Underline basewords and circle suffixes.

- Have students find a multisyllabic word and underline syllables.

WEEK 2

Preparation

- Baby Echo (on a pointer or ruler)
- Large Chart Paper with the story from Week 1
- Copy BRAD'S LOST GLASSES story for each student from the Fluency Kit (in the Stories tab).

Instruct Students

Ask the students to read the title silently. Have them try to remember the "movie" in their mind. Have someone describe the story by retelling it. Read chorally as you point with Baby Echo and determine if the retelling was accurate.

Next disseminate the story to the students. Have them draw pictures for each page and cut on the dotted lines. Staple these into booklets for the students to bring home.

Drill Sounds

a - apple - /ă/	b - bat - /b/
c - cat - /k/	d - dog - /d/
e - Ed - /ĕ/	f - fun - /f/
g - game - /g/	h - hat - /h/
i - itch - /ĭ/	j - jug - /j/
k - kite - /k/	l - lamp - /l/
m - man - /m/	n - nut - /n/
o - octopus - /ŏ/	p - pan - /p/
qu - queen - /kw/	r - rat - /r/
s - snake - /s/	s - bugs - /z/
t - top - /t/	u - up - /ŭ/
v - van - /v/	w - wind - /w/
x - fox - /ks/	y - yellow - /y/
z - zebra - /z/	sh - ship - /sh/
ck - sock - /k/	wh - whistle - /w/
th - thumb - /th/	ch - chin - /ch/
all - ball - /ŏl/	an - fan - /an/
am - ham - /am/	ang - fang - /ang/
ing - ring - /ing/	ong - song - /ong/
ung - lung - /ung/	ank - bank - /ank/
ink - pink - /ink/	onk - honk - /onk/
unk - junk - /unk/	

Echo Sounds

Sounds appear between / /. You say the sound. Students echo the sound and say the letter. Depending on the activity, students then either find or make the letter corresponding to that sound.

CONSONANTS/CONSONANT DIGRAPHS

/b/ - b	/d/ - d	/f/ - f
/g/ - g	/h/ - h	/j/ - j
/k/ - c, k, ck	/l/ - l	/m/ - m
/n/ - n	/p/ - p	/kw/ - qu
/r/ - r	/s/ - s	/t/ - t
/v/ - v	/w/ - w, wh	/ks/ - x
/y/ - y	/z/ - z, s	/ch/ - ch
/sh/ - sh	/th/ - th	

VOWELS

/ă/ - a	/ĕ/ - e	/ĭ/ - i
/ŏ/ - o	/ŭ/ - u	

GLUED/WELDED SOUNDS

/ŏl/ - all	/am/ - am	/an/ - an
/ang/ - ang	/ing/ - ing	/ong/ - ong
/ung/ - ung	/ank/ - ank	/ink/ - ink
/onk/ - onk	/unk/ - unk	

Review Trick Words

the	of	and	to	a	was
is	he	for	as	his	has
I	you	we	they	one	said
from	or	have	were	her	put
there	what	she	been	by	who

Unit 12 Resources

out	so	are	two	about	into
only	other	new	some	could	want
say	do	first	any	my	now
our	over	come	would	after	also
many	how	called	before	your	down
own	each	people	Mr.	Mrs.	should
says	little	years	very	good	because

Current Unit Trick Words

see	work	both	being	under	between

Review Words

shrunk	blast	grunt	blimp
stamp	spend	skunks	stings
brings	branch	chills	shrimp
nutmeg	cobweb	suntan	tiptop
lapdog	sunlit	catnip	bedbug
pinball	index	mascot	whiplash
unzip	laptop	napkin	publish
goblin	picnic	dentist	plastic
himself	insist	contest	chipmunk
splendid	disrupt	insult	admit
invent	absent	sunsets	bedbugs
dishpans	napkins	unzips	tenpins

Sentences

*Write any **bold word** on the board for students to copy. A **bold word** has untaught components.*

The kids had six classes.

The bats are on the benches.

The pup had wet kisses.

I had rashes on my left leg.

Don has glasses to **look through.**

Get well wishes were sent to Ted.

The dresses are pink and red.

Dad had the lost lunches.

Sid rushes to get the bus.

Jack tosses the ball to Fran.

Fill the boxes with the junk.

That thing pinches my neck.

Have students find the unit test pages located at the end of their Composition Books. Dictate the sounds, words and sentences. Have students repeat and then write independently. Encourage them to tap, but they should not use their Student Notebooks.

Dictate The Following Sounds

/z/   /ĕ/   /m/   /th/   /ŭ/

Dictate The Following Words

invents   dresses   shrink   boxes   sunset

benches   squint   crashes   stacks   goblin

Dictate The Following Trick Words

both   work

Dictate The Following Sentences

Did Brad get the glasses?

The branches fell on the path.

Have The Students Do The Following

• Scoop or underline multisyllabic words into syllables.

• If there is a baseword and suffix, underline baseword and circle suffix. (If the word is multisyllabic, just circle the suffix since the baseword is already scooped into syllables.)

Answer Key

SOUNDS

1. z, s   2. e
3. m   4. th
5. u

WORDS

1. in vent(s)
2. dress(es)
3. shrink
4. box(es)
5. sun set
6. bench(es)
7. squint
8. crash(es)
9. stack(s)
10. gob lin

TRICK WORDS

1. both
2. work

SENTENCES

1. Did Brad get the glass(es)?
2. The branch(es) fell on the path.

Unit 13 Level 1

Introduction

In this Unit, you will teach students about two new suffix endings **-ed** and **-ing**.

Look at the words **rented** and **renting**:

rent(ed)   **rent(ing)**

At this point, you will add these suffixes to closed syllable words that **do not change** when the suffix is added. **Do not** add these suffixes to words such as **drip** since you would need to double the **p** to form **dripping** or **dripped**.

Again, **do not** do words that require doubling the consonant.

Also at this point, you will teach only one sound of the suffix **-ed**. You will teach that it says /əd/. In a later Unit, you will teach students that the **-ed** suffix also says /**d**/ and /**t**/. Avoid words with the /**d**/ and /**t**/ sound of this suffix for now.

In order to present the appropriate words, be sure to form the words found in the Resource List provided in this Unit.

PREPARING YOUR MATERIALS

There are no new Standard Sound Cards to be displayed. Have on hand the Blue Word Frames and Yellow Suffix Frames.

Arrange the Standard Sound Card display in the following manner

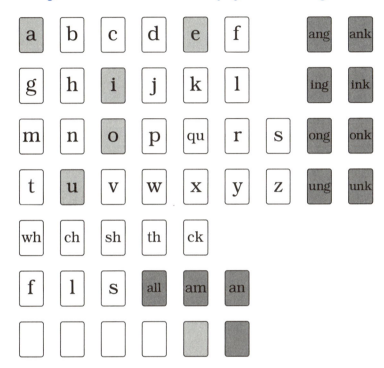

PREPARING YOUR STUDENTS

Students do not add any new Magnetic Letter Tiles to their Letter Boards.

PREPARING FOR HOME SUPPORT

Copy and send home the **Unit 13 Letter and Activity Packet**.

Week 1

DAY ❶	DAY ❷	DAY ❸	DAY ❹	DAY ❺
Drill Sounds	Drill Sounds	Drill Sounds	Drill Sounds	Drill Sounds
Introduce New Concepts	Word of the Day	Word of the Day	Word Talk	Trick Words
Trick Words	Introduce New Concepts	Echo/Find Sounds	Echo/Find Sounds & Words	Word Talk
	Dictation (Composition Book)	Dictation (Dry Erase)	Dictation (Dry Erase)	Storytime
		Make it Fun	Trick Words	Dictation (Day 5 Check-up)

Week 2

DAY ❶	DAY ❷	DAY ❸	DAY ❹	DAY ❺
Drill Sounds	Drill Sounds	Drill Sounds	Drill Sounds	Drill Sounds
Introduce New Concepts	Word of the Day	Word of the Day	Word Talk	Trick Words
Echo/Find Sounds & Words	Trick Words	Dictation (Dry Erase)	Echo/Find Sounds & Words	Word Talk
Dictation (Dry Erase)	Echo/Find Sounds & Words	Make it Fun	Dictation (Dry Erase)	Storytime
	Dictation (Composition Book)		Trick Words	Dictation (Unit Test)

Introduce New Concepts

TEACH THE *-ED* & *-ING* SUFFIXES

The students will now learn more suffixes. Tell them that endings can be added to a baseword to make longer words.

Using the Standard Sound Cards, demonstrate with the word **bug**. Add **s** to form **bugs**.

Say

> Bugs means more than one thing. It is a plural word which means more than one. Bug is the baseword and s is added to it; s is a suffix.
>
> A suffix is an ending that can be added to a baseword.

Reteach that there are two kinds of suffixes: vowel suffixes begin with vowels and consonant suffixes begin with consonants.

Write **ed** on one Yellow Suffix Frame and **ing** on another Frame.

Explain as you display them that the suffixes **-ed** and **-ing** are both **vowel suffixes** because they begin with a vowel.

Write basewords such as **rent** or **inspect** on Blue Word Frames. Add the suffix **-ing**:

Have students read the baseword then read the entire word with the baseword and the suffix together: **rent - renting.**

Ask

> What is the baseword?
>
> What is the suffix?

Do the same with **-ed**. Write words on the Blue Word Frame such as **inspect** and add the yellow **-ed** suffix frame.

Instruct students to read these words naming just the baseword first and then the baseword and suffix. This again helps students solidify the concept and also prepares them for spelling.

Student Notebook Entry

Students add the words **fishing** and **rented** as examples of the **-ed** and **-ing** suffixes to the suffix endings page in the Spelling section of their Student Notebooks.

Teach Students To Mark Words

In the word **fishing**, the letters **ing** are a suffix. Underline the baseword and circle the suffix like this:

fish (**ing**)

If the baseword is multisyllabic, be sure to scoop or underline syllables and then circle the suffix:

ex tend (**ed**)

TEACH SPELLING

Dictate the word, **publishing**. Students must first repeat the word (**publishing**) and name the baseword, (**publish**).

They then say each syllable and spell them:

pub, p-u-b   **lish**, l-i-s-h

Write the syllables on Syllable Frames. Students find the Magnetic Letter Tiles and place them onto the Syllable Overlay. Then ask the students to name the suffix and write it on the Yellow Suffix Frame. Have students add the blank Yellow Suffix Tile to their word.

They should then spell the word orally. It is vital that you establish the habit of naming and spelling the baseword before adding the suffix. Dictate 5-6 unit words and have students build them on their Building Boards. (See Resources.)

 Drill Sounds

Always do the vowel sounds. You can select some consonants, but there is no need to do all of them. (See Unit Resources.)

There are no new sounds. Review previous sounds.

Large Sound Cards

First practice sounds with the Large Sound Cards. Say the letter-keyword-sound and have students echo.

Standard Sound Cards

Next, point to the Standard Sound Cards (on display) with the Baby Echo pointer. You say the letter-keyword-sound and hold up Baby Echo to have students repeat. (Either you or a student can be the drill leader.)

 Word of the Day

Select a Word of the Day from the words below. Make the word using your Standard Sound Card display. Also, write the word on a blank index card and add it to your Word of the Day packet.

Word Resource

WEEK 1

WEEK 2

Review Concepts

Reteach the **-ing** and **-ed** suffixes using the Word of the Day.

Use The Word In A Sentence

Have a student (or students) use the word in a sentence and discuss the word's meaning.

Make Other Words

Then use sound cards to make several other words from this Unit. (See Unit Resources.) Have students tap and read each word.

Student Notebook Entry

Have students add the Word of the Day to the Vocabulary section of their Student Notebooks.

Have students mark up the word by underlining the baseword and circling the suffix.

Write a sentence on the board for students to copy. (This can be done at another time of the day.)

Word Talk

Review the Words of the Day from your Words of the Day index card packet.

Make and Discuss Words

Make 4-5 words with your Standard Sound Card display.

Have students tap and read the words.

Ask a student to use a word in a sentence and another student to explain what the word means.

Read Words

Use your packet of words as flashcards. Have students quickly read them without tapping.

Display Words

Display current and review words. Have students find and read the words as directed.

Instruct Students

Find a word that means "_____."

Find a word with a digraph and a suffix.

Find a word with a blend and a suffix.

Mark the closed syllables in a word, multisyllabic word.

 ## Trick Words

Trick words require lots of practice. Sky write and finger write Trick Words, but **do not** tap them out or make them with the Magnetic Letter Tiles.

Word Resource

WEEK 1

never	another	day

WEEK 2

words	look	through

Students add these words to the Trick Word section of their Student Notebooks. Hold them accountable for the spelling of these words throughout the day. Direct students to look them up in the Trick Word section of their Student Notebooks.

After the introduction of new Trick Words, practice them with sky writing and tracing.

 ## Echo/Find Sounds & Words

Echo/Find Sounds

Say a sound. Have students echo and find the letter on their Letter Board.

There are no new sounds. Review previous sounds.

(See Echo Sounds in Unit Resources for expected student responses.)

Echo/Find Words

(See Review and Current Unit Words in Unit Resources.)

Have students find Magnetic Letter Tiles needed to make words on their Letter Boards. After finding a word, have a student spell it orally. Have students use the Syllable Overlay and the Yellow Suffix Frames as needed.

Dictation

Refer to this Unit's Resource List of Echo Sounds, Words and Sentences.

Proper Dictation Activity procedures are very important. Be sure to follow their demonstration on the CD-ROM.

Note

Be sure students name and spell one syllable at a time for the multisyllabic words. Have them immediately scoop the word into syllables and read it as a proofreading procedure.

DRY ERASE

Dictate 3 sounds, 3 current words and 3 trick words (trick words can be current or review).

Have one student do the multisyllabic words

on your Syllable Frame. Students tap individual sounds only if they get stuck.

Have students "mark up" the review and current words.

COMPOSITION BOOKS

Dictate 3 sounds, 2 review, 2 current words and 2 trick words (trick words can be current or review) and 1 sentence.

Students repeat the word in syllables. They should only tap if needed. Students should immediately scoop multisyllabic words to proofread. Students should write and orally spell trick words with their finger prior to writing them in their Composition Books. Students independently write the sentence and then you lead them through the proofreading procedure.

Have students "mark up" the review and current words.

DAY 5 CHECK-UP

Students do Day 5 Dictation in their Composition Books. Have them check the Check-up box at the top of the page.

Dictate the sound, word, or sentence. Have students repeat and then write independently. Do not have students spell orally. Encourage them to tap as appropriate.

UNIT TEST

Have students find Unit Test pages at the end of their Composition Books.

Dictate the sound, word, or sentence. (See Unit Resources.) Have students repeat and then write independently. Do not have students spell orally. Encourage them to tap as appropriate.

 **Make It Fun**

Preparation

- **s**, **ed**, **ing**, **es** suffix cards in the Appendix of this Manual. Copy and cut into separate cards.
- The Resource List of words (Current And Review).

Suffix Shuffle

This activity will help reinforce spelling words with a suffix.

Instruct Students

Brainstorm all taught suffixes and write them on the board.

s   es   ed   ing

Ask students which suffixes are the vowel suffixes. Distribute suffix cards, one per student. Dictate a word with a suffix. Have all students repeat. Have all students holding the correct suffix stand up and hold up their suffix card. Next, have them all find a place on the board to come up and write the word, including the suffix. They should underline the baseword and circle the suffix.

Storytime

WEEK 1

Preparation

- Baby Echo (on a pointer or ruler)
- Large Chart Paper

THE BIG SPLASH

Write the following story, with the phrases scooped, on chart paper.

The Big Splash

Jess was splashing in the pond

with her pup. Jeff was mad at Jess

and said, "Stop Splashing!"

Next, Jess was jumping in the pond.

Her big jump made a big splash.

Jess insisted that the splash

was not big. Jeff grunted and said,

"Stop splashing!" Jess did stop,

but then she ran on the grass.

She fell on a twig and landed

in the pond. Guess what?

It made a big splash!

Instruct Students

Ask the students to read the title silently. (Tell students to tap words when reading silently, if necessary.) Discuss the title and predict what the story might be about.

Make the word splash with the Standard Sound Cards. Explain that the **s p l** letters are a three letter blend.

Read Sentences

Continue reading one sentence at a time.

- Have students read silently. (Tell students to tap words when reading silently, if necessary.)
- Select a student to come read the sentence with the Baby Echo pointer. Be sure the student uses proper expression and phrasing. If not, model.
- Have the whole class repeat the sentence.

After the story has been read once in this manner, read it altogether with choral reading as you scoop the phrases with Baby Echo.

Make a Movie

Have students "make a movie" in their heads. Tell them to close their eyes and picture The Big Splash.

Ask someone to describe what they see in their movie, discussing each sentence.

Continue with the whole story. Then model retelling the story in your own words and ask a student to retell it in their own words.

Mark Words

Lastly, select students to come mark words as directed.

- Find three words that are closed syllables. Mark them closed.
- Star bonus letters.
- Scoop the multisyllabic baseword that also has a suffix. Circle the suffixes.

WEEK 2

Preparation

- Baby Echo (on a pointer or ruler)
- Large Chart Paper with the story from Week 1
- Copy THE BIG SPLASH story for each student from the Fluency Kit (in the Stories tab)

Instruct Students

Ask the students to read the title silently. Have them try to remember the "movie" in their mind. Have someone describe the story by retelling it. Read chorally as you point with Baby Echo and determine if the retelling was accurate.

Next disseminate the story to the students. Have them draw pictures for each page and cut on the dotted lines. Staple these into booklets for the students to bring home.

Drill Sounds

a - apple - /ă/	b - bat - /b/
c - cat - /k/	d - dog - /d/
e - Ed - /ĕ/	f - fun - /f/
g - game - /g/	h - hat - /h/
i - itch - /ĭ/	j - jug - /j/
k - kite - /k/	l - lamp - /l/
m - man - /m/	n - nut - /n/
o - octopus - /ŏ/	p - pan - /p/
qu - queen - /kw/	r - rat - /r/
s - snake - /s/	s - bugs - /z/
t - top - /t/	u - up - /ŭ/
v - van - /v/	w - wind - /w/
x - fox - /ks/	y - yellow - /y/
z - zebra - /z/	sh - ship - /sh/
ck - sock - /k/	wh - whistle - /w/
th - thumb - /th/	ch - chin - /ch/
all - ball - /ȯl/	an - fan - /an/
am - ham - /am/	ang - fang - /ang/
ing - ring - /ing/	ong - song - /ong/
ung - lung - /ung/	ank - bank - /ank/
ink - pink - /ink/	onk - honk - /onk/
unk - junk - /unk/	

Echo Sounds

Sounds appear between / /. You say the sound. Students echo the sound and say the letter. Depending on the activity, students then either find or make the letter corresponding to that sound.

CONSONANTS/CONSONANT DIGRAPHS

/b/ - b	/d/ - d	/f/ - f
/g/ - g	/h/ - h	/j/ - j
/k/ - c, k, ck	/l/ - l	/m/ - m
/n/ - n	/p/ - p	/kw/ - qu
/r/ - r	/s/ - s	/t/ - t
/v/ - v	/w/ - w, wh	/ks/ - x
/y/ - y	/z/ - z, s	/ch/ - ch
/sh/ - sh	/th/ - th	

VOWELS

/ă/ - a	/ĕ/ - e	/ĭ/ - i
/ŏ/ - o	/ŭ/ - u	

GLUED/WELDED SOUNDS

/ȯl/ - all	/am/ - am	/an/ - an
/ang/ - ang	/ing/ - ing	/ong/ - ong
/ung/ - ung	/ank/ - ank	/ink/ - ink
/onk/ - onk	/unk/ - unk	

Review Trick Words

the	of	and	to	a	was
is	he	for	as	his	has
I	you	we	they	one	said
from	or	have	were	her	put
there	what	she	been	by	who

Unit 13 **Resources**

out   so   are   two   about   into

only   other   new   some   could   want

say   do   first   any   my   now

our   over   come   would   after   also

many   how   called   before   your   down

own   each   people   Mr.   Mrs.   should

says   little   years   very   good   because

see   work   both   being   under   between

Current Unit Trick Words

never   another   day

words   look   through

Review Words

blast	pranks	claps	slams
list	blush	crush	melts
stiff	acts	quilt	band
Batman	sunset	catfish	zigzag
admit	submit	classes	inches
lunches	foxes	glasses	wishes
bunches	kisses	boxes	rashes
ranches	benches	branches	dresses
punches	blesses	pinches	blushes
munches	taxes	crushes	rushes
dashes	waxes	misses	squishes
messes	crashes	tosses	flashes

Current Unit Words

singing	shrinking	flashing
drilling	crossing	jumping
lending	standing	twisting
swinging	insisting	splashing
expanding	publishing	spilling
dusted	rented	hunted
squinted	unlisted	invented
expected	blended	insulted

Sentences

*Write any **bold word** on the board for students to copy. A **bold word** has untaught components.*

Jill is finishing her glass of milk.

Mom is still thinking of her job.

Ken was standing on the hot sand.

The kids are singing a Latin song.

The fishing trip was fantastic.

Chan invented that rocket.

He dented his hotrod in the crash.

Brad disrupted the math class.

Jeff planted the shrubs.

The kids did the job and then rested.

Have students find the unit test pages located at the end of their Composition Books. Dictate the sounds, words and sentences. Have students repeat and then write independently. Encourage them to tap, but they should not use their Student Notebooks.

Dictate The Following Sounds

/ong/   /b/   /p/   /ch/   /kw/

Dictate The Following Words

admit   invented   crashing   drilling   goblin

camping   drifted   disrupted   standing   expected

Dictate The Following Trick Words

words   through

Dictate The Following Sentences

Jeff is squinting in the sun.

Dad trusted the kids.

Have The Students Do The Following

- Underline or scoop syllables and circle suffixes
- Mark all closed syllables

Answer Key

SOUNDS

1. ong   2. b   3. p
4. ch   5. qu

WORDS

1. ăd mĭt
   c   c
2. ĭn vĕnt (ed)
   c   c
3. crăsh (ing)
   c
4. drĭll (ing)
   c
5. gŏb lĭn
   c   c
6. cămp (ing)
   c
7. drĭft (ed)
   c
8. dĭs rŭpt (ed)
   c   c
9. stănd (ing)
   c
10. ĕx pĕct (ed)
    c   c

TRICK WORDS

1. words   2. through

SENTENCES

1. Jĕff is squĭnt (ing) ĭn the
   c   c   c
   sŭn.
   c
2. Dăd trŭst (ed) the kĭd (s).
   c   c   c

Unit 14 Level 1

Introduction

In Unit 14, you will introduce the next syllable pattern:

The **vowel-consonant-e**.

- Has the vowel-consonant-e combination
- The **e** is silent
- The first vowel has a long sound

Examples

bike   ape   stove

Your students will learn the long vowel sound for each vowel, such as /ā/ in **safe**. They will learn that **u** can either say /ū/ as in **mule** or /ü/ as in **rule** when it appears in vowel-consonant-e syllables.

You will also teach that the letter **s** might say /**z**/ between two vowels as in the word **wise**.

Lastly, you will teach your students that the suffix **s** can be added to these words as well.

PREPARING YOUR MATERIALS

There are no new Standard Sound Cards to be displayed.

Have on hand the Large Sound Cards for **a - safe**, **e - Pete**, **i - pine**, **o - home**, **u - mule** and **u - rule**.

Laminate a blank orange vowel Standard Sound Card so that you can write on it, if not already done.

Display the Vowel Sounds Poster with long vowel sounds.

Arrange the Standard Sound Card display in the following manner

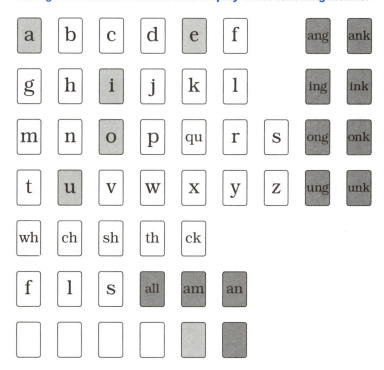

PREPARING YOUR STUDENTS

Students do not add any new Magnetic Letter Tiles to their Letter Boards.

PREPARING FOR HOME SUPPORT

Copy and send home the **Unit 14 Letter and Activity Packet**.

Getting Ready

VIEW THE CD-ROM

LEVEL 1
- Unit 14
  Lesson Activities (see below)

STUDY LESSON ACTIVITIES

Be sure to read the entire Introduce New Concepts thoroughly.

Watch the CD-ROM and practice prior to instruction.

Week 1

DAY ❶	DAY ❷	DAY ❸	DAY ❹	DAY ❺
Introduce New Concepts	Drill Sounds	Drill Sounds	Drill Sounds	Drill Sounds
Trick Words	Introduce New Concepts	Word of the Day	Word Talk	Word Talk
	Echo/Find Sounds & Words	Make it Fun	Trick Words	Storytime
	Dictation (Dry Erase)	Echo/Find Sounds & Words	Dictation (Dry Erase)	

Week 2

DAY ❶	DAY ❷	DAY ❸	DAY ❹	DAY ❺
Drill Sounds	Drill Sounds	Drill Sounds	Drill Sounds	Drill Sounds
Introduce New Concepts	Word of the Day	Word Talk	Word Talk	Storytime
Trick Words	Echo/Find Sounds & Words	Make it Fun	Trick Words	Dictation (Day 5 Check-up)
Echo/Find Sounds & Words	Dictation (Composition Book)	Dictation (Dry Erase)	Dictation (Composition Book)	
Dictation (Dry Erase)				

Week 3

DAY ❶	DAY ❷	DAY ❸	DAY ❹	DAY ❺
Drill Sounds	Drill Sounds	Drill Sounds	Drill Sounds	Drill Sounds
Introduce New Concepts	Word of the Day	Trick Words	Word Talk	Storytime
Echo/Find Sounds & Words	Trick Words	Word of the Day	Echo/Find Sounds & Words	Dictation (Unit Test)*
Dictation (Dry Erase)	Dictation (Composition Book)	Make it Fun	Dictation (Composition Book)	
		Dictation (Dry Erase)		

* If Unit 14 continues for 4 weeks, then do Dictation (Day 5 Check-up) for Week 3, and Dictation (Unit Test) for Week 4.

Introduce New Concepts

WEEK 1 DAY ❶

TEACH LONG VOWEL SOUNDS

Hold up the new vowel Large Sound Cards in order. Tell the students that **a** says /ā/ as in **safe**. Have students repeat letter-keyword-sound: **a - safe** /ā/.

Point out that this long sound is simply the name of the letter. Repeat for every vowel.

When you get to **u**, explain that **u** is the only vowel that has two long sounds: /ū/ as in **mule** or /ü/ as in **rule**. Explain that sometimes it is difficult to get the whole **u** to come out smoothly, so part of the sound /ū/ is "chopped off," and it sounds like /ü/. Have the students listen to hear the difference.

Tap out **rule** and **mule**, stopping at the sound of **u**.

When you tap **mule**, the **u** sounds like /ū/.

When you tap **rule**, the **u** sounds like /ü/.

Discuss what the word **rule** means. The keyword picture for **rule** represents the classroom rule, **Do not chew gum**.

TEACH VOWEL-CONSONANT-E SYLLABLE

Next, review closed syllable with students using the Standard Sound Cards.

Make the word **hop**.

Let the students tap out the sounds and tell how many sounds are in the word (three).

Next, have students listen to you tap the word **hope**. Explain that the word **hope** also has three sounds, but the **o** says its name instead

of /ŏ/ as in **octopus**.

The way to make it say its name is to add an **e**. Add **e** to make the word hope.

Tap the word out again.

Tell students that **e** is **"the busiest letter in the alphabet."** It constantly volunteers to help out and whenever it volunteers, it **"keeps its mouth closed"** while it works.

The **e** in **hope** is silent. It **jumps over** the **p** to give **o** the long sound. **O** says /ō/ when it is long.

Make the word **cap**. Ask students to tap the sounds and name the word.

Ask them what you need to add to make the word into **cape** (add **e**).

Tap out cape: /k/ - /ā/ - /p/. It has only three sounds and the a is long.

Point out the **a-consonant-e**. Tell students that whenever there is a **vowel**, then a **consonant**, then an **e** at the end of the syllable, the **e** is silent and the vowel says its name (the long sound).

The **e** can jump over one sound to change the vowel from a short sound to a long sound.

Use the Standard Sound Cards to practice reading **one-syllable-closed** versus **vowel-consonant-e words**.

Students should practice with both real and nonsense word pairs (**cap - cape**, **fat - fate**, **tap - tape**, **lat - late**, **gobe - gob**, etc.).

Sufficient practice with the Standard Sound Cards is important in every lesson. It is important to have students tap again in order to master the new syllable type.

TEACH THE SOUND /Z/ AS IN *WISE*

Make the word **bugs** with your Large Sound Cards. Ask students to tell you what sound the suffix **-s**, makes (/**z**/).

Show students the words **rise** and **wise**.

Teach that **s** might say /**z**/ between two vowels. Students should be asked, **"When can s say /z/?"** and the response should be, **"As a suffix or when it is between two vowels."**

Say

> Whenever a vowel-consonant-e situation appears in a syllable, it is *not* a closed syllable. This is the second kind of syllable: the vowel-consonant-e syllable.

Teach Students To Mark Words

Mark the new vowel-consonant-e syllable type like this:

First, underline (or scoop) the syllable.

r o p e

Then identify the type of syllable (vowel-consonant-e) by writing **v-e** under the syllable. (The dash (**-**) represents the consonant.)

r o p e
v-e

Lastly, mark the vowel with a macron (¯) to indicate the long sound and slash out the **e** to indicate that it is silent.

r̄ō p e̸
v-e

Be sure to mark the vowel last, emphasizing that if the syllable is vowel-consonant-e, then the vowel is long.

Student Notebook Entry

Students should color the vowel-consonant-e pictures in the Sounds section of their Student Notebooks. Also, have them look up the vowel-consonant-e rule in the Syllable section. Have

them add the following examples:

c̄āv e̸   wīs e̸   plān e̸   līk e̸
 v-e   v-e   v-e   v-e

WEEK 1 DAY ❷

TEACH ECHO/FIND SOUNDS

Teach the response to **"What says /ā/?"** (**a-consonant-e**).

Review with the Standard Sound Cards that **e** helps to change a vowel from a short sound in **hop** to a long sound in **hope**.

Tap it out. The **e** is not heard, but it has to be there to make the **o** say its name.

Ask

> What says /ō/ ?

Demonstrate that **o** says /ō/ when it is followed by a **consonant** (use blank card) and an **e**.

o ☐ e

Explain that the blank card represents a consonant. Cover the blank card with various consonants such as **t**, **m**, **p** or **f** and have the students read: **ote**, **ome**, **ope**, **ofe**.

Return to the blank card and repeat that the blank card stands for a consonant.

Ask

> What says /ī/?

Have students place the appropriate Magnetic Letter Tiles on their Letter Boards.

The oral answer should also be given as the student points to the cards, **"i-consonant-e."**

Demonstrate how to write this: write **i-e**. (The dash (**-**) stands in the place of the blank card or tile and represents the consonant.)

An oral answer should also be given when a student writes **"i-consonant-e."**

Be sure to ask **"What says /ū/?"** and **"What says /ü/?"** The answer to both of these questions is u-e.

TEACH SPELLING

Use the Standard Sound Cards and have students spell current words.

Dictate the word, have the students repeat, and then find the Magnetic Letter Tiles to spell the word. A blank orange tile may be used for the silent **e**.

Be sure to dictate closed syllables as well so that you can teach your students to listen for the long or short vowel sound.

Show students that the letter **k** is used to spell /k/ in vowel-consonant-e words.

Make the word **bike** to demonstrate. Have students add this word to the **Three Ways to Spell /k/** page in the Spelling section of their Student Notebooks.

WEEK 3 DAY ❶

TEACH READING

Use the Standard Sound Cards to demonstrate words with the suffix **-s** added (**cakes, hopes**, etc.).

These should be read **cake-cakes**. The suffix **s** is circled. Do not add **-ing** or **-ed** suffixes to these words.

Make 5-6 Unit words with the Standard Sound Cards and add the suffix **-s**.

TEACH SPELLING

Dictate the word, hopes. Have students repeat the word and then name the baseword. Have a student come find your Standard Sound Cards to spell hope. Then have the student add the Yellow Suffix Frame. Do 3-4 more words.

 Drill Sounds

Referring to the Vowel Sounds Poster, practice short and long vowels.

Say

  a - apple - /ă/

  a - safe - /ā/

Have students repeat.

a - apple - /ă/	→	**a - safe - /ā/**
e - Ed - /ĕ/	→	**e - Pete - /ē/**
i - itch - /ĭ/	→	**i - pine - /ī/**
o - octopus - /ŏ/	→	**o - home - /ō/**
u - up - /ŭ/	→	**u - mule - /ū/**
	→	**u - rule - /ü/**

Large Sound Cards

Next practice sounds with the Large Sound Cards. Say the letter-keyword-sound and have students echo.

Standard Sound Cards

Next, point to the Standard Sound Cards (on display) with the Baby Echo pointer. You say the letter-keyword-sound and hold up Baby Echo to have students repeat. When you point to each vowel, be sure to say all the corresponding sounds. (See above as well as back of card for references).

Ask Students

What are the two long sounds of u?

(/ū/, /ü/)

When does the s say /z/?

(Sometimes when it is a suffix and sometimes between two vowels.)

 ## Word of the Day

Select a Word of the Day from the words below. Make the word using your Standard Sound Card display. Also, write the word on a blank index card and add it to your Word of the Day packet.

Word Resource

WEEK 1

w	i	s	e

WEEK 2

a	p	e	

j	o	k	e

WEEK 3

c	a	v	e	s

n	o	t	e	s

Review Concepts

Reteach the vowel-consonant-e syllable using the Word of the Day.

Use The Word In A Sentence

Have a student (or students) use the word in a sentence and discuss the word's meaning.

Make Other Words

Then use sound cards to make several other words from this Unit. (See Unit Resources.) Have students tap and read each word.

Student Notebook Entry

Have students add the Word of the Day to the Vocabulary section of their Student Notebooks.

Have students mark up the word with the vowel-consonant-e syllable.

Write a sentence on the board for students to copy. (This can be done at another time of the day.)

 ## Word Talk

Review the Words of the Day from your Words of the Day index card packet.

Make and Discuss Words

Make 4-5 words with your Standard Sound Card display.

Have students tap and read the words.

Ask a student to use a word in a sentence and another student to explain what the word means.

Read Words

Use your packet of words as flashcards. Have students quickly read them without tapping.

Display Words

Display current and review words. Have students find and read the words as directed.

Instruct Students

Find the vowel-consonant-e words.

What does the first vowel say? Why?

What letter is silent?

How do you tap this word?

In the words chase and wise, ask "What does s say" and "What else can it say between two vowels?"

Trick Words

Trick words require lots of practice. Sky write and finger write trick words, but **do not** tap them out or make them with the Magnetic Letter Tiles.

WEEK 1

friend	around	circle

WEEK 2

does	nothing	write

WEEK 3

none	color	month

Students add these words to the Trick Word section of their Student Notebooks. Hold them accountable for the spelling of these words throughout the day. Direct students to look them up in the Trick Word section of their Student Notebooks.

After the introduction of new trick words, practice them with sky writing and tracing.

Echo/Find Sounds & Words

Echo/Find Sounds

Say a sound. Have students echo and find the letter on their Letter Board.

Dictate the long sound of the vowels.

(See Echo Sounds in Unit Resources for expected student responses.)

Echo/Find Words

Practice review words. Have students use blank tiles to spell words. They should echo and tap word, find blank tiles and then point to the tiles and name the corresponding letters.

(See Review and Current Unit Words in Unit Resources.)

Have students find Magnetic Letter Tiles needed to make words on their Letter Boards. After finding a word, have a student spell it orally.

Dictation

Refer to this Unit's Resource List of Echo Sounds, Words and Sentences.

Proper Dictation Activity procedures are very important. Be sure to follow their demonstration on the CD-ROM.

DRY ERASE

Dictate 3 sounds, 3 current words and 3 trick words (trick words can be current or review).

This is a teaching time, not a testing time. Be sure students repeat each dictation. They should tap and orally spell the Unit words before writing. Students should write and orally spell trick words with their finger prior to writing them on their Dry Erase Writing Tablets.

Have students "mark up" the review and current words.

COMPOSITION BOOKS

Dictate 3 sounds, 2 review, 2 current words and 2 trick words (trick words can be current or review) and 1 sentence.

This is also a teaching time, not a testing time. Be sure students repeat each thing that you dictate. They should tap and orally spell the review and current Unit words before writing. Students should write and orally spell trick words with their finger prior to writing them in their Composition Books. Students independently write the sentence and then you lead them through the proofreading procedure.

Have students "mark up" the review and current words.

DAY 5 CHECK-UP

Students do Day 5 Dictation in their Composition Books. Have them check the Check-up box at the top of the page.

Dictate the sound, word, or sentence. Have students repeat and then write independently. Do not have students spell orally. Encourage them to tap as appropriate.

UNIT TEST

Have students find Unit Test pages at the end of their Composition Books.

Dictate the sound, word, or sentence. (See Unit Resources.) Have students repeat and then write independently. Do not have students spell orally. Encourage them to tap as appropriate.

 **Make It Fun**

WEEK 1

Preparation

• Strips Of Sturdy Paper.
• Words: not/note, hop/hope, tub/tube, plan/plane, tap/tape

MAKE SPECIAL CARD STRIPS

This activity will help students practice the difference between closed and vowel-consonant-e words.

Instruct Students

See the CD-ROM for a demonstration. Dictate a word below and have a student echo it, tap it out and spell it. Write it on the board. Have students write it in large letters on a strip of paper.

note

Next have them fold over the letter **e**. Have them show the word **note**, then show the word **not**.

WEEKS 2 • 3

Preparation

• Current and Review Word List- Unit Resources
• Word of the Day Packet

STAND UP

This activity helps students distinguish closed and vowel consonant-e words.

Instruct Students

Disseminate cards from the Word of the Day packet, giving one card per student. Write the headings, closed syllable and vowel-consonant-e syllable on the blackboard in two columns.

Closed Syllable   Vowel-Consonant-e Syllable

Call students up in small groups. Have them write their word in the correct column. Read the words in each column.

Erase the words but keep the headings. Next dictate a word from the Unit Resource List. Tell them to stand up if the word you say is a vowel-consonant-e.

Select some review, closed syllable words and some vowel-consonant-e words. Have the students echo the word, and stand. To confirm, write the word under the heading. You can also assign students to teams and tally points.

Storytime

WEEK 1

Preparation

- Baby Echo (on a pointer or ruler)
- Large Chart Paper

THE BIG BASKETBALL GAME

Write the following story, with the phrases scooped, on chart paper.

The Big Basketball Game

Mike was small and Dave was tall.

Mike and Dave went to play basketball.

The kids did not pick Mike to play.

He sat on the side and felt sad.

Then Dave fell and cut his leg.

He was fine, but he did not want to play.

Mike had to go in the game

to play for Dave. Mike got the basketball

and shot it. It went in the net!

Mike was not tall, but his shot still

went in the net. He was glad that he

made a basket in the big game.

Instruct Students

Ask the students to read the title silently. (Tell students to tap words when reading silently, if necessary.) Discuss the title and predict what the story might be about.

Read Sentences

Continue reading one sentence at a time.

- Have students read silently. (Tell students to tap words when reading silently, if necessary.)
- Select a student to come read the sentence with the Baby Echo pointer. Be sure the student uses proper expression and phrasing. If not, model.
- Have the whole class repeat the sentence.

After the story has been read once in this manner, read it altogether with choral reading as you scoop the phrases with Baby Echo.

Make a Movie

Have students "make a movie" in their heads. Tell them to close their eyes and picture The Big Basketball Game.

Ask someone to describe what they see in their movie, discussing each sentence.

Continue with the whole story. Then model re-telling the story in your own words and ask a student to retell it in their own words.

Mark Words

Lastly, select students to come mark words as directed.

- Mark all v-e words.

WEEK 2

Preparation

- Baby Echo (on a pointer or ruler)
- Large Chart Paper with the story from Week 1
- Copy THE BIG BASKETBALL GAME story for each student from the Fluency Kit (in the Stories tab).

Instruct Students

Ask the students to read the title silently. Have them try to remember the "movie" in their mind. Have someone describe the story by re-telling it. Read chorally as you point with Baby Echo and determine if the retelling was accurate.

Next disseminate the story to the students.

Have them draw pictures for each page and cut on the dotted lines. Staple these into booklets for the students to bring home.

WEEK 3

Preparation

- Find a non-fiction book about any animal.
- Chart Paper

Instruct Students

Remind students that some books that have stories that are pretend or make-believe.

Explain that other books tell us facts about things. They teach us things that are true. Show them your non-fiction book and tell the students that it is a book that teaches them true things about (name the subject).

Read the book (or part of the book) to your students. After each page, ask them to name one true fact that they have learned.

Next, tell the students that they will help you write a non-fiction paragraph about (name the subject).

Have the students retell several facts. Write the sentences to create a paragraph. Be sure to indent.

Next have a student come and put an arrow to show the indented first sentence:

→ **Birds build nests.**

Have another student hightlight the punctuation marks.

Tell students that a paragraph has several sentences that all talk about the same topic.

Ask

What do you do at the beginning of the sentence?

(Indent)

What do you put at the end of every sentence?

(a period, a question mark or an exclamation point).

Drill Sounds

a - apple - /ă/	a - safe - /ā/
b - bat - /b/	c - cat - /k/
d - dog - /d/	e - Ed - /ĕ/
e - Pete - /ē/	f - fun - /f/
g - game - /g/	h - hat - /h/
i - itch - /ĭ/	i - pine - /ī/
j - jug - /j/	k - kite - /k/
l - lamp - /l/	m - man - /m/
n - nut - /n/	o - octopus - /ŏ/
o - home - /ō/	p - pan - /p/
qu - queen - /kw/	r - rat - /r/
s - snake - /s/	s - bugs - /z/
t - top - /t/	u - up - /ŭ/
u - mule - /ū/	u - rule - /ü/
v - van - /v/	w - wind - /w/
x - fox - /ks/	y - yellow - /y/
z - zebra - /z/	sh - ship - /sh/
ck - sock - /k/	wh - whistle - /w/
th - thumb - /th/	ch - chin - /ch/
all - ball - /òl/	an - fan - /an/
am - ham - /am/	ang - fang - /ang/
ing - ring - /ing/	ong - song - /ong/
ung - lung - /ung/	ank - bank - /ank/
ink - pink - /ink/	onk - honk - /onk/
unk - junk - /unk/	

Echo Sounds

Sounds appear between / /. You say the sound. Students echo the sound and say the letter. Depending on the activity, students then either find or make the letter corresponding to that sound.

CONSONANTS/CONSONANT DIGRAPHS

/b/ - b	/d/ - d	/f/ - f
/g/ - g	/h/ - h	/j/ - j
/k/ - c, k, ck	/l/ - l	/m/ - m
/n/ - n	/p/ - p	/kw/ - qu
/r/ - r	/s/ - s	/t/ - t
/v/ - v	/w/ - w, wh	/ks/ - x
/y/ - y	/z/ - z, s	/ch/ - ch
/sh/ - sh	/th/ - th	

VOWELS

/ă/ - a	/ā/ - a - e	/ĕ/ - e
/ē/ - e - e	/ĭ/ - i	/ī/ - i - e
/ŏ/ - o	/ō/ - o - e	/ŭ/ - u
/ū/ - u - e	/ü/ - u - e	

GLUED/WELDED SOUNDS

/òl/ - all	/am/ - am	/an/ - an
/ang/ - ang	/ing/ - ing	/ong/ - ong
/ung/ - ung	/ank/ - ank	/ink/ - ink
/onk/ - onk	/unk/ - unk	

Review Trick Words

the	of	and	to	a	was
is	he	for	as	his	has
I	you	we	they	one	said
from	or	have	were	her	put
there	what	she	been	by	who
out	so	are	two	about	into
only	other	new	some	could	want
say	do	first	any	my	now
our	over	come	would	after	also
many	how	called	before	your	down
own	each	people	Mr.	Mrs.	should
says	little	years	very	good	because
see	work	both	being	under	between
never	words	another	day	look	through

Current Unit Trick Words

friend	around	circle	does	nothing
write	none	color	month	

Review Words

plants	winks	thank
next	gifts	blimp
stump	glasses	cramps
disrupt	upset	absent
foxes	inches	index
admit	spills	jumping

singing	shrinking	flashing
drilling	crossing	thinking
expanding	publishing	finishing
spilling	punishing	talented
squinted	invented	expected
blended	insulted	

Current Unit Words

lime	ape	tide	these	cube
whine	lane	wide	cake	line
pole	flame	hose	nine	vase
tube	those	chase	spine	dare
grade	case	vote	file	care
mile	came	bone	cone	wife
smile	note	choke	dime	drive
mine	flute	tape	share	joke
chose	wave	hide	name	pile
close	bite	hope	wine	slope
ride	plane	poke	rule	plate
rise	scrape	throne	spoke	lake
prize	rope	skate	cave	dive
snake	shine	hole	cane	quake
tune	slide	trade	fire	whale
prune	white	bake	like	grape
ripe	globe	mule	kite	wipe
state	home	sale	bike	shake
stone	save	maze	shave	bride
take	strike	base	time	brave

shape	Dave	Steve	Mike	Kate
Jane	Pete	Jake	Duke	June
safe	broke	hate	late	

ropes	games	stripes	whales	rules
rakes	globes	grapes	slides	likes
jokes	grades	votes	tides	whines
flames	cares	bones	cases	shares
scrapes	hides	planes	waves	trades
dives	slopes	game	life	rake
five	plates			

Sentences

*Write any **bold word** on the board for students to copy. A **bold word** has untaught components.*

I like the tune that Kate will sing.

I left the bone on my plate.

Is it safe to ride my bike on that path?

The wise king sat on his throne.

I had the best grade in math class.

I think there is a snake in that hole.

Was Dave late for the dentist?

Mike got the prize at the end of the contest.

Kate will get the shrimp on sale.

Dad **told** a joke that made us all smile.

Sid has a flute to bring to band class.

Beth likes her pink and white pants.

Hank has a limp and must use a cane.

Did the pup choke on that bone?

Mrs. Smith has the best smile.

Dad will drive the kids to class.

We will slide and then go skate.

James will take the flag off the pole.

Calvin will do the quiz in time for lunch.

I will ride my fine bike.

Go to the cave next to the lake.

The bride had a fine time.

Jane must save to get that dress.

It will take a long time to wipe up this mess.

After we skate, we will go home.

James dove into the pond.

We can slide on that hill slope.

That blast made us all jump.

The plum is ripe but the grapes are bad.

My dad has to shave and dress.

Did Mom ask me to shake the rug?

Dad likes to save all this junk.

Ed broke the rules.

The sun shines on the pond.

What are the rules for this game?

The rules in this class are quite **strict**.

Ken slides into home plate.

Ben likes to stroke my cat.

Wipe up the mess and get the plates for lunch.

Have students find the unit test pages located at the end of their Composition Books. Dictate the sounds, words and sentences. Have students repeat and then write independently. Encourage them to tap, but they should not use their Student Notebooks.

Dictate The Following Sounds

/ā/   /ă/   /ī/   /ū/   /ü/

Dictate The Following Words

| mule | brave | joke | expected | glasses |
| pranks | grade | smiles | benches | disrupt |

Dictate The Following Trick Words

friend   circle

Dictate The Following Sentences

Jake had to shave and dress.

Mike invented that fun game.

Have The Students Do The Following

• Scoop the syllables in the multisyllabic words.
• Underline basewords and circle the suffixes.
• Mark the vowel-consonant-e syllables.

Answer Key

SOUNDS

1. a-e   2. a   3. i-e
4. u-e   5. u-e

WORDS

1. <u>mule</u>   2. <u>brave</u>
   v-e   v-e
3. <u>joke</u>   4. expect(ed)
   v-e
5. glass(es)   6. prank(s)
7. <u>grade</u>   8. <u>smile</u>(s)
   v-e   v-e
9. bench(es)   10. <u>dis</u> <u>rupt</u>

TRICK WORDS

1. friend   2. circle

SENTENCES

1. <u>Jake</u> had to <u>shave</u>
   v-e   v-e
   and dress.

2. <u>Mike</u> invented that fun
   v-e
   <u>game</u>.
   v-e

Appendix

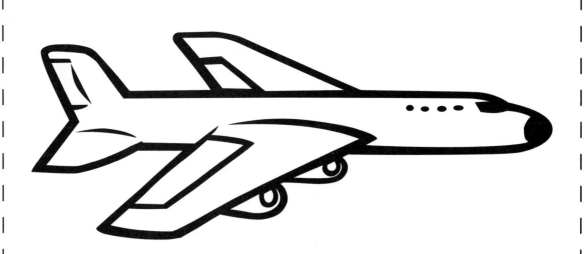

WILSON WRITING GRID OVERHEAD

Aa Bb Cc Dd Ee Ff

Gg Hh Ii Jj Kk Ll

Mm Nn Oo Pp Qq Rr Ss

Tt Uu Vv Ww Xx Yy Zz

Fundations **Letter Formation**

Sky Line Letters

t b f l h k

Plane Line Letters

n m i r u p j

Plane Line Round Letters   Special e

c a o g d s q   e

Plane Line Slide Letters

v w z y x

Fundations **Letter Formation Guide**

Use the following verbalization to direct students in proper letter formation.

Letter Formation for **a**

a is a plane line round letter.

It starts on the (plane line).

1. **Point to the plane line.**
2. **Go back on the plane line then down and around on the grass line,**
3. **and up to the plane line.**
4. **Trace back down to the grass.**

Letter Formation for **b**

b is a sky line letter.

It starts on the (sky line).

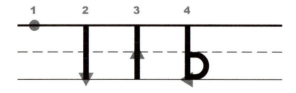

1. **Point to the sky line.**
2. **Go down to the grass line.**
3. **Trace up to the plane line,**
4. **and around to the grass line.**

Letter Formation for **c**

c is a plane line round letter.

It starts on the (plane line).

1. **Point to the plane line.**
2. **Start to fly backwards**
3. **and go down and around to the grass line.**

Letter Formation for **d**

d is a plane line round letter.

It starts on the (plane line) **just like a c.**

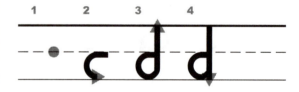

1. **Point to the plane line.**
2. **Go back, down and around to the grass line,**
3. **all the way back up to the sky line.**
4. **Trace back down to the grass line.**

Fundations **Letter Formation Guide**

Use the following verbalization to direct students in proper letter formation.

Letter Formation for **e**

e is a plane line round letter, but it is special. e starts below the plane line.

1 2 3 4

1. Point between the plane line and the grass line.

2. Fly under the plane line.

3. Then go up to the plane line,

4. and around to the grass.

Letter Formation for **f**

f is a sky line letter.

It starts on the (sky line).

1 2 3 4

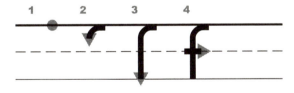

1. Point to the sky line.

2. Trace back on the sky line,

3. and then way down to the grass line.

4. Cross it on the plane line

Letter Formation for **g**

g is a plane line round letter.

It starts on the (plane line) **just like a c.**

1 2 3 4

1. Point to the plane line.

2. Trace back on the plane line,

3. down and around all the way back to the plane line.

4. Trace back down all the way to the worm line and make a curve.

Letter Formation for **h**

h is a sky line letter.

It starts on the (sky line).

1 2 3 4

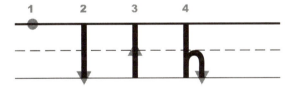

1. Point to the sky line.

2. Go down to the grass line.

3. Trace back up to the plane line,

4. and make a hump.

Fundations **Letter Formation Guide**

Use the following verbalization to direct students in proper letter formation.

Letter Formation for **i**

i is a plane line letter.

It starts on the (plane line).

1. Point to the plane line.

2. Go down to the grass line.

3. Add a dot.

Letter Formation for **j**

j is a plane line letter.

It starts on the (plane line).

1. Point to the plane line.

2. Go all the way down to the worm line, and make a curve.

3. Add a dot.

Letter Formation for **k**

k is a sky line letter.

It starts on the (sky line).

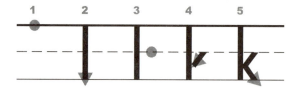

1. Point to the sky line.

2. Go all the way down to the grass line.

3. Point to the plane line and leave a space.

4. Slide over and touch your tall line,

5. and slide back to the grass.

Letter Formation for **l**

l is a sky line letter.

It starts on the (sky line).

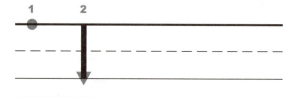

1. Point to the sky line.

2. Go down to the grass and stop.

Fundations **Letter Formation Guide**

Use the following verbalization to direct students in proper letter formation.

Letter Formation for **m**

m is a plane line letter.

It starts on the (plane line).

1. **Point to the plane line.**

2. **Go down to the grass line.**

3. **Trace back up to the plane line,**

4. **and make a hump,**

5. **and then back up to the plane line and make another hump.**

Letter Formation for **n**

n is a plane line letter.

It starts on the (plane line).

1. **Point to the plane line.**

2. **Go down to the grass line.**

3. **Trace back up to the plane line,**

4. **and make a hump.**

Letter Formation for **O**

o is a plane line round letter.

It starts on the (plane line) **just like a c.**

1. **Point to the plane line.**

2. **Trace back, then down to the grass line,**

3. **and around back up to the plane line.**

Letter Formation for **p**

Use the following verbalization to direct students in proper letter formation.

Say

p is a plane line round letter.

It starts on the (plane line).

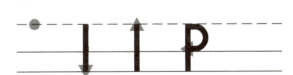

1. **Point to the plane line.**

2. **Go down to the worm line.**

3. **Trace back up to the plane line,**

4. **and curve all the way around to the grass line.**

Fundations **Letter Formation Guide**

Use the following verbalization to direct students in proper letter formation.

Letter Formation for q

q is a plane line round letter.

It starts on the (plane line).

Remember that q is the chicken letter so in the end it wants to point up to its buddy, u.

1. Point to the plane line.

2. Trace back and go down to the grass line around, back to the plane line.

3. Trace back down to the worm line,

4. and point up to his "buddy" u.

Letter Formation for r

r is a plane line letter.

It starts on the (plane line).

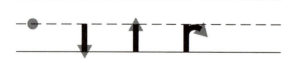

1. Point to the plane line.

2. Go down to the grass line.

3. Trace back up to the plane line,

4. and make a little curve.

Letter Formation for S

s is a plane line round letter.

It starts on the (plane line) just like a c.

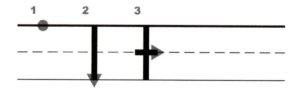

1. Point to the plane line.

2. Trace back and it curves in,

3. and goes back again and lands on the grass.

Letter Formation for t

t is a sky line letter.

It starts on the (sky line).

1. Point to the sky line.

2. Go down to the grass line.

3. Cross it on the plane line.

Fundations **Letter Formation Guide**

Use the following verbalization to direct students in proper letter formation.

Letter Formation for **U**

u is a plane line round letter.

It starts on the (plane line).

1. **Point to the plane line.**
2. **Go down to the grass line.**
3. **Curve up to the plane line,**
4. **and trace straight down to the grass.**

Letter Formation for **V**

v is a plane line slide letter.

It starts on the (plane line) **and** (slides).

1. **Point to the plane line.**
2. **Slide down to the grass line.**
3. **Slide up to the plane line.**

Letter Formation for **W**

w is a plane line slide letter.

It starts on the (plane line) **and** (slides).

1. **Point to the plane line.**
2. **Slide down to the grass line.**
3. **Slide up to the plane line.**
4. **Slide down to the grass line.**
5. **Slide up to the plane line.**

Letter Formation for **X**

x is a plane line slide letter.

It starts on the (plane line) **and** (slides).

1. **Point to the plane line.**
2. **Slide down to the grass line.**
3. **Leave a space and point to the plane line.**
4. **Slide back to the grass line.**

Fundations **Letter Formation Guide**

Use the following verbalization to direct students in proper letter formation.

Letter Formation for **y**

y is a plane line slide letter.

It starts on the (plane line) **and** (slides).

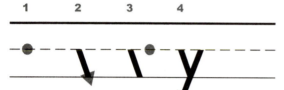

1. Point to the plane line.

2. Slide down to the grass line.

3. Pick up your pencil (finger) and leave a space and point to the plane line.

4. Slide back - all the way to the worm line.

Letter Formation for **Z**

z is a plane line slide letter, but it doesn't slide right away.

Where does it start? (On the plane line).

Before it slides, the z goes on the plane line.

1. Point to the plane line.

2. Go on the plane line.

3. Slide back to the grass line.

4. Then go on the grass line.

Fundations® **Pencil Grip**

Use these Keyword Pictures to make a Vowel Extension activity as described in the Lesson Activity Plan. This activity helps students extend their vowel sounds.

1 _____   2 _____

3 _____   4 _____

5 _____   6 _____

7 _____   8 _____

9 _____   10 _____

s	ed	ed	ing	ing	es
s	ed	ed	ing	ing	es
s	ed	ed	ing	ing	es
s	ed	ed	ing	ing	es
s	ed	ed	ing	ing	es
s	ed	ed	ing	ing	es

Name: _____ Today's Date: _____ *Check-up* ☐

Sounds

1   2   3

Review Words

1   2

Current Words

1   2

Trick Words

1   2

Sentence

1

❶ Closed Syllable

- Ends in a consonant and only has one vowel.
- The vowel in a closed syllable is short.

Examples

up   hat   ship   last

Mark-up Sample

lăst
   c

❷ Vowel-Consonant-e Syllable

- Has the vowel-consonant-e combination.
- The **e** is silent.
- The first vowel has a long sound.

Examples

bike   ape   stove

Mark-up Sample

stōve
  v-e

❸ Open Syllable

- Ends with a single vowel (this might be the **only** letter in the syllable).
- The vowel has a long sound.

Examples

I   be   shy   hi

Mark-up Sample

hī
 o

❹ Consonant-le Syllable

- Contains a consonant-le.
- Occurs at the end of a word.
- The **e** is silent (it is present only because every syllable needs a vowel).
- Only the consonant and the **l** are sounded.

Examples

cradle   little   bubble

Mark-up Sample

bub ble
   -le

❺ R-Controlled Syllable

- Contains a vowel combined with an **r** (**ar**, **er**, **ir**, **or**, **ur**).
- The vowel is neither long nor short; its sound is controlled by the r.

Examples

start   fir   hurt   art

Mark-up Sample

ar t
 r

❻ Double Vowel - "D" Syllable

- Contains a diphthong or vowel digraph.

Examples

beat   feel   eight   new

Mark-up Sample

n ew
  d

Unit 1 **Test Recording Form**   Level **K**

Student _____   **Date** _____

Record successful responses with a check ☑. Answers, when provided, appear in italics.

Examiner _____

Student Correctly Identifies Lower-Case Letters

*Using the student's Letter Board and Letter Tiles, point to letters and have student name each letter. Ask , "What letter is this?" If student is unable to **name** the letters, have student **find** letters. Say, "Find the letter **a**." Note if student can find letters but not yet name them.*

a ☐	r ☐	z ☐	b ☐	g ☐
j ☐	k ☐	e ☐	o ☐	v ☐

Score: _____ *out of 10 (Naming Letters)*   _____ *out of 10 (Finding Letters)*

Student Correctly Identifies Letter Corresponding to Sound

*Using the student's Letter Board and Letter Tiles, say sound and have student point to corresponding letters. Ask, "What says /**s**/?"*

/s/ s ☐	/n/ n ☐	/ĭ/ i ☐	/kw/ q ☐	/f/ f ☐
/z/ z ☐	/h/ h ☐	/l/ l ☐	/p/ p ☐	/v/ v ☐

Score: _____ *out of 10*

Student Correctly Forms Lower-Case Letters

*Using the student's Dry Erase Board, dictate letters and have student write the lower-case letter on the Writing Grid. Say, "Write the letter **t**."*

t ☐	c ☐	g ☐	m ☐	x ☐
p ☐	e ☐	d ☐	h ☐	f ☐

Score: _____ *out of 10*

Unit 2 **Test Recording Form**

Level **K**

Student _____

Date _____

Record successful responses with a check ☑. Answers, when provided, appear in italics.

Examiner _____

Student Correctly Identifies Beginning Sounds

*Say a word and ask student to tell you the sound at the beginning of the word. Provide an example: "What is the first sound in the word **sink**?" Student responds: /s/*

meat	/m/	☐	talk	/t/	☐	sip	/s/	☐	door	/d/	☐	clap	/k/	☐
bang	/b/	☐	face	/f/	☐	zebra	/z/	☐	lion	/l/	☐	wagon	/w/	☐

Score: _____ **out of 10**

Student Correctly Identifies Upper-Case Letters

*Point to upper-case letters (see Unit 2 Test in Teacher's Manual) and have student name each letter. Ask , "What letter is this?" If student is unable to **name** the letters, have student **find** letters. Say, "Find the letter **A**." Note if student can find letters but not yet name them.*

A	☐	E	☐	W	☐	B	☐	D	☐
Q	☐	G	☐	M	☐	N	☐	R	☐

Score: _____ **out of 10 (Naming Letters)**   _____ **out of 10 (Finding Letters)**

Student Correctly Forms Upper-Case Letters

*Using the student's Dry Erase Board, dictate letters and have student write the upper-case letter on a Writing Grid. Say, "Write the upper-case letter **G**."*

G	☐	N	☐	Z	☐	P	☐	H	☐
T	☐	F	☐	X	☐	B	☐	V	☐

Score: _____ **out of 10**

Student _____

Date _____

Record successful responses with a check ☑. Answers, when provided, appear in italics.

Examiner _____

Student Correctly Identifies Ending Sounds

*Say a word and ask student to tell you the sound at the end of the word. Provide an example: "What is the last sound in the word **bat**?" Student responds: /t/*

sharp	*/p/*	☐	lick	*/k/*	☐	stuff	*/f/*	☐	phone */n/* ☐ bag */g/* ☐
lend	*/d/*	☐	fuzz	*/z/*	☐	drum	*/m/*	☐	sheet */t/* ☐ talk */k/* ☐

Score: _____ **out of 10**

Student Correctly Blends Sounds to Form Words

Say sounds one at a time and have student blend to form word. Say, "I will say sounds slowly. Blend them together and tell me the word."

/s/ /ă/ /t/ *sat* ☐	/f/ /ĭ/ /t/ *fit* ☐	/l/ /ŏ/ /g/ *log* ☐	/m/ /ă/ /t/ *mat* ☐	/n/ /ă/ /p/ *nap* ☐

Score: _____ **out of 5**

Student Correctly Reads C-V-C Words

Form words using the student's Letter Board and Letter Tiles and have student tap and read the words. Say, "Tap these sounds and tell me the word that I made."

nap	☐	sit	☐	rob	☐	mud	☐	net	☐

Score: _____ **out of 5**

Student Correctly Names Letters in Alphabetical Order

Ask student to place Letter Tiles onto Letter Board and to recite the alphabet in order.

☐ Yes	☐ No	Comments:

Unit 4 **Test Recording Form** Level **K**

Student _____   **Date** _____

Record successful responses with a check ☑. Answers, when provided, appear in italics.

Examiner _____

Student Correctly Identifies Vowel Sounds

*Say a word and have student say the vowel sound. Provide an example: "What vowel sound is in the word **pat**?"*
Student responds: /ă/

tag	/ă/	☐	pit	/ĭ/	☐	log	/ŏ/	☐	pen	/ĕ/	☐	mud	/ŭ/	☐

Score: _____ *out of 5*

Student Correctly Taps and Reads Words

Form words using the student's Letter Board and Letter Tiles and have student tap and read the words. Say, "Tap these sounds and tell me the word that I made."

top	☐	gum	☐	dip	☐	bet	☐	wax	☐

Score: _____ *out of 5*

Student Correctly Segments a Word into Its Sounds

*Say a word and have student say its sounds. Provide an example: "Tell me each sound in the word **cup**." Student responds: /k/ /ŭ/ /p/*

tap	/t/ /ă/ /p/	☐	rug	/r/ /ŭ/ /g/	☐	job	/j/ /ŏ/ /b/	☐	dig	/d/ /ĭ/ /g/	☐	nut	/n/ /ŭ/ /t/	☐
bat	/b/ /ă/ /t/	☐	bib	/b/ /ĭ/ /b/	☐	pet	/p/ /ĕ/ /t/	☐	cot	/k/ /ŏ/ /t/	☐	led	/l/ /ĕ/ /d/	☐

Score: _____ *out of 10*

Student Correctly Taps and Spells Words

Say a word and have student repeat the word, tap it and then find corresponding Letter Tiles to spell the word on the student's Letter Board.

sit	☐	job	☐	pet	☐	mad	☐	bug	☐

Score: _____ *out of 5*

Student Successfully Retells a Story

Using one of the stories from a Storytime activity, see if student can retell the story with the pictures as a guide.

☐ Yes	☐ No	☐ Yes, with assistance

Unit 5 **Test Recording Form**

Level **K**

Student _____ **Date** _____

Record successful responses with a check ☑. Answers, when provided, appear in italics.

Examiner _____

Student Correctly Identifies Trick Words

Present trick words on flashcards and have student read them. (Do not tap trick words.)

the	☐	is	☐	was	☐	of	☐	and	☐

Score: _____ *out of 5*

Student Successfully Reads a Sentence

*Using your Blue Sentence Frames, write the following sentence and have student read it: **The rat had a nap.** Note which words student reads correctly.*

The	☐	rat	☐	had	☐	a	☐	nap	☐

Score: _____ *out of 5*

Student Successfully Completes a Sentence

*Using your Blue Sentence Frames, write the following sentence with noted omissions: **Deb is on the mat.** (Make sure to leave off the punctuation square for the period.) Have student complete the sentence and note which items are completed successfully. Say, "I will say a sentence. Repeat the sentence and finish making it for me."*

[ ]	is	on	the	[ ]		student correctly spells *Deb*	☐
						student uses capital *D*	☐
						student correctly spells *mat*	☐
						student adds the period	☐

Score: _____ *out of 4*

Student Successfully Relates Events in a Narrative

Using a fiction and a non-fiction book from Storytime, ask the following questions.

Which of these books tells a make-believe story? ☐	Which of these books tells true facts? ☐
What happened first? ☐	Can you tell me two true facts? ☐
What happened next? ☐	
What happened at the end? ☐	

Score: _____ *out of 6*